D0941020

QUOTATIONS
for
SPECIAL OCCASIONS

QUOTATIONS *for* SPECIAL OCCASIONS

By
MAUD VAN BUREN

NEW YORK
THE H. W. WILSON COMPANY
1938

First Printing 1938
Second Printing 1949
Third Printing 1955
Fourth Printing 1961

Printed in the United States of America

Library of Congress Catalog Card No. 38-27833

To my fellow-librarians everywhere and particularly to Clara Frances Baldwin whose wise leadership for nearly forty years was an inspiration to Minnesota librarians.

Preface

"Never enough!"—the plaint of librarians oftenest heard in any discussion of SPECIAL DAY resources. As for quotations, there are enough, certainly, scattered through many volumes old and new. This book is an effort to bring together in small compass the best of these widely-scattered thoughts, for that ever-increasing demand upon libraries, from schools, churches, clubs and the ever-growing number of organizations of every imaginable interest.

The resources of many public and college libraries have been drawn upon for this volume. I am specially indebted to Miss Genevieve M. Macdonald and Miss Alice I. Branham of the Minneapolis Public Library, Miss Helen K. Starr and Miss Helen Rugg of the James Jerome Hill Reference Library of St. Paul, and to Miss Eleanor Herrmann and Miss Elsie Baker of the St. Paul Public Library, for generous aid in research.

MAUD VAN BUREN

Owatonna, Minnesota
December 20, 1937

Acknowledgments

The following have generously contributed to this work: American Humane Association; American Humane Education Society; National Humane Review; Annals of the American Academy of Political and Social Science; National Safety Council; Boy Scouts of America; Ford Motor Company; Oxford University Press: "The Gray Book"; Good Housekeeping: Kate Randle Menefee; Charles Scribner's Sons: Eugene Field, Henry van Dyke, Robert Louis Stevenson; Liberty Hyde Bailey: "The Miracle"; Robert Bridges ("Droch"); Witter Bynner; Robert P. Tristram Coffin; Hermann Hagedorn; Henry Herbert Knibbs; Edwin Markham (works copyrighted by the author and used by his permission); Christopher Morley: "Songs for a Little House," "Mince Pie"; Frederick A. Stokes Co.: Alfred Noyes; Grantland Rice; Lew Sarett; Robert Haven Schauffler; Charles Hanson Towne; Carolyn Wells; Margaret Widdemer; Richard Burton: "The Blue Bird," "Columbus" from Collected Poems published by Bobbs, Merrill Company, Indianapolis; Harper & Brothers: Grace Noll Crowell; Rev. Philip Gregory; Anna Blake Mezquida; Angela Morgan; New York Times; Jessie B. Rittenhouse from "Debt" from the collection "The Door of Dreams," Houghton, Mifflin Co.; Macmillan Co.: John Kendrick Bangs, "My Dog"; Beacon Press: "New Hymnal for American Youth"; Mrs. W. W. Christman: Poems of W. W. Christman; Mrs. Rudyard Kipling: from "The Seven Seas" by Rudyard Kipling, copyright, 1893, 1921, reprinted by permission from Doubleday, Doran & Co. Inc., Rudyard Kipling's Verses, Inclusive edition, 1885-1932, by Rudyard Kipling, copyright, 1891, 1934, reprinted by permission from Doubleday, Doran & Co.; and the following: From "Trees and Other Poems" by Joyce Kilmer, copyright, 1914, by Doubleday, Doran & Co. Inc., "Main Street and Other Poems" by Joyce Kilmer, copyright, 1917, by Doubleday Doran & Co. Inc., "Poems, Essays & Letters," vol. I, by Joyce Kilmer, copyright, 1914, by Doubleday, Doran & Co. Inc.

While the greatest diligence has been used to ascertain the owners of the rights and to secure the necessary permissions to include the quotations in this volume, the editor and publisher desire to offer their apologies in any possible case of accidental infringement.

Contents

Quotations for Special Occasions

ARBOR DAY

The grass is green, buds on the bushes throng,
The glory of the leaf is on the wood.
—*Agathias Scholasticus*

Now dandelions in the short, new grass,
Through all their rapid stages daily pass.
—*John Albee*

Faint murmurs from the pine-tops reach my ear,
As if a harp-string—touched in some far sphere—
Vibrating in the lucid atmosphere,
Let the soft south wind waft its music here.
—*Thomas Bailey Aldrich*

Wild-flowers are fringing the dusty lanes.
—*Thomas Bailey Aldrich*

. . . .I wish I were an elm-tree,
A great, lofty elm-tree, with green leaves gay!
The winds would set them dancing,
The sun and moonshine glance in,
The birds would house among the boughs,
And ever sweetly sing!
—*William Allingham*

Pluck not the wayside flower;
It is the traveler's dower.
—*William Allingham*

The oaks and the pines, and their brethren of the wood, have seen so many suns rise and set, so many seasons come and go, and so many generations pass into silence, that we may well wonder what "the story of the trees" would be to us if they had tongues to tell it, or we ears fine enough to understand.
—*Anon.*

Loud through the air resounds the woodman's stroke,
When, lo! a voice breaks from the groaning oak,
"Spare, spare my life! a trembling virgin spare!
Oh, listen to the Hamadryad's prayer!
No longer let that fearful axe resound;
Preserve the tree to which my life is bound.
See, from the bark my blood in torrents flows;
I faint, I sink, I perish from your blows."
—*Apollonius Rhodius*

Blossom of the almond trees,
April's gift to April's bees,
Birthday ornament of spring.
—*Edwin Arnold*

Oft thou hast given them store
Of flowers—the frail-leaf'd, white anemone—
Dark bluebells drench'd with dews of summer eves—
And purple orchises with spotted leaves.
—*Matthew Arnold*

To the great tree-loving fraternity we belong. We love trees with universal and unfeigned love, and all things that do grow under them or around them—the whole leaf and root tribe. Not alone when they are in their glory, but in whatever state they are—in leaf, or rimed with frost, or powdered with snow, or crystal-sheathed in ice, or in severe outline stripped and bare against a November sky—we love them.
—*Henry Ward Beecher*

Flowers are the sweetest things that God ever made and forgot to put a soul into.
—*Henry Ward Beecher*

Daffodil and eglantine,
And woodbine,
Lily, violet, and rose
Plentiful in April fair,
To the air,
Their pretty petals do unclose.
—*Remy Belleau*

Earth's tall sons, the cedar, oak, and pine,
Their parent's undecaying strength declare.
—*Sir Richard Blackmore*

Gay little Dandelion
Lights up the meads,
Swings on her slender foot,
Telleth her beads.
—*Helen Barron Bostwick*

In the wide and rocky pasture where the cedar trees are gray,
The briar rose was growing with the blueberry and bay.
—*Anne Hempstead Branch*

Such a starved bank of moss
Till, that May-morn,
Blue ran the flash across:
Violets were born!
—*Robert Browning*

The groves were God's first temples.
—*William Cullen Bryant*

This mighty oak—
By whose immovable stem I stand and seem
Almost annihilated—not a prince
In all that proud old world beyond the deep
E'er wore his crown as loftily as he
Wears the green coronal of leaves with which
Thy hand has graced him.
—*William Cullen Bryant*

When beechen buds begin to swell,
And woods the blue-bird's warble know,
The yellow violet's modest bell
Peeps from the last year's leaves below.
—*William Cullen Bryant*

Come, let us plant the apple-tree.
Cleave the tough greensward with the spade;
Wide let its hollow bed be made;
There gently lay the roots, and there
Sift the dark mould with kindly care.
—*William Cullen Bryant*

Thou didst look down
Upon the naked earth, and, forthwith, rose
All these fair ranks of trees.
—*William Cullen Bryant*

What does he plant who plants a tree?
He plants the friend of sun and sky.
. . . .
A nation's growth from sea to sea
Stirs in his heart who plants a tree.
—*Henry Cuyler Bunner*

How friendly the pine-tree is to man—so docile and available as timber and so warm and protective as shelter. Its balsam is salve to his wounds, its fragrance is long life to his nostrils; an abiding, perennial tree, tempering the climate, cool as murmuring waters in summer and like a wrapping of fur in winter.
—*John Burroughs*

The pine is the tree of silence. Who was the Goddess of Silence? Look for her altars amid the pines—silence above, silence below.
—*John Burroughs*

Daisies and buttercups, lo, they surpass
Coined gold of kings.
—*Richard Burton*

There is pleasure in the pathless woods.
—*Lord Byron*

Weary travelers, journeying west,
In the shade of the trees find pleasant rest;
And often they start, with glad surprise,
At the rosy fruit that round them lies.
—*Lydia Maria Child*

For me the jasmine buds unfold
And silver daisies star the lea,
The crocus hoards the sunset gold,
And the wild rose breathes for me.
—*Florence Earle Coates*

We are the Trees.
Our dark and leafy glade
Bands the bright earth with softer mysteries.
Beneath us changed and tamed the seasons run;
In burning zones, we build against the sun
Long centuries of shade.
—*Mary Colborne-Veel*

There's something in a noble tree—
What shall I say? a soul?
For 'tis not form, or aught we see
In leaf or branch or bole.
Some presence, though not understood,
Dwells there alway, and seems
To be acquainted with our mood,
And mingles in our dreams.
—*Samuel Valentine Cole*

And here were forests ancient as the hills,
Enfolding sunny spots of greenery.
—*Samuel Taylor Coleridge*

Young meadows hasting their green laps to fill
With golden dandelion and daffodil:
These are fit sights for spring.
—*Clarence Chatham Cook*

Oh, the green things growing, the green things growing,
The faint sweet smell of the green things growing!
I should like to live, whether I smile or grieve,
Just to watch the happy life of my green things growing.
—*Dinah Maria Mulock Craik*

God wrote His lovliest poem on the day
He made the first tall silver poplar tree.
—*Grace Noll Crowell*

A tree which has lost its head will never recover it again, and will survive only as a monument of the ignorance and folly of its Tormentor. —*George William Curtis*

Buttercup's lanterns are lighted about me,
Burly red clover's warm cheek presses mine. —*Margaret Deland*

Then came the cowslip,
Like a dancer in the fair,
She spread her little mat of green,
And on it danced she.
—*Sydney Dobell*

There is no blue like the blue cup
The tall delphinium holds up.
—*Louise Driscoll*

The monarch oak, the patriarch of the trees,
Shoots slowly up, and spreads by slow degrees;
Three centuries he grows, and three he stays
Supreme in state, and in three more decays.
—*John Dryden*

Behold the trees unnumber'd rise,
Beautiful, in various dyes;
The gloomy pine, the poplar blue,
The yellow beech, the sombre yew,
The slender fir that taper grows,
The sturdy oak with broad-spread boughs.
—*John Dyer*

Across the homestead to the rookery elms,
Whose tall old trunks had each a grassy mound,
So rich for us, we counted them as realms
With varied products: here were earth-nuts found,
And here the Lady-fingers in deep shade.
—*George Eliot*

I see my trees repair their boughs.
—*Ralph Waldo Emerson*

For pleasant shade of branches high:
For fragrant air and cooling breeze:
For beauty of the blooming trees,
Father in Heaven, we thank Thee!
—*Ralph Waldo Emerson*

Beneath my feet
The ground-pine curled its pretty wreath,
Running over the club-moss burrs:
I inhaled the violet's breath;
Around me stood the oaks and firs.
—*Ralph Waldo Emerson*

The apple bough of white
That at my open window rocks and sways,
Against the pane its dewy blossom lays.
—*Gustav Falke*

It is difficult to realize how great a part of all that is cheerful and delightful in the recollections of our own life is associated with trees. —*Wilson Flagg*

Upon the gray old forest's rim
I snuffed the crab-tree's sweet perfume;
And farther, where the light was dim,
I saw the bloom
Of May-apples, beneath the tent
Of umbrel leaves above them bent.
—*William Davis Gallagher*

Dark grow the pine-woods, dark and drear—
The woods that bring the sunset near.
—*Richard Watson Gilder*

If I knew I should die tomorrow, I would plant a tree today. —*Stephen Girard*

The hawthorne bush, with seats beneath the shade,
For talking age and whispering lovers made.
—*Oliver Goldsmith*

Bronzed and moulded by wind and sun,
Maddening, gladdening every one
With a gypsy beauty full and fine,—
A health to the crimson columbine!
—*Elaine Goodale*

How tender and how slow, in sunset's cheer,
Far on the hill, our quiet treetops fade!
A broidery of northern seaweed, laid
Long in a book, were scarce more fine and clear.
—*Louise Imogen Guiney*

A pine-tree standeth lonely
In the North on an upland bare:
It standeth whitely shrouded
With snow, and sleepeth there.
—*Heinrich Heine*

Each violet peeps from its dwelling
To gaze at the bright stars above.
—*Heinrich Heine*

I come, I come! ye have called me long—
I come o'er the mountains with light and song!
Ye may trace my step o'er the wakening earth,
By the winds which tell of the violet's birth,
By the primrose stars in the shadowy grass,
By the green leaves opening as I pass.
—*Felicia Hemans*

Lo, all about me—violets!
—*Ella Higginson*

Softer than silence, stiller than still air
Float down from high pine-boughs the slender leaves.
—*Thomas Wentworth Higginson*

A forest murderously ruined by the lumberman's axe is like a field of battle when the fighting is over—a sight to make humanity weep.
—*Frank A. Hill*

It is easy to say, "It is only a poplar," and so much harder to replace its living cone than to build a granite obelisk!
—*Oliver Wendell Holmes*

What are these maples and beeches and birches but odes and idyls and madrigals? What are these pines and firs and spruces but holy hymns, too solemn for the many-hued raiment of their gay deciduous neighbors?
—*Oliver Wendell Holmes*

When we plant a tree, we are doing what we can to make our planet a more wholesome and happier dwelling-place for those who come after us, if not for ourselves. As you drop the seed, as you plant the sapling, your left hand hardly knows what your right hand is doing. But Nature knows, and in due time the Power that sees and works in secret will reward you openly.
—*Oliver Wendell Holmes*

It is something to make two blades of grass grow where only one was growing, it is much more to have been the occasion of the planting of an oak which shall defy twenty scores of winters, or of an elm which shall canopy with its green cloud of foliage half as many generations of mortal immortalities.
—*Oliver Wendell Holmes*

Glad earth perceives, and from her bosom pours
Unbidden herbs and voluntary flowers:
Thick, new-born violets a soft carpet spread,
And clust'ring lotus swelled the rising bed;
And sudden hyacinths the earth bestrow,
And flamy crocus made the mountain glow.
—*Homer*

I remember, I remember
The roses, red and white,
The violets, and the lily-cups—
Those flowers made of light!
The lilacs where the robin built,
And where my brother set
The laburnum on his birthday,—
The tree is living yet!
—*Thomas Hood*

There are rich counsels in the trees.
—*Herbert P. Horne*

Loveliest of trees, the cherry now
Is hung with bloom along the bough.
—*Alfred Edward Housman*

The black haw is in flower again,
The red bud's rosy tide
Splashes the wood and stains the shade
Where dog-tooth violets hide.
—*Margaret Belle Houston*

Rose and white, the apple blossom
Hides you from the sultry sky—
Let it flutter, blown and scatter'd,
On the meadows by-and-by!
—*Henrik Ibsen*

In vestments green the pines about me gleamed
Like priests that tend the sacrificial fire.
—*John Hall Ingham*

I found a yellow flower in the grass,
A tiny flower with petals like a bell,
And yet, methought, more than a flower it was,—
More like a miracle.
—*John Hall Ingham*

He who plants an oak looks forward to future ages, and plants for posterity. Nothing can be less selfish than this. He cannot expect to sit in its shade nor enjoy its shelter; but he exults in the idea that the acorn which he has buried in the earth shall grow up into a lofty pile, and shall keep on flourishing and increasing, and benefiting mankind long after he shall have ceased to tread his paternal fields. —*Washington Irving*

There is something nobly simple and pure in a taste for the cultivation of forest trees. It argues, I think, a sweet and generous nature, to have this strong relish for the beauties of vegetation, and this friendship for the hardy and glorious sons of the forest.
—*Washington Irving*

The poppies, lithe and fleet
Seem running, fiery torchmen, to and fro
To mark the shore.
—*Helen Hunt Jackson*

I know the lands are lit
With all the autumn blaze of Golden Rod;
And everywhere the Purple Asters nod
And bend and wave and flit.
—*Helen Hunt Jackson*

By day or by night, summer or winter, beneath trees the heart feels nearer to that depth of life which the far sky means.
—*John Richard Jefferies*

Open afresh your round of starry folds,
Ye ardent marigolds!
—*John Keats*

Through brakes of the cedar and sycamore bowers
Struggles the light that is love to the flowers.
—*Henry C. Kendall*

I think that I shall never see
A poem lovely as a tree.
. . . .
Poems are made by fools like me,
But only God can make a tree.
—*Joyce Kilmer*

Glooms of the live-oaks, beautiful-braided and woven
With intricate shades of the vines that myriad-cloven
Clamber the forks of the multiform boughs.
—*Sidney Lanier*

Heaven and earth help him who plants a tree
And his work his own reward shall be.
—*Lucy Larcom*

He who plants a tree
Plants a hope.
—*Lucy Larcom*

Every tree gives answer to some different mood:
This one helps you, climbing; that for rest is good:
Beckoning friends, companions, sentinels, they are;
Good to live and die with, good to greet afar.
—*Lucy Larcom*

Spring came with tiny lances thrusting,
And earth was clad in peeping green;
In russet bark, the twigs incrusting,
Tenderest blossom-points were seen.
—*Wilbur Larremore*

Happy is the man who loves the woods and waters,
Brother to the grass, and well-beloved of Pan.
—*Richard Le Gallienne*

This is the forest primeval. The murmuring pines and the hemlocks,
Bearded with moss, and in garments green, indistinct in the twilight,
Stand like Druids of eld, with voices sad and prophetic,
Stand like harpers hoar, with beards that rest on their bosoms.

—*Longfellow*

I hear the wind among the trees
Playing celestial symphonies;
I see the branches downward bent,
Like keys of some great instrument.

—*Longfellow*

The cowslip startles in meadows green,
The buttercup catches the sun in its chalice,
And there's never a leaf or a blade too mean
To be some happy creature's palace.

—*James Russell Lowell*

The maple-swamps glow like a sunset sea,
Each leaf a ripple with its separate flush.

—*James Russell Lowell*

I care not how men trace their ancestry,
To ape or Adam; let them please their whim;
But I in June am midway to believe
A tree among my far progenitors,
Such sympathy is mine with all the race,
Such mutual recognition vaguely sweet
There is between us.

—*James Russell Lowell*

I willingly confess to so great a partiality for trees as tempts me to respect a man in exact proportion to his respect for them.

—*James Russell Lowell*

The reckless and wanton destruction of forests has ruined some of the richest countries on earth. —*Sir John Lubbock*

Hath not the oak stored up the song of bird,
Whisper of wind and rain-lisp?

—*Charles Henry Luders*

There is no unbelief.
Whoever plants a seed beneath the sod
And waits to see it push away the clod,
Trusts in God.

—*Bulwer-Lytton*

Can we conceive what humanity would be if it did not know the flowers?

—*Maurice Maeterlinck*

The green of May is edging all the boughs,
The shy arbutus glimmers in the wood.

—*Edwin Markham*

How could such sweet and wholesome hours
Be reckoned but with herbs and flowers?

—*Andrew Marvell*

Now the bright crocus flames, and now
The slim narcissus takes the rain,
And, straying o'er the mountain's brow,
The daffodillies bud again.

—*Meleager*

The flow'ry May, who from her green lap throws
The yellow cowslip, and the pale primrose.

—*John Milton*

Cedar, and pine, and fir, and branching palm,
A sylvan scene! and as the ranks ascend,
Shade above shade, a woody theatre
Of stateliest view.

—*John Milton*

Bring the rathe primrose that forsaken dies,
The tufted crow-toe, and pale jessamine,
The white pink, and the pansy freaked with jet,
The glowing violet,
The musk-rose, and the well-attired woodbine,
With cowslips wan that hang the pensive head,
And every flower that sad embroidery wears.

—*John Milton*

The asters cast
Their purple coronets, and below
The brown ferns shiver in the blast.

—*S. Weir Mitchell*

There is nevertheless, a certain respect and a general duty of humanity that ties us, not only to beasts that have life and sense, but even to trees and plants.

—*Michael de Montaigne*

Woodman, spare that tree!
Touch not a single bough!
In youth it sheltered me,
And I'll protect it now.

—*George P. Morris*

Plant thou a tree whose griefless leaves shall sing
Thy deed and thee, each fresh, unfolding spring.

From Memorial Tablet,
Mt. Rubidoux, California

During a man's life only saplings can be grown, in the place of the old trees—tens of centuries old—that have been destroyed. It took more than three thousand years to make some of the trees in these Western woods—trees that are still standing in perfect strength and beauty, waving and singing in the mighty forests of the Sierra. Through all the wonderful, eventful centuries since Christ's time—and long before that—God has cared for these trees, saved them from drought, disease, avalanches and a thousand straining, leveling tempests and floods; but He cannot save them from fools—only Uncle Sam can do that.

—*John Muir*

I know, I know, where violets blow
Upon a sweet hillside,
And very bashfully they grow
And in the grasses hide.
—Robert Louis Munger

Trees that erst were gray to view
Now their verdant robes renew;
In their shade
Nests are made;
Thence the toll of May is paid.
—Sir Neidhart von Reuental

The still, bright forests, massed and green
Like painted woodlands glow
In shade and shine; and belts of pine
Climb up to meet the snow.
—Isabel Maud Peacocke

A tree is a nobler object than a prince in his coronation robes. *Alexander Pope*

The pine wishes herself a shrub
When the axe is at her root.
—Proverb

Willows are weak, yet they bind other wood.
—Proverb

Never a daisy that grows, but a mystery guideth the growing. *—Richard Realf*

Along the pastoral ways I go,
To get the healing of the trees.
—Lizette Woodworth Reese

For when the Maker set its crown of beauty,
And for its home ordained the torrid ring,
Assigning unto each its place and duty,
He made the Palm a King.
—Tracy Robinson

These little firs today are things
To clasp into a giant's cap,
Or fans to suit his lady's lap.
—Dante G. Rossetti

Long, sparkling aisles of steel-stemmed trees
Bending to counterfeit a breeze.
—James R. Russell

God His manual sign hath set
In the tender violet.
—Margaret E. Sangster

It is said that the Aztecs always planted a tree when an infant came into the world, and gave it the child's own name. And the old Mexican Indians plant trees on certain days of the year, under the full moon, naming them after their children.
—Robert Haven Schauffler

To heal mine aching moods,
Give me God's virgin woods.
—Clinton Scollard

'Tis merry in greenwood, thus runs the old lay,
In the gladsome month of lively May,
When the wild bird's song on stem and spray
Invites to forest bower:
Then rears the ash his airy crest,
Then shines the birch in silver vest,
And the beech in glistening leaves is drest,
And dark between shows the oak's proud breast,
Like a chieftain's frowning tower.
—Sir Walter Scott

I know a bank whereon the wild thyme blows,
Where oxlips, and the nodding violet grows;
Quite over-canopied with lush woodbine,
With sweet musk-roses, and with eglantine.
—William Shakespeare

Here's flowers for you;
Hot lavender, mints, savory, majoram;
The marigold, that goes to bed with the sun,
And with him rises weeping.
—William Shakespeare

Oh, Rosalind, these trees shall be my books,
And in their barks my thoughts I'll character,
That every eye which in this forest looks,
Shall see thy virtue witnessed everywhere.
—William Shakespeare

Awake! arise! and come away!
To the wild woods and the plains,
To the pools where winter rains
Image all their roof of leaves,
Where the pine its garland weaves
Of sapless green, and ivy dun,
Round stems that never kiss the sun.
—Percy Bysshe Shelley

If you are a notable, and wish to be remembered, better plant a tree than build a city or strike a medal—it will outlast both.
—Alexander Smith

All sorts of flowers the which on earth do spring,
In goodly colors gloriously arrayed.
—Edmund Spenser

The violet, pallid blue,
The little daisy, that at evening closes,
The virgin lily, and the primrose true.
—Edmund Spenser

The trees are God's great alphabet:
With them He writes in shining green
Across the world His thoughts serene.
—Leonora Speyer

Along our path the woods are bold,
And glow with ripe desire;
The yellow chestnut showers its gold,
The sumachs spread their fire.
—Edmund Clarence Stedman

O, my proud palms! my royal palms that stood
In stately groups, a queenly sisterhood!
—Charles Warren Stoddard

ARMISTICE DAY

Splendid it was that you were willing to die for us—how much more desirable had you been permitted to live for us.
—Cyrus Adler

At 11 o'clock on the morning of November 11, 1918, an entire world, weary, worn and bent under the disaster of the World War, knelt in thanks to God. The guns ceased booming. A new note was in the air. A new hope was in every heart, a hope and a prayer that the fighting of nation against nation, of people against people, had ended for all time. We want to go back in spirit to that grand moment. We want to recall the purpose common to everyone at that moment to do each his or her share to make impossible, ever again, such a disaster.
To the American Legion from its Commander, 1921

O silent host of soldier dead, of
wistful shadow men,
Our pledge, to ease the watch you
tread: *"It shall not be again!"*
—S. Omar Barker

We told that boy when he marched away that he was fighting a war to end all wars. He fell, believing. *—Bruce Barton*

The unshaken soul they sought, possessed in
peace.
What seek we now, and hazard all on the
aim? *—Laurence Binyon*

Have we died in vain, in vain? Is our dream
denied?
You men who live on the earth we bought
with our woe,
Will ye stand idly by while they shape new
wars?
Or will ye rise, who are strong, to fulfill our
dream,
To silence the demagogue's voice, to crush
the fools
Who play with the blood-stained toys that
crowd new graves? *—William E. Brooks*

They have signed the Armistice
in the Forest of Compiègne—
The task is just beginning. . . .
—Dana Burnet

O lithe young limbs and radiant,
grave young eyes,
Now have you taught us beauty
cannot fade.
—Maxwell Struthers Burt

Be not afraid, O Dead, be not afraid:
We have not lost the dreams that once were
flung
Like pennons to the world.
—Maxwell Struthers Burt

Three hundred cannon threw up their emetic,
And thirty thousand muskets flung their pills
Like hail, to make a bloody diuretic;
Mortality! thou hast thy monthly bills!
—Lord Byron

We pledge them that . . . we shall yet build anew a temple of human civilization, a temple of peace, of brotherhood and of justice for all nations of the earth. Of that temple thy marble shall be the cornerstone, the memory of thee shall fill it with a glory of sacrificial radiance, and from its pulpit thy silent spirit shall so speak to unborn generations with the accents of compelling eloquence, that this day shall no longer be spoken in terms of war as armistice day, but as peace day, the beginning of an enduring peace and amity among the children of men.
—Rabbi Edward N. Calisch

"Armistice" is a sinister word. Is that all we have—an armed truce? Our country hoped to help the world to a better condition than that. And she can yet do this—and do it best by resolutely being herself. Imitating the desperate make-shifts of crumbling systems but weakens her power to help mankind. . . Nothing can be good for America, nothing can enlarge her helpfulness, that is bought at the price of her moral identity.
—W. J. Cameron

No more may his wished sight return.
His golden lamp no more can burn,
Quenched is all his flame,
His hoped fame
Now hath left him nought but name.
—Thomas Campion

Above them, as they slumber in graves that
none may number
Dawns grow to day, days dim to dusk, and
dusks in darkness pass.
—Guy Wetmore Carryl

Of all their grim campaigning no sight or
sound remaining,
The memory of them mutely to greater
glory grows. *—Guy Wetmore Carryl*

And with them went our yesterdays,
The bitter need, the words unsaid:
Back to the rim beyond the night,
One with the unforgotten dead.
—Eleanor Alletta Chaffee

Armistice Day! with the war behind,
But how is it ended for one made blind?
—Edmund Vance Cooke

Armistice Day! with its petty pride!
And the wars are ended—for those who died!
—Edmund Vance Cooke

Rest on, O heroes! in your silent slumber!
Hail and farewell, ye mighty, moveless dead!
—Rose Terry Cooke

Toll for the brave!
The brave that are no more!
—William Cowper

We treasure them in memory:
Our country's sacrifice.
—Norman H. Crowell

When we have bled at every pore,
Shall we still strive for gear and store?
—Austin Dobson

Make this thing plain to us, O Lord!
That not the triumph of the sword—
Not that alone—can end the strife,
But reformation of the life—
But full submission to Thy Word!
—Austin Dobson

"Behold all Europe writhing on the rack,
The sins of fathers grinding down the sons,
How long, O Lord!" He sends no answer back,
But still I hear the mutter of the guns.
—Arthur Conan Doyle

They battled, they endured, they died
To make a new Apocalypse.
—John Drinkwater

Faith with the Dead kept through our living faith;
In this alone the true remembrance lies.
—Basil Ebers

Alone with God, where no wind blows,
And Death, his shadow—doom'd, he goes.
That God is there the shadow shows.
—Ebenezer Elliott

Spirit that made those heroes dare
To die, and leave their children free,
Bid Time and Nature gently spare
The shaft we raise to them and thee.
—Emerson

I gave my life for freedom—This I know;
For those who bade me fight had told me so.
—W. N. Ewer

Far they lie, forever dumb,
Those brave young lives for noble years so meet;
Lost to the Future, never more to greet
The morns with gladness.
—W. P. F. Ferguson

To the young dead we consecrate
These lives that now we dedicate.
—Annie Fields

To drum-beat and heart-beat
A soldier marches by;
There is color in his cheek,
There is courage in his eye.
—Francis Miles Finch

Armistice Day, the 11th of November, should be made sacred throughout the entire civilized world. It is the day when we think of the noble sacrifice made by the hero dead, of the brilliant records of duty performed left on the field of battle by those wounded, of the spirit of patriotism and bravery shown by those who, fortunately, escaped shot and shell. *—Ferdinand Foch*

Arouse in the whole body of the people an adventurous willingness, as they sacrificed greatly for war, so, also, for international good-will, to dare bravely, think wisely, decide resolutely and to achieve triumphantly.
—Harry Emerson Fosdick

Leave not the hereafter
Of mankind to war, as though I had not died.
—John Galsworthy

For the youth they gave and the blood they gave,
We must render back the due.
—Theodosia Garrison

All glory we would give them, pales beside
The eternal splendor of those men, who thought
But of the sacred cause for which they fought.
—Charles Buxton Going

Their vision was a world secure and just
Won by their victory—their only task
To crush one hideous foe; and in that trust
They sped with eager feet, and paid the price
Unstinting, of the last great sacrifice.
—Charles Buxton Going

Here rests his head upon the lap of Earth
A Youth, to Fortune and to Fame unknown.
—Thomas Gray

In love, in grief, in pride, we yield our sons.
—Hermann Hagedorn

There where the oaks loom, dark and high,
Over the sombre hill,
Body on body, cold and still,
Under the stars they lie.
—Hermann Hagedorn

But to the hero, when his sword
Has won the battle for the free,
Thy voice sounds like a prophet's word;
And in its hollow tones are heard
The thanks of millions yet to be.
—Fitz-Greene Halleck

For thou art freedom's now, and fame's—
One of the few, the immortal names,
That were not born to die.
—Fitz-Greene Halleck

Our part is to atone for the losses of the heroic dead by making a better republic for the living. *—Warren Gamaliel Harding*

Too young, too many far, they seemed,
To be so soon, so grimly, dead.
—John Helston

Youth and beauty, dauntless will,
Dreams that life could ne'er fulfil.
Here lie buried,—here in peace
Wrongs and woes have found release.
—*Thomas Wentworth Higginson*

Hallow the urn that is nameless,
Reverence the fallen head,
The memory, speechless and blameless,
The graves of the Unknown Dead!
—*Thomas Wentworth Higginson*

"SOMEWHERE in France"—we know not where—he lies,
Mid shuddering earth and under anguished skies!
—*John Hogben*

Green be the graves where her martyrs are lying!
Shroudless and tombless they sunk to their rest.
—*Oliver Wendell Holmes*

Proud stands his country, bared and bowed of head,
While safe he sleeps among the deathless dead.
—*M. A. DeWolfe Howe*

And they have thrust our shattered dead away in foreign graves,
Exiled forever from the port the homesick sailor craves!
—*Rupert Hughes*

Proudly you gathered, rank on rank to war,
As who had heard God's message from afar;
All you had hoped for, all you had, you gave
To save mankind—yourselves you scorned to save.
—*Hymn sung at the Tomb of the Unknown Soldier*

We beseech Thee, Lord of Compassion, shelter them forevermore under the cover of Thy wings, and let their souls be bound up in the bond of eternal life, with the souls of Righteousness who are ever with Thee.
—*Jewish Welfare Board*

Comrades true, born anew, peace to you!
Your souls shall be where the heroes are
And your memory shine like the morning-star.
—*Joyce Kilmer*

They will touch the hearts of the living with a flame that sanctifies,
A flame that they took with strong young hands from the altar-fires of God.
—*Joyce Kilmer*

Lord God of Hosts, be with us yet
Lest we forget! Lest we forget!
—*Rudyard Kipling*

The battle's rage was o'er,
And many a one came home no more.
—*Detlev von Liliencron*

Fear not that ye have died for naught,
The torch ye threw to us we caught.
—*R. W. Lillard*

The legion of the living, who came back to us from the flaming front, will bind us forever to the voiceless slopes of Verdun, to the inarticulate hum of the Argonne, to the murmuring meadows of the Marne.
—*Martin Wilie Littleton*

Is true Freedom but to break
Fetters for our own dear sake,
And, with leathern hearts, forget
That we owe mankind a debt?
No! true Freedom is to share
All the chains our brothers wear,
And, with heart and hand, to be
Earnest to make others free!
—*James Russell Lowell*

Armistice Day . . . . . is to remind us of the supreme need of justice in the relations of men and nations, and of the duty that still belongs to us—not less than it belongs to others—to give our best thought and effort to the establishment of peace upon true foundations.
—*Alma Lundman*

If ye break faith with us who die
We shall not sleep, though poppies grow
In Flanders fields.
—*John McCrae*

How shall we honor them, our Deathless Dead?
How keep their mighty memories alive?
In him who feels their passion, they survive!
Flatter their souls with deed, and all is said!
—*Edwin Markham*

They went like Kings in a pageant to the imminent death.
—*John Masefield*

They have given their lives, with bodies bruised and broken,
Upon their Country's altar they have bled.
—*J. Corson Miller*

They fought for peace, for peace they fell.
—*Joaquin Miller*

He sleeps at last—a hero of his race.
Dead! —and the night lies softly in his face,
While the faint summer stars, like sentinels,
Hover above his lonely resting-place.
—*George Edgar Montgomery*

A soldier, yet less soldier than a man,
Who gave to justice what a soldier can.
—*George Edgar Montgomery*

Wreathe pride now for his granite brow, lay love on his breast of stone.
—*William Vaughn Moody*

How shall we rank thee upon glory's page?
—*Thomas Moore*

And the dead men plead their cause,
And the crippled men implore:
"Go, fashion the Future's laws
That war shall be no more."
—*Angela Morgan*

Toll the bells; greet the Unnamed, the Unknown!
Hushed be each murmur of mirth!
Bend in prayer, you, the forgetful of earth!
—*Louis I. Newman*

What we suggest for the fitting theme of this day of commemoration is the long, slow and endless task of strengthening justice and right in the world.
New York Herald Tribune, November 11, 1926

After battle sleep is best,
After noise, tranquility.
—*Roden Berkeley Wriothesley Noel*

On fame's eternal camping ground
Their silent tents are spread,
And Glory guards with solemn round
The bivouac of the dead.
—*Theodore O'Hara*

Pause for a moment, forgetting the day's occupation,
Offer a prayer—a tear.
—*Vilda Sauvage Owens*

He is the youth of America, taken untimely;
Symbol of countless thousands who perished young;
Sinew and bone of a Nation, crusht in the making;
The poet, his song half sung.
—*Vilda Sauvage Owens*

Peace. Shake out the folds of the flag and tell over the story of the Armistice. Count the stars of gold and the crosses in Flanders. Teach that the glory of war is a lie and that Peace has come out of Gethsemane, purchased with price and with crosses.
—*Angelo Patri*

We pay silent and grateful tribute to-day to those gallant sons of America who have given their lives that the great principles of liberty and justice might endure.
—*General Pershing*

Spare of your flowers to deck the stranger's grave,
Who died for a lost cause:—
A soul more daring, resolute, and brave,
Ne'er won a world's applause.
—*Henry Peterson*

For their spirits are the glory of the dayspring overhead,
And their bugles blow Reveillé at the golden gates of morn.
—*Eden Phillpotts*

Bid us remember in what hours they gave
All that mankind may give
That we might live.
—*Majorie L. C. Pickthall*

He sleeps alone;—the mountain cloud
That night hangs round him, and the breath
Of morning scatters, is the shroud
That wraps his martial form in death.
—*John Pierpont*

Not hate, but glory, made these chiefs contend;
And each brave foe was in his soul a friend.
—*Alexander Pope*

No name to bid us know
Who rests below,
No word of death or birth,
Only the grass's wave,
Over a mound of earth,
Over a nameless grave.
—*Adelaide A. Procter*

Are the gleaming snows and the poppies red
All that is left of the brave of yore?
—*Edna Dean Proctor*

The wind today is full of ghosts with ghostly bugles blowing
Where shadows steal across the world, as silent as the dew,
Where golden youth is yellow dust, by haunted rivers flowing,
Through valleys where the crosses grow, as harvest wheat is growing,
And only dead men see the line that passes in review.
—*Grantland Rice*

Let me kneel
And pay my tribute to the myriad dead,
Who counted not the blood that they have shed
Against the goal their valor shall reveal.
—*Corinne Roosevelt Robinson*

Their greatest greatness is unknown—
Earth knows a little—God, the rest.
—*Abram Joseph Ryan*

Youthful and buoyant and blithe they went into battle,
Fresh as Olympian athletes strung for the prize:
Aged and broken and done they dragged from the victory,
All with that look, that terrible look in their eyes.
—*Robert Haven Schauffler*

Let not a whisper fall
That we have died in vain!
—*Clinton Scollard*

And so, while the dead are laurelled, the brave of the elder years,
A song, we say, for the men of to-day who have proved themselves their peers.
—Clinton Scollard

Master of Life, we thank Thee
That they were what they were.
—Duncan Campbell Scott

A weary road these men have trod;
O house them in the home of God!
—Frederick George Scott

Soldier, rest! thy warfare o'er,
Sleep the sleep that knows not breaking;
Dream of battled fields no more,
Days of danger, nights of waking.
—Sir Walter Scott

Here pause: these graves are all too young as yet
To have outgrown the sorrow which consigned
Its change to each.
—Percy Bysshe Shelley

Have we kept faith with those who made
For us their rendezvous with death?
—James T. Shotwell

By recalling the high hopes of those who poured out the rich wine of their youth upon the high altars we may become the more keenly aware of the great work still left undone. We shall be reminded that the dead are summoning us to take up the torch which their hands carried in glory and honor through the great tribulations of war; that they are demanding of us to safeguard the spiritual legacies which they have bequeathed unto us, and to make real that for which they gave all that life held dear.
—Abba Hillel Silver

(Round them sea and barren land, over them the sky,
Oh, we're leaving them, leaving them, quiet where they lie!) *—C. Fox Smith*

But, Almighty God, futile will have been our observance of this sacred day, of no avail will have been all the sufferings of our martyrs if there be not born in us the conviction that wars must no longer afflict mankind—wars with all their terrors—wars in which the hand of one man is turned against his brother! *—Rabbi Hyman Solomon*

The history of a soldier's wound beguiles the pain of it. *—Laurence Sterne*

Over their graves rang once the bugle's call,
The searching schrapnel and the crashing ball;
The shriek, the shock of battle.
—Henry Jerome Stockard

For thee, O now a silent soul, my brother,
Take at my hands this garland, and farewell.
—Algernon Charles Swinburne

Content thee, howe'er, whose days are done;
There lies not any troublous thing before,
Nor sight nor sound to war against thee more,
For whom all winds are quiet as the sun,
All waters as the shore.
—Algernon Charles Swinburne

Earth, that all too soon hath bound him,
Gently wrap his clay!
Linger lovingly around him,
Light of dying day!
Softly fall, ye summer showers;
Birds and bees among the flowers
Make the gloom seem gay.
—John Randolph Thompson

Hosts of the martyred dead!
In dreams I see them pass—
Pale, wistful shadows.
—Edythe C. Toner

They dared to die, let us who live
Dare to have pity and forgive.
—Lucia Trent

Old griefs that once I knew can cause no pain
Since I remember
The tramp of feet that came not home again
In November.
—Sophie Tunnell

That day the guns fell silent at a word,
And instant bells awoke, and every hill
Rang high with song, till heaven itself was stirred:
Only the dead lay still,
The weary dead.
—Nancy Byrd Turner

They will attain, even through war on wars,
What they had lost in peace.
—Louis Untermeyer

They bore our country's great word across the rolling sea,
"America swears brotherhood with all the just and free."
They wrote that word victorious on fields of mortal strife,
And many a valiant lad was proud to seal it with his life. *—Henry van Dyke*

Our youth has stormed the hosts of hell and won;
Yet we who pay the price of their oblation
Know that the greater war is just begun
Which makes humanity the nations' Nation.
—Willard Wattles

And always we shall walk with the young dead. *—Edith Wharton*

Ah send anew
The spirit that once flamed so high and bright,
When, by your graves, we bade you brave adieu. *—Curtis Wheeler*

Immortal youth shall crown their deathless fame. *—Seymour W. Whiting*

"Put up the sword!" The voice of Christ once more
Speaks, in the pauses of the cannon's roar,
O'er fields of corn by fiery sickles reaped
And left dry ashes; over trenches heaped
With nameless dead; o'er cities starving slow
Under a rain of fire; through wards of woe
Down which a groaning diapason runs
From tortured brothers, husbands, lovers, sons
Of desolate women in their far-off homes,
Waiting to hear the step that never comes!
O men and brothers! let that voice be heard.
War fails, try peace; put up the useless sword!

—*Whittier*

Of man for man the sacrifice,
All that was theirs to give, they gave.

—*Whittier*

The present and all that it holds belongs to the nations and the peoples who preserve self-control and the orderly processes of their governments; the future to those who prove themselves the true friends of mankind. To conquer with arms is to make only a temporary conquest; to conquer the world by earning its esteem is to make permanent conquest.

—*Woodrow Wilson*

And things there be too stern and dark
To live in any outward mark;
The things that they alone can tell,
Like Dante, who have walk'd in hell.

—*E. Armine Wodehouse*

Oh, not in vain the millions bled
If we be worthy of our dead!

—*David McKee Wright*

BE KIND TO ANIMALS WEEK

As long as we tolerate the ownership and control of animals by people of known vicious propensities under conditions that are bound to result in cruelty, we are not striking at the root of cruelty to animals.
—Anti-Cruelty Society

Humane work must be lifted out of the realms of emotion and be placed, together with other modern benevolent work, upon a scientific basis. *—Anti-Cruelty Society*

Therefore fear God in whatsoe'er ye deal
With the dumb peoples of the wing and hoof.
—Edwin Arnold

And even dumb animals have fallen in love with men. *—Athenaeus*

The dashing dog, and stealthy stepping cat,
Hawk, bull, and all that breathe, . . .
Were made in love and made to be beloved.
—Philip James Bailey

I have no dog, but it must be
Somewhere there's one belongs to me—
A little chap with wagging tail,
And dark brown eyes that never quail,
But look you through, and through, and through,
With love unspeakable, but true.
—John Kendrick Bangs

The greatest attribute of heaven is mercy.
—Beaumont and Fletcher

To Mercy, Pity, Peace, and Love,
All pray in their distress,
And to these virtues of delight
Return their thankfulness.
—William Blake

He who hurts the little wren
Shall never be beloved by men.
—William Blake

A robin red breast in a cage
Puts all Heaven in a rage.
—William Blake

A horse misused upon the road
Calls to heaven for human blood.
—William Blake

Kindness to animals is not mere sentiment, but a requisite of even a very ordinary education. *—Mrs. R. Fleming Bowden*

God made all the creatures and gave them our love and our fear,
To give sign, we and they are His children, one family here.
—Robert Browning

Wee, sleekit, cow'rin, tim'rous beastie,
O what a panic's in thy breastie!
Thou need na start away sae hasty,
Wi' bickering brattle!
I wad be laith to rin and chase thee
Wi' murd'ring pattle!
—Robert Burns

Personally, I would not give a fig for any man's religion whose horse, cat and dog do not feel its benefits. Life in any form is our perpetual responsibility. Its abuse degrades those who practice it. Its rightful usage is a signal token of genuine manhood.
—S. Parkes Cadman

In a world as cursed by prejudice and hate as ours we cannot afford to relinquish any heartfelt preferences and attachments of man or beast. Still less can we afford to treat them scurvily or vilely.
—S. Parkes Cadman

Beyond domestic animals and our response to their fealty and affection, we have a peculiar charge concerning the wild animals which supply our clothes, food and adornments.
—S. Parkes Cadman

I love thee, pious ox; a gentle feeling
Of vigor and of peace thou giv'st my heart;
How solemn, like a monument, thou art!
—Giosué Carducci

I am the mule—the butt of countless jokes—
But since time was my neck has known the yokes
Of labor merciless, of crushing tasks which tell
Of human cruelty which breeds a human hell.
—Will Chamberlain

My mother, I know,
Would sorrow so,
Should I be stolen away;
So I'll speak to the birds
In my softest words,
Nor hurt them in my play.
—Lydia Maria Child

He prayeth well who loveth well
Both man and bird and beast.
—Samuel Taylor Coleridge

He prayeth best, who loveth best
All things both great and small;
For the dear God who loveth us,
He made and loveth all.
—Samuel Taylor Coleridge

Of course it is the brave who are merciful.
—Stephen Coleridge

Sport on, fair flocks, at pleasure,
Nip Vesta's flow'ring treasure;
I myself will duly hark,
When my watchful dog doth bark;
From wolf and fox I will defend ye.
—Henry Constable

We called him "Rags." He was just a cur,
But twice, on the Western Line,
That little old bunch of faithful fur
Had offered his life for mine.
—Edmund Vance Cooke

Detested sport, that owes its pleasures to another's pain. *—William Cowper*

Ye therefore who love mercy, teach your sons
To love it too.
—William Cowper

I would not enter on my list of friends
(Though graced with polished manners and fine sense,
Yet wanting sensibility) the man
Who needlessly sets foot upon a worm.
—William Cowper

Man has done much for the animals; the animal kingdom has done a thousand times more for man. Let us not forget the debt.
—Richard C. Craven

I tell ye, the song o' the fire and the chirruping hiss o' the tea,
The roar of the wind in the chimbly, they sound dreadful cheerful to me.
But they'd harrer me, plague me, and fret me, unless as I set here i knew
That the critters are munchin' their fodder and bedded and comf'table, too.
These biskits are light as a feather, but, boy, they'd be heavier 'n lead
If I thought that my hosses was shiv'rin', if I thought that my cattle warn't fed.
—Holman F. Day

I am quite sure he thinks that I am God—
Since He is God on whom each one depends
For life, and all things that His bounty sends—
My dear old dog, most constant of all friends.
—William Croswell Doane

Folk will know how large your soul is,
By the way you treat a dog!
—Charles F. Doran

"Exerce justice with mercy and conscience;
And let no small beast suffer scaith nor scorns

....

And let no bogle with his busteous horns
The meek plough-ox oppress, for all his pride,
But in the yoke go peaceable him beside."
—William Dunbar

While humane service may hold further economic value by prolonging life and improving the quality of animals, the spiritual values far supersede these material benefits.
—George H. Earle

Animals are such agreeable friends—they ask no questions, they pass no criticisms
—George Eliot

How beautiful a day can be
When kindness touches it!
—George Elliston

Hast thou named all the birds without a gun? *—Ralph Waldo Emerson*

I ain't afeard uv snakes, or toads, or bugs, or worms, or mice,
An' things 'at girls are skeered uv I think are awful nice!
—Eugene Field

The woods were made for the hunters of dreams,
The brooks for the fishers of song;
To the hunters who hunt for the gunless game
The streams and the woods belong.
—Sam Walter Foss

All earthly things I had the making of
Were numbered and were measured then by Me;
And each was ordered to its end by Love.
—Francis of Assisi, Saint

You creatures wild, of field and air,
Keep far from men, where'er they go!
—John Galsworthy

Kindness to animals is a financial asset in that it prolongs their lives, increases their fitness for service and improves the quality of their products. But the greater assets are in the spiritual values of life. Mercy uplifts the soul and purifies the life.
—A. W. S. Garden

No herds that roam the valley free
To slaughter I condemn,
Taught by that Power that pities me,
I learn to pity them.
—Oliver Goldsmith

We are all in the same boat, both animals and men. You cannot promote kindness to one without benefiting the other.
—Edward Everett Hale

"Why should throughout this land of historied rights
Mild creatures, despot-doomed, bewildered, plead
Their often hunger, thirst, pangs, prisonment,
In deep dumb gaze more eloquent
Than tongues of widest heed?"
—Thomas Hardy

Our relation to the animals is a part and parcel of our human morality, and is interwoven with it and inseparable from it. Our duties toward our lower helpmates form part of our duties toward our fellow-beings, for they in a sense are our fellow-beings. Man can only regard himself as the advance guard of a vast army of living, sentient beings and his natural function is to use, protect and improve this wondrous and complex brotherhood.

—*Frederic Harrison*

From beasts we scorn as soulless,
In forest, field and den,
The cry goes up to witness
The soullessness of men.

—*M. Frida Hartley*

I'm with animals just as I am with children. I should as soon think of hurting one as another. —*Childe Hassam*

Is there not something in the pleading eye
Of the poor brute that suffers, which arraigns
The law that bids it suffer?

—*Oliver Wendell Holmes*

Our long and difficult upward climb from savagery is measured not only by our treatment of our fellowmen but by our treatment of the "brutes of the field" who are our servants. —*Honolulu Star-Bulletin*

And in that day will I make a covenant for them with the beasts of the field, and with the fowls of heaven, and with the creeping things of the ground: and I will break the bow, and the sword, and the battle out of the earth, and will make them to lie down safely. —*Hosea 2:18*

Do you know the little woodmouse
That pretty little thing,
That sits among the forest leaves,
Or by the forest spring?

—*Mary Howitt*

Deliberate cruelty to our defenceless and beautiful little cousins is surely one of the meanest and most detestable vices of which a human being can be guilty.

—*William Ralph Inge*

I am strongly convinced that to make a pleasure of killing harmless beasts and birds is a barbarous thing, now that we know what science has taught us about our kinship with them. —*William Ralph Inge*

Darwin and his fellow-workers proved that all life in the world springs from one root, and that the lower animals are literally our distant cousins. There is nothing to be ashamed of in the relationship. But we can hardly suppose that the other animals, if they are able to think, admit our superiority. If they were capable of formulating a religion, they might differ considerably as to the shape of the beneficent Creator, but they would nearly all agree that the Devil must be very like a big white man.

—*William Ralph Inge*

The wolf also shall dwell with the lamb, and the leopard shall lie down with the kid; and the calf, and the young lion, and the fatling together; and a little child shall lead them. —*Isaiah II:6*

Religion to be adequate for life must dominate all of life. Hence it should be vitally concerned with the movement to promote kindness to animals. . . They merit the kindness and we cannot avoid the practice of it without stultifying our souls and negating our Christian principles. —*Charles W. Jeffras*

My feeling toward the animal is that he is our younger brother, and that we *are* our brother's keeper. —*Mary Johnston*

Cruelty to dumb animals is one of the distinguishing vices of the lowest and basest of the people. Wherever it is found, it is a certain mark of ignorance and meanness.

—*Jones of Nayland*

What is this life we take so wantonly?
A spark of God's great love so stamped upon
Because we have the craft and lust to kill!
What Golden Rule is made for man alone?
The beast looks in your eyes and cries you shame. —*Charles Keeler*

If indeed thy heart were right, then would every creature be to thee a mirror of life, and a book of holy doctrine.

—*Thomas à Kempis*

Buy a pup and your money will buy
Love unflinching that cannot lie.

—*Rudyard Kipling*

Perhaps, when the Hand that fashioned all shall strike, and the earth be dumb
Out of the dim and the voiceless vast—back to their own again—
Herd and band and the mated beasts, fearless and free, shall come,
Knowing naught of the ancient fear of a tribe that were named as men.

—*Henry Herbert Knibbs*

My dog! the difference between thee and me
Knows only our Creator. —*Lamartine*

And the brown thrush keeps singing, "A nest do you see
And five eggs, hid by me in the juniper-tree?
Don't meddle! Don't touch! little girl, little boy,
Or the world will lose some of its joy!
Now I'm glad! now I'm free!
And I always shall be,
If you never bring sorrow to me."

—*Lucy Larcom*

Your "sport" of hunting brings to the weaker creatures of your common earth the shadow of fear and death, where with your superior strength and wisdom you might bring joy and life instead. —*William J. Long*

Among the noblest in the land,
Though he may count himself the least,
That man I honor and revere,
Who, without favor, without fear,
In the great city dares to stand
The Friend of every friendless Beast.
—*Longfellow*

"What fair renown, what honor, what repute
Can come to you from starving this poor brute?
He who serves well and speaks not, merits more
Than they who clamor loudest at the door.
Therefore the law decrees that as this steed
Served you in youth, henceforth you shall take heed
To comfort his old age, and to provide
Shelter in stall, and food and field beside."
—*Longfellow*

Of all the beasts he learned the language,
Learned their names and all their secrets,
How the beavers built their lodges,
Where the squirrels hid their acorns,
How the reindeer ran so swiftly,
Why the rabbit was so timid,
Talked with them whene'er he met them,
Called them "Hiawatha's Brothers."
—*Longfellow*

They are slaves who fear to speak
For the helpless and the weak.
—*James Russell Lowell*

How much more interesting would every walk in the country be, if Man would but treat other animals with kindness, so that they might approach us without fear, and we might have the constant pleasure of watching their winning ways.
—*Sir John Lubbock*

Fie on us! we who hunt and kill,
Voracious, but unsated still;
Who ransack earth, and sea, and air,
And slay all creatures for our fare.
—*Charles Mackay*

Blessed are the merciful: for they shall obtain mercy. —*Matthew 5:7*

The person who has a disregard for the suffering of animals can be set down as one indifferent in a large measure to the plight of his fellow man in misfortune. Suffering is suffering and it is not easy to see where a distinction can be made which will render an individual indifferent to suffering in any quarter.
—*Minneapolis Tribune April 21, 1931*

Fear God in respect of animals: ride them when they are fit to be ridden, and get off when they are tired. —*Mohammed*

Verily there are rewards for our doing good to dumb animals. —*Mohammed*

We sufficiently discover in most of their works how much animals excel us, and how unable our art is to imitate them. . . As to fidelity, there is no animal in the world so treacherous as man. —*Montaigne*

Humaneness has a practical value as well as an ethical one.
—*Editorial. National Humane Review, May 1935*

The humane movement, in addition to benefiting children and animals, has an important psychological bearing on the proper relations of man to man.
—*National Humane Review, May, 1935*

There is something so very dreadful, so Satanic in tormenting those who have never harmed us, and who cannot defend themselves, who are utterly in our power.
—*Cardinal Newman*

And the Lord opened the mouth of the ass, and she said unto Balaam, What have I done unto thee, that thou hast smitten me these three times? —*Numbers 22:28*

Come hither, sweet Robin,
And be not afraid,
I would not hurt even a feather;
Come hither, sweet Robin,
And pick up some bread,
To feed you this very cold weather.
—*Nursery Rhyme*

And you each gentle animal
In confidence may bind,
And make them follow at your will,
If you are only kind.
—*Nursery Rhyme*

I had a little pony,
His name was Dapple-grey;
I lent him to a lady,
To ride a mile away.
She whipped him, she slashed him,
She rode him through the mire;
I would not lend my pony now
For all the lady's hire.
—*Nursery Rhyme*

A man of kindness to his beast is kind,
Brutal actions show a brutal mind,
Remember, He who gave thee speech and reason
Made the brute and formed him mute—
He can't complain, but God's omniscient eye
Beholds thy cruelty, He hears his cry,
He was destined thy servant and thy drudge,
But know this—his Creator is thy Judge.
—*Old Stanza*

Man could not be altogether cleared from injustice in dealing with beasts as he now does. —*Plutarch*

A good man will take care of his horses and dogs, not only while they are young, but when old and past service. . . Were it only to learn benevolence to human kind, we should be merciful to other creatures. For my own part, I would not sell even an old ox that had labored for me. —*Plutarch*

Just how much misery has been caused by inhumaneness can never be told since the dumb animal has no language in which to record its suffering but we do know that gentleness, mercy and kindness toward the dumb and helpless are attributes of true nobility. —*Mrs. H. Clay Preston*

Go to the ant, thou sluggard: consider her ways, and be wise. —*Proverbs 6:6*

A righteoeus man regardeth the life of his beast. —*Proverbs 12:10*

When kindness and regard are shown to "the beasts which perish," these never fail to give them back tenfold.
—*Louise De La Ramé*

If our mind exceeds the mind of animals and birds in much, theirs exceeds ours at least in some things, as their sight, scent, and hearing far surpass ours.

When we remember also that these other races are absolutely alone, are never aided by man, are only, on the contrary, hindered by him, opposed, thwarted, and persecuted by him, their achievements are, relatively to their opportunities, much more wonderful than any of his. The elements which are his great foes are likewise theirs; they have to encounter and suffer all the woes of tempest, hurricane, flood, the width of barren seas, the hunger on solitary shores; and they have also in his ruthless and unceasing spite an enemy more cruel than any with which he himself has to contend.
—*Louise De La Ramé*

We may refuse to agree with Mr. Shaw that a cockroach suffering the pangs of unrequited affection is an object pitiful enough to blight the joy of living; but we have learned to recognize emotional qualities in beasts we know, or know about. We see in them the signs and tokens of feelings that are akin to our affections and to our animosities, to our confidences and to our withdrawals. —*Agnes Repplier*

A child when cruel is morally hurt, and a moral hurt is greater than a physical one.
—*Harriet C. Reynolds*

Spare all the harmless creatures of the earth:
Spare, and be spared—or who shall plead for thee?
—*Christina G. Rossetti*

The last and least of things,
That soar on quivering wings,
Or crawl among the grass blades out of sight,
Have just as clear a right
To their appointed portion of delight
As queens or kings.
—*Christina G. Rossetti*

Nothing more rapidly refines, uplifts, exalts both mind and heart than generous, gracious, unselfish ministrations to others, whether those others be our own fellow-men or the creatures below us. —*Francis H. Rowley*

Whosoever is not actively kind, is cruel.
—*John Ruskin*

Speak gently, Spring, and make no sudden sound;
For in my windy valley yesterday I found
Newborn foxes squirming on the ground—
Speak gently.
—*Lew Sarett*

We and the beasts are kin. Man has nothing that the animals have not at least a vestige of; the animals have nothing that man does not in some degree share. Since then the animals are creatures with wants and feelings differing in degree only from our own, they surely have their rights.
—*Ernest Thompson Seton*

Wilt thou draw near the nature of the gods? Draw near them then in being merciful; sweet mercy is nobility's true badge.
—*Shakespeare*

Nature teaches beasts to know their friends.
—*Shakespeare*

Mine enemy's dog,
Though he had bit me, should have stood that night
Against my fire.
—*Shakespeare*

I do not dare to kill, and I have killed the desire to kill for sport. Living and letting live is better sport. —*Dallas Lore Sharp*

The behavior of men to the lower animals, and their behavior to each other, bear a constant relationship. —*Herbert Spencer*

Shield the nests where'er they be,
On the ground or on the tree.
—*James Stephens*

The underlying principles of the anticruelty cause are justice for the helpless, succor for the suffering, consideration for the weak, compassion for the unfortunate and kindness as the corner stone of character.
—*William O. Stillman*

The surest index of a gentleman is his treatment of those who are weaker and less able to care for themselves. The brightest phase of life during the last few tragic years has been that society has cared for those caught in paths of calamity. But it is even more significant that we live in a day when humane societies attempt so successfully to make kindness even to dumb animals a part of life's pattern. —*A. J. Stoddard*

Is there a beast that lives, and will not move
Toward our poor love with a more lovely love?
—*Arthur Symons*

Kind hearts are more than coronets,
And simple faith than Norman blood.
—*Alfred Tennyson*

Kitty and terrier, biddy and doves,
All things harmless Gustava loves.
The shy, kind creatures 'tis joy to feed,
And oh, her breakfast is sweet indeed
To happy little Gustava!
—*Celia Thaxter*

Why should man expect his prayer for mercy to be heard by What is above him when he shows no mercy to what is under him? —*Prince Pierre Troubetskoy*

The one absolutely unselfish friend that a man can have in this selfish world, the one that never deserts him, and the one that never proves ungrateful or treacherous, is his dog. —*George G. Vest*

Men will turn again with renewed interest to the animal world. In these disordered days a stupid, uncontrollable massacre of animal species goes on—from certain angles of vision it is a thing almost more tragic than human miseries. —*H. G. Wells*

"Whom God's creatures love," the angel fair
Murmured, "God doth bless with angels' care."
—*Thomas Westwood*

Down came squirrel eager for his fare,
Down came bonny blackbird, I declare.
Little Bell gave each his honest share,
Ah the merry three!
—*Thomas Westwood*

I think I could turn and live with animals, they are so placid and self-contain'd,
I stand and look at them long and long.
—*Walt Whitman*

Oh for boyhood's painless play,
Sleep that wakes in laughing day,
Health that mocks the doctor's rules,
Knowledge never learned of schools,
Of the wild bee's morning chase,
Of the wild flower's time and place,
Flight of fowl and habitude
Of the tenants of the wood;
How the tortoise bears his shell,
How the woodchuck digs his cell,
And the ground-mole sinks his well;
How the robin feeds her young,
How the oriole's nest is hung;
Where the whitest lilies blow,
Where the freshest berries grow,
Where the ground-nut trails its vine,
Where the wood-grape's clusters shine;
Of the black wasp's cunning way,
Mason of his walls of clay,
And the architectural plans
Of gray hornet artisans!
For, eschewing books and tasks,
Nature answers all he asks;
Hand in hand with her he walks,
Face to face with her he talks,
Part and parcel of her joy—
Blessings on the barefoot boy!
—*Whittier*

The sooner we recognize the fact that the mercy of the All-Merciful extends to every creature endowed with life, the better it will be for us as men and Christians. —*Whittier*

For the wonderful brain of man,
However mighty its force,
Had never achieved its lordly plan
Without the aid of the horse.
—*Ella Wheeler Wilcox*

The bird that constructs its beautiful nest with nature's materials is greater than the wanton hand that destroys it, though less powerful. —*Ella Wheeler Wilcox*

I am humbled and full of repentance
For my race's enmity,
That these gentle-eyed wood-creatures
Should whir from their hostelry;
And I fain would make their acquaintance
That they should reverse the sentence
And not be afraid of me.
—*Florence Wilkinson*

Mercy for the beast is but an aspect of that larger kindness without which mercy to man is incomplete. —*L. C. Williams*

The life of all creatures is brave and pitiful
Whether they be men, with dark thoughts to vex them,
Or birds, wheeling in the swift joys of flight,
Or brittle ephemerids, spinning to death in the haze
Of gold that quivers on dim evening waters.
—*Francis Brett Young*

For all those weak and lowly
Depending on man solely,
By all we hold most holy,
Hear us, we beseech Thee.
—*Freda Elton Young*

BIRD DAY

Birds in the shady cypress ply their song,
  Tending the dewy nestlings of their brood:
The finches twitter shrill: the turtle dove
  Coos from the shelter of his leafy choir.
—Agathias Scholasticus

When in the misty Southern ways
Oriole and jay have flown,
And of all sweet birds, alone
The robin stays.
—Thomas Bailey Aldrich

O lonesome sea-gull, floating far
  Over the ocean's icy waste,
Aimless and wide thy wandering are,
  Forever vainly seeking rest:—
  Where is thy mate, and where thy nest?
—Elizabeth Akers Allen

Within a budding grove,
In April's ear sang every bird his best.
—William Allingham

"Phoebe!" is all it has to say
  In plaintive cadence o'er and o'er,
Like children who have lost their way,
  And know their names, and nothing more.
—Anon.

The singing white-throat poured my gladness out,
And spread my golden wonder through the trees.
—Anon.

The swift wild duck, the beautiful thing!
The strength of the sun in his yellow feet,
  The purple of night asleep on his breast,
  The green of a thousand Junes on his crest,
The bank of the heavens across his wing!
—Anon.

Yellow-hammer's rat-tat-too on the orchard bough;
  That's the sound that used to break through my morning dreams.
—Anon.

Gallant and gay in their doublets gray,
  All at a flash like the darting of flame,
Chattering Arabic, African, Indian—
  Certain of springtime, the swallows came!
—Edwin Arnold

Hark! ah, the Nightingale!
  The tawny-throated!
Hark! from that moonlit cedar what a burst!
What triumph! hark!—what pain!
—Matthew Arnold

Was it, as the Grecian sings,
Birds were born the first of things,
Before the sun, before the wind,
Before the gods, before mankind,
Airy, ante-mundane throng—
  Witness their unworldly song!
—Matthew Arnold

Under the yew-tree's heavy weight
The owls stand in their sullen fashions,
Like Pagan gods of Pagan passions
They dart their eyes and meditate.
—Charles Baudelaire

Birds delight
Day and night;
Nightingale
In the dale,
Lark in sky,
Merrily,
Merrily, merrily, to welcome in the year.
—William Blake

Circling on high, in cloudless sky,
The shadowed hawk with passioned eye
In widening orbits floats, a spy,
Circling on high.
—Francis Brooks

My birds, come back! the hollow sky
  Is weary for your note.
—Alice Brown

That's the wise thrush; he sings each song twice over,
Lest you should think he never could recapture
The first fine careless rapture!
—Robert Browning

Merrily swinging on brier and weed
  Near to the nest of his little dame,
Over the mountain-side or mead,
  Robert of Lincoln is telling his name:
    Bob-o'-link, bob-o'-link,
    Spink, spank, spink.
—William Cullen Bryant

There are notes of joy from the hang-bird and wren,
And the gossip of swallows through all the sky.
—William Cullen Bryant

The feather'd people you might see,
Perch'd all around on every tree,
In notes of sweetest melody
  They hail the charming Chloe.
—Robert Burns

The bird as a piece of living nature is what interests me, having vital relations to all out-of-doors, and capable of linking my mind to itself and its surroundings with threads of delightful associations. The live bird is a fellow passenger; we are making the voyage together, and there is a sympathy between us that quickly leads to knowledge. . . . The observer of bird life in the open has heaven and earth thrown in. —*John Burroughs*

When nature made the blue-bird she wished to propitiate both the sky and the earth, so she gave him the color of the one on his back and the hue of the other on his breast.
—*John Burroughs*

In the very spring,
Nay, in the bluster of March, or haply before,
The bluebird comes, and a-wing
Or alight, seems evermore
For song that is sweet and soft.
—*Richard Burton*

Jubilant the music through the fields a-ringing,—
Carol, warble, whistle, pipe,—endless ways of singing,
Oriole, bobolink, melody of thrushes.
—*Frances Louisa Bushnell*

Along the sea-edge, like a gnome
Or rolling pebble in the foam,
As though he timed the ocean's throbbing,
Runs a piper, bobbing, bobbing.
—*Witter Bynner*

Now do a choir of chirping minstrels bring
In triumph to the world the youthful spring!
—*Thomas Carew*

From hazel bushes came songs of thrushes
And blackbirds—sweeter than harper's lay.
—*Michael Cavanagh*

And the loveliest lyric I ever heard
Was the wildwood strain of a forest bird.
—*Madison Cawein*

While the bluebird sits on the locust-bough
Whose shadow is painted across thy brow,
And carols his welcome so sad and sweet
To the Spring that comes and kisses his feet.
—*William Ellery Channing*

The geese drive northward
In a long gray harrow;
Spring has come back,
And brings the sweet fox sparrow.
—*W. W. Christman*

Sweet is the hermit's evening bell,
And sweet the mellow canticle
Of the wood thrush; but more I love
The murmur of the mourning dove.
—*W. W. Christman*

Within a thick and spreading hawthorn bush,
That overhung a mole-hill large and round,
I heard from morn to morn a merry thrush
Sing hymns of rapture, while I drank the sound
With joy.
—*John Clare*

The cheeriest note of winter comes rollicking oft to me
Like the voice of a song-struck sunbeam:
"Chickadee dee dee! Chickadee!"
—*Martha Haskell Clark*

But calm, white calm, was born into a swan.
—*Elizabeth Coatsworth*

It would take an angel's eye
To see the humming-bird's hot wings.
He stands raptly on thin air
At his banquetings
—*Robert P. Tristram Coffin*

Do you ask what the birds say? The Sparrow, the Dove,
The Linnet, and Thrush say, "I love and I love!"
—*Samuel Taylor Coleridge*

Closer to God art thou than I:
His minstrel thou, whose brown wings fly
Through silent ether's summer climes.
—*Mortimer Collins*

A meadow lark sang at the drooping of dusk;
Its silvery notes with the sea seemed in tune.
—*Charles Commerford*

The rook sits high, when the blast sweeps by,
Right pleased with his wild see-saw:
And though hollow and bleak be the fierce wind's shriek,
It is marked by his loud caw-caw.
—*Eliza Cook*

Sweet, sweet, sweet! O happy that I am!
(Listen to the meadow-larks, across the fields that sing!)
Sweet, sweet, sweet!
—*Ina Coolbrith*

"So the Bluebirds have contracted, have they, for a house?
And a nest is under way for little Mr. Wren?
Hush, dear, hush! Be quiet, dear; quiet as a mouse.
These are weighty secrets, and we must whisper them."
—*Susan Coolidge*

When Nature had made all her birds,
With no more cares to think on,
She gave a rippling laugh, and out
There flew a Bobolinkon.
—*Christopher P. Cranch*

The mocking bird is music-mad tonight,
He thinks the stars are notes;
That he must sing each spattered star, and be
A choir of many throats.
—*Grace Noll Crowell*

Hail, ye plebeian underwood!
Where the poetic birds rejoice,
And for their quiet nests and plenteous food,
Pay with their grateful voice.
—*Abraham Crowley*

The rooks shall stalk the plough, larks mount the skies,
Blackbirds and speckled thrushes sing aloud.
—*John Davidson*

And far and away o'er the bending corn,
We see the swarming swallows flash.
—*Richard Dehmel*

Upon this leafy bush
With thorns and roses in it,
Flutters a thing of light,
A twittering linnet!
—*Walter de la Mare*

Thou, red-breast, singest the old song over,
Though many a time thou hast sung it before.
—*Aubrey de Vere*

At morning the pale pigeons come in a band,
Shining and fleet.
—*George Dillon*

A bird that stays in wintry days;
A friend indeed is he;
And better than all other birds
I love the chickadee!
—*Marian Douglas*

Here are humming birds that come
To seek the tall delphinium—
Songless bird and scentless flower
Communing in a golden hour.
—*Louise Driscoll*

I thought the sparrow's note from heaven,
Singing at dawn on the alder bough;
I brought him home, in his nest, at even;
He sings the song, but it cheers not now,
For I did not bring home the river and sky;—
He sang to my ear,—they sang to my eye.
—*Ralph Waldo Emerson*

Know'st thou what wove yon woodbird's nest
Of leaves, and feathers from her breast?
—*Ralph Waldo Emerson*

O birds, your perfect virtues bring,
Your song, your forms, your rhythmic flight,
Your manners for the heart's delight,
Nestle in hedge, or barn, or roof,
Here weave your chamber weather-proof.
—*Ralph Waldo Emerson*

The sky-lark warbles high
His trembling thrilling ecstacy!
—*Thomas Gray*

Blackbird and thrush in every bush,
Stare, linnet, and cock-sparrow!
—*Thomas Heywood*

Wake from thy nest, robin red-breast!
Sing, birds, in every furrow!
—*Thomas Heywood*

But oh, but oh, the meadow-lark!
And oh, the song he sang!
—*Ella Higginson*

Birds have their nests; they rear their eager young,
And flit on errands all the livelong day.
—*Thomas Wentworth Higginson*

Happy Song-sparrow, that on the woodland side
Or by the meadow sits, and ceaseless sings
His mellow roundelay in russet pride.
—*Henry Beck Hirst*

Bird of the wilderness,
Blithesome and cumberless,
Sweet be thy matin o'er moorland and lea!
—*James Hogg*

Hear! hear! hear!
Listen! the word
Of the mocking bird!
—*Richard Hovey*

Hurrah, the swallow is back from his flight,
With his back of jet and his breast of white,
The summer's earliest harbinger!
—*Richard Hovey*

Oh, the white Sea-gull, the wild Sea-gull,
A joyful bird is he,
As he lies like a cradled thing at rest
In the arms of a sunny sea!
—*Mary Howitt*

I'll tell a secret that I heard—
The perfect way to catch a bird.
Just get a bird book, called a guide,
And with field-glasses at your side
Go out into the woods and see
The bird perched up in some tall tree;
Stop, too, and hear his melody—
You've got him!
—*Leland B. Jacobs*

The robin in the apple-tree,
The brown thrush in the wood,
The meadow larks, all called to me;
I understood.
—*Charles Frederick Johnson*

As from out the tuneful throat
Came the sweetest, springlike note,
And I truly heard an English sparrow sing.
—*Bertha Johnston*

The red-breast whistles from a garden-croft;
And gathering swallows twitter in the skies.
—*John Keats*

Sometimes goldfinches one by one will drop
From low-hung branches; little space they stop,
But sip, and twitter, and their feathers sleek,
Then off at once, as in a wanton freak;
Or perhaps, to show their black and golden wings,
Pausing upon their yellow flutterings.
—*John Keats*

Thou wast not born for death, immortal Bird!
No hungry generations tread thee down;
The voice I hear this passing night was heard
In ancient days by emperor and clown.
—John Keats

Carols of gladness ring from every tree.
—Frances Anne Kemble

A bird appears a thoughtless thing;
He's ever living on the wing,
And keeps up such a carolling,
That little else to do but sing
A man would guess had he.
—Charles and Mary Lamb

And up the leafless tree
The nut-hatch runs, and nods, and clings;
The bluebird dips with flashing wings,
The robin flutes, the sparrow sings,
And the swallows float and flee.
—Archibald Lampman

Superb and sole, upon a plumëd spray
That o'er the general leafage boldly grew,
He summ'd the woods in song.
—Sidney Lanier

O little bird, a speck thou art
'Mid blue infinities of sky;
Thou hast a compass and a chart
Within that bright and anxious eye.
—Augusta Larned

Within the oak a throb of pigeon wings
Fell silent!
—Francis Ledwidge

Speak it with rapture—buds will break
Along the limbs that thrushes shake
With song for love's and lovers' sake.
—Mary Sinton Leitch

A flock of crows high from the Northland flies,
On their dark wings the evening sunshine plays.
—Detlev von Liliencron

Do you ne'er think what wondrous beings these?
Do you ne'er think who made them, and who taught
The dialect they speak, where melodies
Alone are the interpreters of thought?
Whose household words are songs in many keys,
Sweeter than instrument of man e'er caught!
Whose habitations in the tree-tops even
Are half-way houses on the road to heaven!
—Longfellow

The purple finch,
That on wild cherry and red cedar feeds,
A winter bird, comes with his plaintive whistle.
—Longfellow

Listen! the choir is singing; all the birds,
In leafy galleries beneath the eaves,
Are singing! listen, ere the sound be fled,
And learn there may be worship without words.
—Longfellow

Then the little Hiawatha
Learned of every bird its language,
Learned their names and all their secrets,
How they built their nests in Summer,
Where they hid themselves in Winter,
Talked with them where'er he met them,
Called them "Hiawatha's Chickens."
—Longfellow

The grackles have come.
The smoothness of the morning is puckered with their incessant chatter.
—Amy Lowell

June's bridesman, poet o' the year,
Gladness on wings, the bobolink, is here;
Half-hid in tip-top apple-blooms he swings,
Or climbs against the breeze with quiverin' wings,
Or, givin' way to't in a mock despair,
Runs down, a brook o' laughter, through the air.
—James Russell Lowell

The little bird sits at his door in the sun,
Atilt like a blossom among the leaves,
And lets his illumined being o'errun
With the deluge of Summer it receives.
—James Russell Lowell

Hark, hark, with what a pretty throat
Poor robin redbreast tunes his note!
Hark how the jolly cuckoos sing
Cuckoo! to welcome in the spring!
Cuckoo! to welcome in the spring!
—John Lyly

Crescent-winged, sky-clean
Hermit of pastures wild,
Upland plover, shy-souled lover
Of field ways undefiled!
—Percy MacKaye

A strange thing, that a lark and robin sky
Should drop a wild duck on a little pond
Where cattle drink!
—Leroy McLeod

Here's a health to the birds one and all!
A health to the birds great and small!
—Seumas MacManus

The bluebird, stained with earth and sky,
Shouts from a blowing bough
In green aerial freedom, wild and high.
—Edwin Markham

The bobolink,
Out on the uncertain brink
Of swaying alder, swings,
Loosing his song out, link by golden link.
—Edwin Markham

The wild ducks floating by in flocks;
The flying geese with phantom scream;
The heron on the rocks.

—Lloyd Mifflin

To hear the Lark begin his flight,
And singing startle the dull night,
From his watch-tower in the skies,
Till the dappled dawn doth rise;
Then to come in spite of sorrow,
And at my window bid good-morrow.

—John Milton

That green-gold flash was a vireo,
And yonder flame where the marsh-flags grow
Was a scarlet tanager.

—William Vaughn Moody

God, when you patterned a bird song,
Flung on a silver string,
How did you know the ecstasy
That crystal call would bring?

—Angela Morgan

The wild geese, flying in the night, behold
Our sunken towns lie underneath a sea,
Which buoys them on its billows.

—James Herbert Morse

I've plucked the berry from the bush,
The brown nut from the tree,
But heart of happy little bird
Ne'er broken was by me.

—William Motherwell

Sing on, sing on, blithe bird! and fill
My heart with summer gladness.

—William Motherwell

In every street these tunes our ears do greet—
Cuckoo, jug-jug, pu-we, to-witta-woo!
Spring, the sweet Spring!

—Thomas Nashe

Soar, bird, fling wide
That song of birds in deserts born!

—Friedrich Wilhelm Nietzsche

A jaybird blew his clarinet,
A brown thrush tried to trill.

—Cotton Noe

Carols of light
From a lovlier kingdom,
On earth unheard,
Gleams of a music
Scattered like dew
By the careless wayside,
Pour through the lifted
Throat of a bird.

—Alfred Noyes

Listen, the sweet birds jargoning
From tree to tree.

—Jean Passerat

Thou glorious mocker of the world! I hear
Thy many voices ringing through the glooms
Of these green solitudes; and all the clear,
Bright joyance of their song enthralls the ear,
And floods the heart.

—Albert Pike

Ha! what a burst was that! The Æolian strain
Goes floating through the tangled passages
Of the still woods; and now it comes again,
A multitudinous melody, like a rain
Of glassy music under echoing trees,
Close by a ringing lake.

—Albert Pike

Up and down!—up and down!
From the base of the wave to the billow's crown,
And amidst the flashing and feathery foam
The stormy petrel finds a home.

—Bryan Waller Procter

In the hollow tree, in the old grey tower,
The spectral owl doth dwell;
Dull, hated, despised in the sunshine hour,
But at dusk he's abroad and well.

—Bryan Waller Procter

Alone from out the stubble piped the quail,
And croaked the crow through all the dreamy gloom;
Alone the phesant, drumming in the vale,
Made echo to the distant cottage loom.

—Thomas Buchanan Read

And every little brownbird that doth sing,
Hath something greater than itself, and bears
A living word to every living thing.

—Richard Realf

Winter has planted the field black with crows.
In frustrate flocks they cark and scream and caw.

—Cale Young Rice

Consider
The birds, that have no barn nor harvest-weeks.

—Christina G. Rossetti

The little wild birds have come flying
From beyond the sea, the blue sea;
The little birds go fluttering
About the bushes, over the open field:
All have their mates and rejoice in love.

—Russian

They'll come again to the apple tree—
Robin and all the rest—
When the orchard branches are fair to see,
In the snow of the blossom dressed;
And the prettiest thing in the world will be
The building of the nest.

—Margaret E. Sangster

Chant then, O bird, tilt back your bill;
And, perched upon the balsam's nodding cones,
From out the plum-blue shadows spill
Your pebbly silver tones.
—*Lew Sarett*

There is abundant proof that birds and men for the most part can dwell together if the birds are invited; and more and more as their part in human existence is understood, are they being invited. —*Dallas Lore Sharp*

Far, far above the sea-stretch
And the lance-grass salt with spray,
The pelicans are flying
Against the golden day!
—*Rena Sheffield*

Day had awakened all things that be,
The lark, and the thrush, and the swallow free.
—*Percy Bysshe Shelley*

Hail to thee, blithe Spirit!
Bird thou never wirt!—
That from Heaven, or near it,
Pourest thy full heart
In profuse strains of unpremeditated art.
—*Percy Bysshe Shelley*

Come, summer visitant, attach
To my reed roof your nest of clay,
And let my ear your music catch.
—*Charles Smith*

The time of the singing of birds is come.
—*Song of Solomon 2:12*

Hark! how the cheerful birds do chaunt their lays,
And carol of love's praise:
The merry lark her matins sings aloft;
The thrush replies; the mavis descant plays;
The ouzell shrills; the ruddock warbles soft.
—*Edmund Spenser*

Yes, daw and owl, curlew and crested hern,
Kingfisher, mallard, water-rail and tern,
Chaffinch and greenfinch, wagtail, stonechat, ruff,
Whitethroat and robin, fly-catcher and chough,
Missel-thrush, magpie, sparrow-hawk and jay,
Built, those far ages gone, in this year's way.
—*J. C. Squire*

The sweetest sound our whole year round—
'Tis the first robin of the spring!
The song of the full orchard choir
Is not so fine a thing.
—*Edmund Clarence Stedman*

A lark sang up from the breezy land,
A lark sang down from a cloud afar.
—*James Stephens*

Kildees call from the fields where now
The banding blackbirds follow the plow.
—*George Sterling*

Long before the eagle furls his pinion on the pine-top,
Long before the bluebird gleams in sapphire through the glen,
Long before the lily blots the shoal with golden apples,
Leaves the loon his southern sun to sail the lake again.
—*Alfred Billings Street*

Hush!
With sudden gush
As from a fountain sings in yonder bush
The Hermit Thrush.
—*John Banister Tabb*

"Summer is coming, summer is coming,
I know it, I know it, I know it.
Light again, leaf again, life again, love again,
Yes, my wild little Poet.
—*Alfred Tennyson*

The woods were filled so full with song
There seemed no room for sense of wrong.
—*Alfred Tennyson*

I sit and hear the blithe song-sparrow sing
His strain of rapture not to be suppressed.
—*Celia Thaxter*

No sadder sound salutes you than the clear,
Wild laughter of the loon.
—*Celia Thaxter*

Oriole—athlete of the air—
Of fire and song a glowing core.
—*James Maurice Thompson*

Where water-grass grows overgreen
On damp cool flats by gentle streams,
Still as a ghost and sad of mien,
With half-closed eyes the heron dreams.
—*James Maurice Thompson*

The robin's chuckling note
Bubbles in his throat.
—*Earl D. Todd*

The oriole flashes by; and, look!
Into the mirrow of the brook,
Where the vain bluebird trims his coat,
Two tiny feathers fall and float.
—*John Townsend Trowbridge*

Quickly before me runs the quail,
Her chickens skulk behind the rail;
High up the lone wood-pigeon sits,
And the woodpecker pecks and flits.
—*John Townsend Trowbridge*

Hear the notes
Of birds with sunset shaking on their throats.
—*Louis Untermeyer*

There's magic in that small bird's note—
See, there he flits—the yellow-throat:
A living sunbeam, tipped with wings,
A spark of light that shines and sings
"*Witchery—witchery—witchery.*"
—*Henry van Dyke*

He that hath found some fledged bird's nest may know
At first sight if the bird be flown;
But what fair well or grove he sings in now,
That is to him unknown.
—Henry Vaughan

And now a miraculous gurgling gushes
Like nectar from Hebe's Olympian bottle,
The laughter of tune from a rapturous throttle!
—William Henry Venable

Those little nimble musicians of the air, that warble forth their curious ditties, with which nature hath furnished them to the shame of art. *—Izaak Walton*

I know a vale where the oriole swings
Her nest to the breeze and the sky.
—Albert D. Watson

And the blackbird piped; you never heard
Half so gay a song from any bird;—
Full of quips and wiles,
Now so round and rich, now soft and slow.
—Thomas Westwood

In the swamp in secluded recesses,
A shy and hidden bird is warbling a song.
—Walt Whitman

Oh then comes the blue-bird, the herald of spring!
And hails with his warblings the charms of the season.
—Alexander Wilson

And hark! how blithe the Throstle sings!
He, too, is no mean preacher:
Come forth into the light of things,
Let nature be your teacher.
—William Wordsworth

The Eagle, he was lord above.
—William Wordsworth

O cuckoo! shall I call thee bird,
Or but a wandering voice?
—William Wordsworth

Art thou the bird whom Man loves best,
The pious bird with the scarlet breast,
Our little English Robin?
—William Wordsworth

BOOK WEEK

Books are the legacies that a great genius leaves to mankind, which are delivered down from generation to generation, as presents to the posterity of those who are yet unborn.
—Addison

That is a good book which is opened with expectation and closed with profit.
—Amos Bronson Alcott

A man is known by the company his mind keeps. To live continually with noble books, with "high-erected thoughts seated in the heart of courtesy," teaches the soul good manners. *—Thomas Bailey Aldrich*

Old friends to trust! old books to read!
—Alonzo of Aragon

For friends . . . do but look upon good Books: they are true friends, that will neither flatter nor dissemble. *—Francis Bacon*

Some books are to be tasted, others to be swallowed, and some few to be chewed and digested. *—Francis Bacon*

He that loveth a book, will never want a faithful friend, a wholesome counsellor, a cheerful companion, an effectual comforter.
—Isaac Barrow

Without books, God is silent, justice dormant, natural science at a stand, philosophy lame, letters dumb, and all things involved in Cimerian darkness. *—Thomas Bartholin*

That place that does contain
My books, the best companions, is to me
A glorious court, where hourly I converse
With the old sages and philosophers;
And sometimes, for variety, I confer
With kings and emperors, and weigh their counsels.
—Beaumont and Fletcher

Filling a bookcase is like gathering a social circle.
—May Lamberton Becker

A book is a garden, an orchard, a storehouse, a party, a company by the way, a counsellor, a multitude of counsellors.
—Henry Ward Beecher

Books are the compasses and telescopes and sextants and charts which other men have prepared to help us navigate the dangerous seas of human life. *—Jesse Lee Bennett*

I love my books as drinkers love their wine;
The more I drink, the more they seem divine.
—Francis Bennoch

With a book for every mood—the old books that have fired the imagination and blazed the trails for one's dreams, and the new ones that breathe the spirit of the modern age and yet keep it within bounds—the child has a heritage that will make its future safe.
—William Frederick Bigelow

Libraries are not made, they grow.
—Augustine Birrell

Of all odd crazes, the craze to be forever reading new books is one of the oddest.
—Augustine Birrell

Books are embalmed minds. *—Bovee*

Books are men of higher stature,
And the only men that speak aloud for future times to hear.
—Elizabeth Barrett Browning

No man can be called friendless who has God and the companionship of good books.
—Elizabeth Barrett Browning

When a book raises your spirit and inspires you with noble and manly thoughts, seek for no other test of its excellence. It is good and made by a good workman. *—Bruyere*

Now may this little Book a blessing be
To those that love this little Book and me:
And may its buyer have no cause to say,
His money is but lost or thrown away.
—Bunyan

Nothing ought to be more weighed than the nature of books recommended by public authority. So recommended, they soon form the character of the age . . . if education takes in *vice* as any part of its system, there is no doubt but that it will operate with abundant energy, and to an extent indefinite.
—Edmund Burke

Some books are lies frae end to end.
—Robert Burns

You, O Books, are the golden vessels of the temple . . . burning lamps to be held ever in the hand. *—Richard de Bury*

The assembled souls of all men held wise, imprisoned until some one takes them down from a shelf and reads them.
—Samuel Butler the Younger

'Tis pleasant, sure, to see one's name in print;
A book's a book, although there's nothing in't.
—Lord Byron

But words are things, and a small drop of ink,
Falling like dew upon a thought, produces
That which makes thousands, perhaps millions, think.

—Lord Byron

Of all the things which man can do or make here below, by far the most momentous, wonderful, and worthy are the things we call books. *—Carlyle*

In books lies the soul of the whole Past Time: the articulate audible voice of the Past, when the body and material substance of it has altogether vanished like a dream.

—Carlyle

The true University of these days is a Collection of Books. *—Carlyle*

There are men that will make you books, and turn them loose into the world, with as much dispatch as they would do a dish of fritters. *—Cervantes*

God be thanked for books! they are the voices of the distant and the dead, and make us heirs of the spiritual life of past ages.

—W. E. Channing

Books are the true levellers.

——W. E. Channing

And out of old bookes, in good faithe,
Cometh al this new science that men lere.

—Geoffrey Chaucer

Due attention to the inside of books, and due contempt for the outside, is the proper relation between a man of sense and his books.

—Lord Chesterfield

A book is the only immortality.

—Rufus Choate

A room without books is as a body without a soul. *—Cicero*

Books are the food of youth, the delight of old age; the ornament of prosperity, the refuge and comfort of adversity; a delight at home, and no hindrance abroad; companions by night, in travelling, in the country.

—Cicero

Next to acquiring good friends, the best acquisition is that of good books.

—Charles Caleb Colton

Books are not seldom talismans and spells.

—Cowper

Books cannot always please, however good;
Minds are not ever craving for their food.

—George Crabbe

From my point of view, a book is a literary prescription put up for the benefit of someone who needs it. *—S. M. Crothers*

A precious book is a foretaste of immortality.

—T. L. Cuyler

O blessed letters! that combine in one
All ages past, and make one live with all.

—Samuel Daniel

The monument of vanish'd minds.

—Sir William D'Avenant

We've found that fairyland is everywhere—
You open up a book and, why, you're there!

—Mary Carolyn Davies

Books should to one of these four ends conduce:
For wisdom, piety, delight, or use.

—Sir John Denham

There are books of which the backs and covers are by far the best parts.

—Charles Dickens

Whoever has read the best books has acquired not only information but a method of thinking. Intelligence is as contagious as gracefulness and wit used to be in the eighteenth century. This is not all. Doctrines are tested and developed, methods are improved, views are completed, the work of the whole world becomes the property of each individual seeker who cares to annex its results. *—Ernest Dimnet*

Golden volumes! richest treasures!
Objects of delicious pleasures!

—Isaac D'Israeli

Who, without books, essays to learn,
Draws water in a leaky urn.

—Austin Dobson

Uncertain whose the narrower span,
The clown unread, or half-read gentleman.

—Dryden

Of making many books there is no end.

—Ecclesiastes 12:12

Bad books are like intoxicating drinks; they furnish neither nourishment nor medicine.

—Tryon Edwards

Books are the quietest and most constant of friends; they are the most accessible and wisest of counsellors, and the most patient of teachers. *—Charles W. Eliot*

Consider what you have in the smallest chosen library. A company of the wisest and wittiest men that could be picked out of all civil countries, in a thousand years, have set in the best order the results of their learning and wisdom. *—Emerson*

Until we have discovered that certain books grow with our maturing experience and other books do not, we have not learned how to distinguish a great book from a book.

—John Erskine

A book is to me like a hat or coat—a very uncomfortable thing until the newness has been worn off. —*Charles B. Fairbanks*

If the crowns of all the kingdoms of Europe were laid down at my feet in exchange for my books and my love of reading, I would spurn them all. —*Fénelon*

A thousand years hence they are what you find them today, speaking the same words, holding forth the same comfort.
—*Eugene Field*

That place that does
Contain my books, the best companions, is
To me a glorious court, where hourly I
Converse with the old sages and philosophers.
—*John Fletcher*

Something very significant has happened to a man when he realizes that in books the greatest souls of the world will come to call on him as though there were no one else on earth whom they had to call upon.
—*Harry Emerson Fosdick*

Why, except for some special reason, read an inferior book, at the very time you might be reading one of the highest order?
—*John Foster*

Books make up no small part of human happiness. —*Frederick the Great*

A book that is shut is but a block.
—*Thomas Fuller*

To divert, at any time, a troublesome fancy, run to thy Books. They presently fix thee to them, and drive the other out of thy thoughts. They always receive thee with the same kindness. —*Thomas Fuller*

A taste for books is the pleasure and glory of my life. I would not exchange it for the riches of the Indies. —*Gibbon*

The first time I read an excellent book, it is to me just as if I had gained a new friend. When I read over a book I have perused before, it resembles the meeting with an old one. —*Oliver Goldsmith*

I armed her against the censures of the world; showed her that books were sweet unreproaching companions to the miserable, and that if they could not bring us to enjoy life, they would at least teach us to endure it.
—*Oliver Goldsmith*

From every book invisible threads reach out to other books; and as the mind comes to use and control those threads the whole panorama of the world's life, past and present, becomes constantly more varied and interesting, while at the same time the mind's own powers of reflection and judgment are exercised and strengthened.
—*Helen E. Haines*

Books impart deepened sensitiveness to ideals, to beauty, to pleasure, to the best emotions of life. —*Helen E. Haines*

Formal education applies its patterns to the mind; but only through books does the mind itself enrich, deepen, apply, modify, and develop those patterns in individual life fulfillment. —*Helen E. Haines*

If I have not read a book before, it is, to all intents and purposes, new to me, whether it was printed yesterday or three hundred years ago. —*W. C. Hazlitt*

Thou art a plant sprung up to wither never,
But, like a laurel, to grow green forever.
—*Robert Herrick*

Old books, as you well know, are books of the world's youth, and new books are fruits of its age. —*Oliver Wendell Holmes*

The best of a book is not the thought which it contains, but the thought which it suggests; just as the charm of music dwells not in the tones but in the echoes of our hearts.
—*Oliver Wendell Holmes*

My books kept me from the ring, the dog-pit, the tavern, and the saloon.
—*Thomas Hood*

Through his reading a man comes to the cities of the mind. —*Lynn Harold Hough*

It is books that teach us to refine our pleasures when young, and which, having so taught us, enable us to recall them with satisfaction when old. —*Leigh Hunt*

The proper study of mankind is books.
—*Aldous Huxley*

Every man who knows how to read has it in his power to magnify himself, to multiply the ways in which he exists, to make his life full, significant and interesting.
—*Aldous Huxley*

The scholar only knows how dear these silent, yet eloquent, companions of pure thoughts and innocent hours become in the season of adversity. When all that is worldly turns to dross around us, these only retain their steady value.
—*Washington Irving*

Seek ye out of the book of the Lord, and read. —*Isaiah 34:16*

There is no worse robber than a bad book.
—*Italian Proverb*

A blessed companion is a book,—a book that, fitly chosen, is a lifelong friend, . . . a book that, at a touch, pours its heart into our own. —*Douglas Jerrold*

Dear, human books,
With kindly voices, winning looks!
Enchant me with your spells of art,
And draw me homeward to your heart.
—*Lionel Johnson*

A man ought to read just as inclination leads him; for what he reads as a task will do him little good. —*Samuel Johnson*

There may be some men are born only to suck out the poison of books.
—*Ben Jonson*

Books! What though cloth or morocco bound?
Between their covers lies magic ground.
—*Theda Kenyon*

Except a living man there is nothing more wonderful than a book! A message to us from the dead,—from human souls whom we never saw, who lived perhaps thousands of miles away; and yet these, on those little sheets of paper, speak to us, teach us, comfort us, open their hearts to us as brothers.
—*Charles Kingsley*

We cannot, then, silence evil books, but we can turn away our eyes from them; for we can take care that what we read, and what we let others read, should be good and wholesome. —*Charles Kingsley*

I love to lose myself in other men's minds. . . Books think for me. —*Charles Lamb*

The Love of Books, the Golden Key
That opens the Enchanted Door.
—*Andrew Lang*

Here stand my books, line upon line
They reach the roof, and row by row,
They speak of faded tastes of mine,
And things I did, but do not, know.
—*Andrew Lang*

How vast an estate it is that we came into as the intellectual heirs of all the watchers and searchers and thinkers and singers of the generations that are dead! What a heritage of stored wealth! What perishing poverty of mind we should be left in without it!
—*J. N. Larned*

What we ought to seek everywhere in books is escape from the commonplace—the commonplace in thought and the commonplace in character with which our daily life surrounds us. —*J. N. Larned*

Medicine for the soul.
—*Library at Thebes (Inscription over the door)*

Get books and read and study them carefully.
—*Abraham Lincoln*

Books are sepulchres of thought;
The dead laurels of the dead.
—*Longfellow*

The love of learning, the sequestered nooks,
And all the sweet serenity of books.
—*Longfellow*

For books are more than books, they are the life
The very heart and core of ages past.
—*Amy Lowell*

What a sense of security in an old book which time has criticized for us!
—*James Russell Lowell*

We may sit in our library and yet be in all quarters of the earth. —*Sir John Lubbock*

Every great book is an action.
—*Martin Luther*

Far more seemly were it for thee to have thy study full of books, than thy purse full of money. —*John Lyly*

There is no Past, so long as Books shall live!
—*Bulwer-Lytton*

Hark! the world so loud,
And they, the movers of the world, so still!
—*Bulwer-Lytton*

The book of the moment often has immense vogue, while the book of the age, which comes in its company from the press, lies unnoticed; but the great book has its revenge. It lives to see its contemporary pushed up shelf by shelf until it finds its final resting-place in the garret or the auction room.
—*Hamilton Wright Mabie*

I would rather be a poor man in a garret with plenty of books than a king who did not love reading.
—*Thomas Babington Macauley*

A house without books is like a room without windows. —*Horace Mann*

If we have no other benefit by the multitude of books that are written, we have this benefit,—an opportunity to observe the various workings of the same spirit about the same truths. —*Thomas Manton*

He fed his spirit with the bread of books.
—*Edwin Markham*

Old books to read!
Ay, bring those nodes of wit,
The brazen-clasped, the vellum writ,
Time-honored tomes!
—*Robert Hinckley Messinger*

Man's books are but man's alphabet,
Beyond and on his lessons lie—
The lessons of the violet,
The large gold letters of the sky.
—*Joaquin Miller*

A good book is the precious life-blood of a master-spirit, embalmed and treasured up on purpose to a life beyond life. —*Milton*

As good almost kill a man as kill a good book; who kills a man kills a reasonable creature, God's image; but he who destroys a good book kills reason itself. —*Milton*

The one invincible thing is a good book; neither malice nor stupidity can crush it.
—*George Moore*

Silent companions of the lonely hour,
Friends who can never alter or forsake.
—*Caroline E. S. Norton*

Books are part of man's prerogative;
In formal ink they thought and voices hold,
That we to them our solitude may give,
And make time present travel that of old.
—*Sir Thomas Overbury*

The books which help you most are those which make you think the most.
—*Theodore Parker*

A book, like a person, has its fortunes with one; is lucky or unlucky in the precise moment of its falling in our way, and often by some happy accident counts with us for something more than its independent value.
—*Walter Pater*

To desire to have many books, and never to use them, is like a child that will have a candle burning by him, all the while he is sleeping. —*Henry Peacham*

I have friends whose society is delightful to me; they are persons of all countries and of all ages; distinguished in war, in council, and in letters; easy to live with, always at my command. —*Petrarch*

Wear the old coat and buy the new book.
—*Austin Phelps*

For the price of one ticket to an ephemeral entertainment, you can secure a book that will give strength and leisure to your mind all your life. —*William Lyon Phelps*

Books are immortal sons deifying their sires.
—*Plato*

Even in life the best friendships are based not so much on propinquity and contact as on the touching of minds and spirits, and this is almost completely obtainable in a book.
—*Mary Wright Plummer*

We ought to regard books as we do sweetmeats, not wholly to aim at the pleasantest, but chiefly to respect the wholesomest; not forbidding either, but approving the latter most. —*Plutarch*

Most wondrous book! bright candle of the Lord! —*Robert Pollock*

As much company as I have kept, and as much as I love it, I love reading better, and would rather be employed in reading than in the most agreeable conversation. —*Pope*

To buy books only because they were published by an eminent printer, is much as if a man should buy clothes that did not fit him, only because made by some famous tailor.
—*Pope*

And he had in his hand a little book open.
—*Revelations 10:2*

Bread of flour is good; but there is bread, sweet as honey, if we would eat it, in a good book. —*Ruskin*

I love a book,—its throbbing heart!
—*Clinton Scollard*

A book! oh, rare one! —*Shakespeare*

That book in many's eyes doth share the glory
That in gold clasps locks in the golden story.
—*Shakespeare*

My library was dukedom large enough.
—*Shakespeare*

While you converse with lords and dukes,
I have their betters here—my books.
—*Thomas Sheridan*

Give me the room whose every nook
Is dedicated to a book.
—*Frank Dempster Sherman*

Live always in the best company when you read. —*Sydney Smith*

Talk of the happiness of getting a great prize in the lottery! What is that to the opening of a box of books!
—*Robert Southey*

My days among the Dead are passed,
Around me I behold,
Where'er these casual eyes are cast,
The mighty minds of old:
My never-failing friends are they,
With whom I converse day by day.
—*Robert Southey*

When we are collecting books, we are collecting happiness. —*Vincent Starrett*

The virtue which we gather from a fable, or an allegory, is like the health we got by hunting; as we are engaged in an agreeable pursuit that draws us on with pleasure, and makes us insensible of the fatigues that accompany it. —*Sir Richard Steele*

I often derive a peculiar satisfaction in conversing with the ancient and modern dead,—who yet live and speak excellently in their works.—My neighbours think me *often alone*,—and yet at such times I am in company with more than five hundred mutes—each of whom, at my pleasure, communicates his ideas to me by dumb signs—quite as intelligently as any person living can do by uttering of words.
—*Laurence Sterne*

Books are like the windows of a great tower. They let light in.
—*William L. Stidger*

Most books, like their authors, are born to die; of only a few books can it be said that death hath no dominion over them; they live, and their influence lives forever.
—*J. Swartz*

Books, the children of the brain.
—*Swift*

Books give the same turn to our thoughts that company does to our conversation, without loading our memories, or making us even sensible of the change. —*Swift*

Books, like proverbs, receive their chief value from the stamp and esteem of the ages through which they have passed.
—*Sir William Temple*

Let your bookcases and your shelves be your gardens and your pleasure-grounds. Pluck the fruit that grows therein, gather the roses, the spices, and the myrrh.
—*Judah Ibn Tibbon*

A good book is the best of friends, the same today and for ever.
—*Martin Farquhar Tupper*

Opening a book is like opening a door,
Turning a leaf's like a bend in the lane.
—*Nancy Byrd Turner*

Here is the best solitary company in the world: and in this particular chiefly excelling any other, that in my study I am sure to converse with none but wise men; but abroad it is impossible for me to avoid the society of fools. —*Sir William Waller*

For a good book is a solid thing.
—*Pearl Buck Walsh*

I conceive that a knowledge of books is the basis on which all other knowledge rests.
—*George Washington*

Books are lighthouses erected in the great sea of time. —*E. P. Whipple*

Books are the glass of council to dress ourselves by. —*Bulstrode Whitlock*

The lords of thought await our call!
—*Whittier*

O for a Booke and a shadie nooke, eyther in-a-doore or out;
With the grene leaves whisp'ring overhede, or the Streete cryes all about.
Where I maie Reade all at my ease, both of the Newe and Olde;
For a jollie goode Booke whereon to looke is better to me than Golde.
—*John Wilson*

What holy cities are to nomadic tribes—a symbol of race and a bond of union—great books are to the wandering souls of men: they are the Meccas of the mind.
—*G. E. Woodberry*

Dreams, books, are each a world; and books, we know,
Are a substantial world, both pure and good:
Round these, with tendrils strong as flesh and blood,
Our pastime and our happiness will grow.
—*William Wordsworth*

Books are yours,
Within whose silent chambers treasure lies
Preserved from age to age; more precious far
Than that accumulated store of gold
And orient gems which, for a day of need,
The Sultan hides deep in ancestral tombs.
These hoards of truth you can unlock at will.
—*William Wordsworth*

CHRISTMAS DAY

Over earth's shadows are ringing yet
The notes of celestial song;
The voices of angels and men are met,
And praises high prolong;
Oh, love untold,
Hope manifold,
Joy of each Christmas morn!

—Anon.

He rides to the East, and he rides to the West,
Of his goodies he touches not one;
He eateth the crumbs of the Christmas feast
When the dear little folks are done.
Old Santa Claus doeth all that he can;
This beautiful mission is his;
Then, children, be good to the little old man,
When you find who the little man is.

—Anon.

Once in Royal David's city
Stood a lowly cattle shed,
Where a mother laid her baby
In a manger for His bed.
Mary was that mother mild,
Jesus Christ that little child.

—Anon.

The merry Christmas, with its generous boards,
Its fire-lit hearths, and gifts and blazing trees,
Its pleasant voices uttering gentle words,
Its genial mirth, attuned to sweet accords,
Its holiest memories!
The fairest season of the passing year—
The merry, merry Christmas time is here.

—George Arnold

Oh, the Shepherds in Judea!—
Do you think the Shepherds know
How the whole round earth is brightened
In the ruddy Christmas glow?

—Mary Austin

Remember
This December,
That love weighs more than gold!

—Josephine Dodge Daskam Bacon

O Night, the chosen of nights,
Longing and dream of the years,
Blessèd thou art.

—Katharine Lee Bates

O holy Child of Bethlehem!
Descend to us, we pray;
Cast out our sin, and enter in,
Be born in us today.

—Phillips Brooks

And Christmas once is Christmas still;
The gates through which He came,
And forests wild and murmuring rill,
And fruitful field and breezy hill,
And all that else the wide world fill
Are vocal with His name.

—Phillips Brooks

The earth has grown old with its burden of care,
But at Christmas it always is young.

—Phillips Brooks

Loud, underneath the great blue sky,
My heart shall paean sing,
The gold and myrrh of meekest love
Mine only offering. *—Alice Brown*

O Father, may that holy star
Grow every year more bright,
And send its glorious beams afar
To fill the world with light.

—William Cullen Bryant

No trumpet-blast profaned
The hour in which the Prince of Peace was born;
No bloody streamlet stained
Earth's silver rivers on that sacred morn;
But, o'er the peaceful plain,
The war-horse drew the peasant's loaded wain.

—William Cullen Bryant

The Eve is here, with merriment for all,
And Santa Claus, with merry marvels fraught,
Before the dawn across the roofs comes stealing.

—Gelett Burgess

A cattle manger was sufficient service that first Christmas. Now it has grown into hospitals, and refuges for children, and schools, and myriad works of mercy and enlightenment ranging in ever-widening circles through the world; and from these have flowed the sciences and social insight and good will that steadily beat back the frontiers of ignorance, evil and distress. Beginning like a silver rill, that First Christmas has flowed through lurid ages and dark ages, through centuries of renaissance and generations of discovery, broadening as it ran, until now its oceanic waters touch every shore and every interest of mankind. Is that Christmas over?

—W. J. Cameron

Christmas is the gentlest, loveliest festival of the revolving year—and yet, for all that, when it speaks, its voice has strong authority.

—W. J. Cameron

There has been only one Christmas—the rest are anniversaries—and *it* is not over yet. One cattle shed could house all the people who knew of that First Christmas, and now whole nations, peoples of all creeds and tongues feel the compulsions of the time.

—W. J. Cameron

O Christmas Sun! What holy task is thine!
To fold a world in the embrace of God!
—*Guy Wetmore Carryl*

This happy day, whose risen sun
Shall set not through eternity,
This holy day when Christ the Lord,
Took on him our humanity.
—*Phoebe Cary*

Who has not loved a little child, he knows not Christmas Day.
—*Martha Haskell Clark*

Then sing to the holly, the Christmas holly,
That hangs over peasant and king.
—*Eliza Cook*

Here comes old Father Christmas,
With sound of fife and drums;
With mistletoe about his brows,
So merrily he comes!
His arms are full of all good cheer,
His face with laughter glows,
He shines like any household fire
Amid the cruel snows.
—*Rose Terry Cooke*

For we bear the sweetest story
That the glad year ever tells;
How He loved the little children,—
He who brought the Christmas bells!
Ding, dong! ding, dong, Christmas bells!
—*George Cooper*

"And so we shake
The snowy flake
From cedar and myrtle fair,
And the boughs that nod
On the hills of God
We raise to His glory there."
—*Arthur Cleveland Coxe*

God rest ye, little children; let nothing you affright,
For Jesus Christ, your Savior, was born this happy night;
Along the hills of Galilee the white flocks sleeping lay,
When Christ, the Child of Nazareth, was born on Christmas day.
—*Dinah Maria Mulock Craik*

Great little One! whose all-embracing birth
Lifts Earth to Heaven, stoops Heaven to Earth.
—*Richard Crashaw*

To Thee, meek Majesty, soft King
Of simple graces and sweet loves!
Each of us his lamb will bring,
Each his pair of silver doves!
—*Richard Crashaw*

Whatever else be lost among the years,
Let us keep Christmas still a shining thing.
—*Grace Noll Crowell*

Those good people will exhibit the most of the spirit of our Blessed Master who practice Christmas-giving and cheerful, unselfish and zealous Christmas-living through all the circling year. —*T. L. Cuyler*

Garland the Yule log; scatter the wheat—
Feast for the starving birds to eat.
—*Walter de la Mare*

With finger on her solemn lip,
Night hushed the shadowy earth,
And only stars and angels saw
The little Saviour's birth.
—*Margaret Deland*

Happy, happy Christmas, that can win us back to the delusions of our childish days, that can recall to the old man the pleasures of his youth, and transport the sailor and the traveler, thousands of miles away, back to his own fireside and his quiet home!
—*Charles Dickens*

I have always thought of Christmas time as a good time; a kind, forgiving, charitable, pleasant time; the only time I know of, in the long calendar of the year, when men and women seem by one consent to open their shut-up hearts freely. . . . .

And therefore, though it has never put a scrap of gold or silver in my pocket, I believe that it *has* done me good, and *will* do me good; and I say, God bless it!
—*Charles Dickens*

Oh, the nearness of the Christ Child,
When, for a sacred space,
He nestles in our very homes—
Light of the human race!
—*Mary Mapes Dodge*

It *is* the calm and silent night!
A thousand bells ring out, and throw
Their joyous peals abroad, and smite
The darkness, charm'd and holy now.
—*Alfred Domett*

Yet have I brought a gift the Child
May not despise, however small;
For here I lay my heart today,
And it is full of love for all.
Take Thou the poor but loyal thing,
My only tribute, Christ, my king!
—*Eugene Field*

Star of the East, the night were drear
But for the tender grace
That with thy glory comes to cheer,
Earth's loneliest, darkest place,
For by that charity we see
Where there is hope for all and me.
—*Eugene Field*

Peace to all that have goodwill!
God, who heaven and earth doth fill,
Comes to turn us away from ill,
And lies so still
Within the crib of Mary.
—German

He came among us at Christmas tide,
At Christmas tide,
In Bethlehem;
Men shall bring Him from far and wide
Love's diadem:
Jesus, Jesus,
Lo, He comes, and loves, and saves, and frees us! *—German*

Oh, see the air is shaken with white and heavenly wings—
This is the Lord of all the earth, this is the King of Kings.
—Richard Watson Gilder

Silent night, holy night,
All is calm, all is bright
Round yon Virgin Mother and Child,
Holy Infant so tender and mild.
—Franz Gruber

Brightest and best of the Sons of the morning!
Dawn on our darkness and lend us thine aid!
Star of the East, the horizon adorning,
Guide where our Infant Redeemer is laid!
—Reginald Heber

Oh! lovely voices of the sky
Which hymned the Saviour's birth,
Are ye not singing still on high,
Ye that sang, "Peace on earth"?
—Felicia Hemans

The shepherds sing; and shall I silent be?
My God, no hymn for Thee?
My soul's a shepherd, too; a flock it feeds
Of thoughts and words and deeds;
My pasture is Thy Word; the streams Thy grace,
Enriching all the place.
—George Herbert

What sweeter musick can we bring,
Than a Caroll, for to sing
The Birth of this our heavenly King?
Awake the Voice! awake the String!
Heart, Eare, and Eye, and every thing
Awake!
—Robert Herrick

The Darling of the world is come,
And fit it is we finde a roome
To welcome Him. The nobler part
Of all the house here, is the heart,
Which we will give Him; and bequeath
This Hollie, and this Ivie Wreath,
To do Him honour; who's our King,
And Lord of all this Revelling.
—Robert Herrick

Never we needed Thee so sore
Since the first day began.
—Katharine Tynan Hinkson

In the light of that star
Lie the ages impearled;
And that song from afar
Has swept over the world.
Every hearth is aflame, and the Beautiful sing
In the homes of the nations that Jesus is King.
—Josiah Gilbert Holland

Good luck unto old Christmas,
And long life let us sing,
For he doth more good unto the poor
Than many a crownéd king!
—Mary Howitt

Fail not to call to mind, in the course of the twenty-fifth of this month, that the Divinest Heart that ever walked the earth was born on that day; and then smile and enjoy yourselves for the rest of it; for mirth is also of Heaven's making. *—Leigh Hunt*

Christmas is here,
Merry old Christmas,
Gift-bearing, heart-touching, joy-bringing Christmas,
Day of grand memories, king of the year!
—Washington Irving

When mother-love makes all things bright,
When joy comes with the morning light,
When children gather round their tree,
Thou Christmas Babe,
We sing of Thee!
—Tudor Jenks

"For sweetness of thy birth
Every little bird and beast,
Wind and wave and forest tree,
Praises God exceedingly,
Exceedingly."
—Sophie Jewett

What comfort by Him do we win,
Who made Himself the prince of sin,
To make us heirs of Glory?
To see this babe, all innocence,
A martyr born in our defence,
Can man forget this story?
—Ben Jonson

I sing the birth was born tonight,
The author both of life and light;
The angels so did sound it,
And, like the ravished shepherds said,
Who saw the light, and were afraid,
Yet searched, and true they found it.
—Ben Jonson

For who hath nought to give but love,
Gives all his heart away,
And giving all, hath all to give,
Another Christmas Day.
—Charles W. Kennedy

Unlock the door this evening
And let your gate swing wide,
Let all who ask for shelter
Come speedily inside.
What if your yard be narrow?
What if your house be small?
There is a Guest is coming
Will glorify it all.

—*Joyce Kilmer*

Oh, blessed day, which giv'st the eternal lie
To self, and sense, and all the brute within;
Oh, come to us, amid this war of life;
To hall and hovel, come; to all who toil,
In senate, shop, or study; . . .
Come to them, blest and blessing, Christmas Day.
Tell them once more the tale of Bethlehem;
The kneeling shepherds, and the Babe Divine:
And keep them men indeed, fair Christmas Day.

—*Charles Kingsley*

Back over the black mystery of old years, forward into the black mystery of the years to come, shines ever more confident the golden kindliness of Christmas.

—*Winifred Kirkland*

Oh, children of the village choir,
Your carols on the midnight throw!
Oh, bright across the mist and mire,
Ye ruddy hearths of Christmas glow!

—*Andrew Lang*

O earth, O heart, be glad on this glad morn!
God is with man! Life, life to us is born!

—*Lucy Larcom*

Christmas, prithee, be thou dressed
In thy best—
Snowy wimple, snowy gown—
Laying down
Flooring pure and white, to greet
Jesu's feet.
Gloria in Excelsis.

—*Lady Anne Lindsay*

Except the Christ be born again tonight
In dreams of all men, saints and sons of shame,
The world will never see his kingdom bright.

—*Vachel Lindsay*

Three Kings came riding from far away,
Melchior and Gaspar and Baltasar;
Three Wise Men out of the East were they,
And they travelled by night and they slept by day,
For their guide was a beautiful, wonderful star.

—*Longfellow*

Then pealed the bells more loud and deep:
"God is not dead, nor doth He sleep!
The Wrong shall fail,
The Right prevail,
With peace on earth, good-will to men!"

—*Longfellow*

Within the hall are song and laughter,
The cheeks of Christmas glow red and jolly,
And sprouting is every corbel and rafter
With lightsome green of ivy and holly;
Through the deep gulf of the chimney wide
Wallows the Yule log's roaring tide.

—*James Russell Lowell*

Oh, where should we be when the Christmas bells ring
If it weren't for supplies of brown paper and string?

—*E. V. Lucas*

Good news from heaven the angels bring,
Glad tidings to the earth they sing:
To us this day a child is given,
To crown us with the joy of heaven.

—*Martin Luther*

Blessed is the season which engages the whole world in a conspiracy of love!

—*Hamilton Wright Mabie*

What was the first prophetic word that rang
When down the starry sky the angels sang,
That night they came as envoys of the Birth—
What word but peace, "peace and good will on earth"?

—*Edwin Markham*

"Glory to God: good-will to men!"
Come! Feel it, show it, give it then!

—*Edward Sandford Martin*

Good Christmas, whom our children love,
We love you, too! Lift us above
Our cares, our fears, our small desires!
Open our hands and stir the fires
Of helpful fellowship within us,
And back to love and kindness win us!

—*Edward Sandford Martin*

The years have drifted down a misty way
Since Magi came along Judean hills;
But love and loyalty live on today,
Like shining wreaths upon our window sills.

—*Kate Randle Menefee*

This Infant of mankind, this One,
Is still the little welcome Son.

—*Alice Meynell*

When all the tinsel has been laid away,
The tree is stripped, the fevered rush is past—
You still have trees, a hill, a child at play,
And love, and prayer, and fadeless things that last.

—*Anna Blake Mezquida*

Dear day of all days in the year;
Dear day of song, goodwill and cheer;
'Tis golden Christmas morning!

—*Joaquin Miller*

Ring out, ye crystal spheres!
Once bless our human ears,
If ye have power to touch our senses so;
And let your silver chime
Move in melodious time,
And let the bass of Heaven's deep organ blow,
And with your ninefold harmony
Make up full consort to the angelic symphony.
—John Milton

This is the month, and this the happy morn,
Wherein the Son of Heaven's eternal King,
Of wedded maid and virgin mother born,
Our great redemption from above did bring,
For so the holy sages once did sing,
That He our deadly forfeit should release,
And with His Father work us a perpetual peace.
—John Milton

'Twas the night before Christmas, when all through the house
Not a creature was stirring,—not even a mouse;
The stockings were hung by the chimney with care,
In hopes that St. Nicholas soon would be there.
—Clement C. Moore

"News of a fair and marvellous thing,
The snow in the street, and the wind on the door,
Nowell, Nowell, Nowell, we sing.
Minstrels and maids, stand forth on the floor.
From far away we come to you,
To tell of great tidings, strange and true."
—William Morris

At the joyous table,
Think of those who've none,—
The orphan and the widow,
Hungry and alone.
Bountiful your offerings,
To the altar bring;
Let the poor and needy
Christmas carols sing.
—William A. Muhlenberg

We hear the beating of wings over Bethlehem and a light that is not of the sun or of the stars shines in the midnight sky. Let the beauty of the story take away all narrowness, all thought of formal creeds. Let it be remembered as a story that has happened again and again, to men of many different races, that has been expressed through many religions, that has been called by many different names. Time and space and language lay no limitations upon human brotherhood.
—New York Times, Dec. 25, 1937

Only in souls the Christ is brought to birth,
And there He lives and dies.
—Alfred Noyes

All you that to feasting and mirth are inclined,
Come, here is good news for to pleasure your mind,
Old Christmas is come for to keep open house,
He scorns to be guilty of starving a mouse.
—Old Carol

The holly and the ivy,
Now both are full well grown,
Of all the trees that are in the wood,
The holly bears the crown.
—Old Carol

And all the bells on earth shall ring
On Christmas day, on Christmas day;
And all the bells on earth shall ring
On Christmas day in the morning.
—Old Carol

Praise the day with joy and mirth, love and exaltation,
When our Saviour came to earth, bringing man salvation.
—Old Catalan Nativity Song

As Joseph was a-walking,
He heard an angel sing,
"This night shall be the birth-time
Of Christ, the heavenly king.
He neither shall be born
In housen nor in hall,
Nor in the place of Paradise,
But in an ox's stall."
—Old English

Then be ye glad, good people,
This night of all the year,
And light ye up your candles,
For His star it shineth clear.
—Old English

We bring in the holly, the ivy, the pine,
The spruce and the hemlock together we twine;
With evergreen branches our walls we array
For the keeping of Christmas, our high holiday.
Glory to God in the highest we sing,
Peace and good-will are the tidings we bring.
—Old English

Peace on earth, good will to men—
Oh, dim and holy light! . . . . .
Little King of all the world,
I share Thy dream tonight!
—Catherine Parmenter

With holly and ivy
So green and so gay,
We deck up our houses
As fresh as the day,
With bays and rosemary,
And laurel complete,
And everyone now
Is a king in conceit.
—Poor Richard's Almanack

O, to have dwelt in Bethlehem
When the star of the Lord shone bright!
To have sheltered the holy wanderers
On that blessèd Christmas night;
To have kissed the tender wayworn feet
Of the Mother undefiled,
And, with reverent wonder and deep delight,
To have tended the Holy Child!
—Adelaide A. Procter

But the star that shone in Bethlehem
Shines still, and shall not cease,
And we listen still to the tidings,
Of Glory and of Peace.
—Adelaide A. Procter

What can I give Him,
Poor as I am?
If I were a shepherd
I would bring a lamb;
If I were a wise Man,
I would do my part,—
Yet what I can I give Him,
Give my heart.
—Christina G. Rossetti

The shepherds had an angel,
The wise men had a star;
But what have I, a little child,
To guide me home from far,
Where glad stars sing together,
And singing angels are?
—Christina G. Rossetti

Of all dear days is Christmas Day
The dearest and the best.
—Margaret E. Sangster

That is the glory of the spirit of Christmas. It triumphs over all obstacles; it breaks down all barriers; it flourishes in all countries and in every heart. For the spirit of Christmas fulfils the greatest hunger of mankind.
—Loring A. Schuler

Each age has deemed the new-born year
The fittest time for festal cheer. . .
And well our Christian sires of old
Loved when the year its course had rolled
And brought blithe Christmas back again,
With all his hospitable train.
—Sir Walter Scott

Heap on more wood!—the wind is chill;
But let it whistle as it will,
We'll keep our Christmas merry still.
—Sir Walter Scott

It came upon the midnight clear
That glorious song of old,
From angels bending near the earth
To touch their harps of gold:
"Peace on the earth, good will to men
From heaven's all-gracious King"—
The world in solemn stillness lay
To hear the angels sing.
—Edmund Hamilton Sears

This day shall Christian lips be mute,
And Christian hearts be cold?
—Edmund Hamilton Sears

Some say that ever 'gainst that season comes
Wherein our Savior's birth is celebrated,
The bird of dawning singeth all night long;
And then, they say, no spirit can walk abroad;
The nights are wholesome; then no planets strike,
No fairy takes, nor witch hath power to charm;
So hallow'd and so gracious is the time.
—Shakespeare

I send my thoughts afar, and let
Them paint your Christmas Day at home.
—Edward Rowland Sill

Oh, the little stars sang down to Him,
And the moon she gave a crown to Him,
And the snow a silver carpet for His throne;
And the oxen by the manger
Did homage to the Stranger,
As to King who claimeth fealty from His own;
And there whispered then the wind to Him,
As one who would be kind to Him,
Making music, angel music, from on high.
—Charles William Stubbs

Bid our peace increase,
Thou that madest morn;
Bid oppressions cease,
Bid the night be peace,
Bid the day be born.
—Algernon Charles Swinburne

Rise, happy morn; rise, holy morn;
Draw forth the cheerful day from night;
O Father, touch the east, and light
The light that shone when Hope was born.
—Alfred Tennyson

The time draws near the birth of Christ;
The moon is hid; the night is still;
The Christmas bells from hill to hill
Answer each other in the mist.
—Alfred Tennyson

As fits the holy Christmas birth,
Be this, good friends, our carol still—
Be peace on earth, be peace on earth,
To men of gentle will.
—William Makepeace Thackeray

And we—are we not wise
To cling with avid eyes
To the old tale, and be
Moved by its memory?
Unutterably dim
Our bright world, lacking Him.
—Charles Hanson Towne

At Christmas be merry and thank God of all,
And feast thy poor neighbours, the great and the small.
Yea, all the year long have an eye to the poor,
And God shall send luck to keep open thy door.
—Thomas Tusser

In the climes of the icy North,
And the lands of the cane and the palm,
By the Alpine cotter's blazing hearth,
And in tropic belts of calm,
Men list tonight the welcome swells,
Sweet and clear, of Christmas Bells!

—*Unknown*

Are you willing to believe that love is the strongest thing in the world—stronger than hate, stronger than evil, stronger than death—and that the blessed life which began in Bethlehem nineteen hundred years ago is the image and brightness of the Eternal Love? Then you can keep Christmas,

And if you keep it for a day, why not always?
But you can never keep it alone.

—*Henry van Dyke*

Awake, glad heart! Get up, and sing!
It is the birthday of thy King.
Awake! Awake!

—*Henry Vaughan*

It is impossible to conceive of any holiday that could take its place, nor indeed would it seem that human wit could invent another so adapted to humanity.

—*Charles Dudley Warner*

See the kinder shepherds round Him,
Telling wonders from the sky!
Where they sought Him, there they found Him,
With His Virgin mother by.

—*Isaac Watts*

Shepherds, rejoice, lift up your eyes,
And send your fears away;
News from the region of the skies!
Salvation's born today.

—*Isaac Watts*

There smiles Christmas, holly-crown'd
With his blithest coronet:
Friendship's face he loveth well:
'Tis a countenance whose spell
Sheds a balm o'er every mead and dell.
Where we used to fret.

—*Theodore Watts-Dunton*

Hark! the herald angels sing,
Glory to the new-born King;
Peace on earth and mercy mild,
God and sinners reconciled!
Joyful, all ye nations, rise,
Join the triumph of the skies;
With the angelic host proclaim,
Christ is born in Bethelehem.

—*Charles Wesley*

Blow bugles of battle, the marches of peace;
East, west, north and south, let the long quarrel cease;
Sing the song of great joy that the angels began,
Sing of glory to God and of good-will to man!

—*John Greenleaf Whittier*

Sound over all waters, reach out from all lands,
The chorus of voices, the clasping of hands;
Sing hymns that were sung by the stars of the morn,
Sing songs of the angels when Jesus was born!
With glad jubilations
Bring hope to the nations!

—*John Greenleaf Whittier*

Who gives to whom hath naught been given
His gift in need, though small indeed,
As is the grass-blade's wind-blown seed,
Is large as earth and rich as heaven.

—*John Greenleaf Whittier*

God bless the master of this house,
Likewise the mistress too;
And all the little children
That round the table go.

—*Yorkshire*

COLUMBUS DAY

In all parts of the Old World, as well as of the New, it was evident that Columbus had kindled a fire in every mariner's heart. That fire was the harbinger of a new era, for it was not to be extinguished.
—*Charles Kendall Adams*

He was forever obeying his illusions.
—*Editorial. Atlantic Monthly March 1892*

It is not at all difficult to show that many more than Columbus, in his age, perceived *a priori* the evidence of a Cathay lying to the westward, to be reached by sailing in that direction. But Columbus put the evidence to the test; and the very obstacles which he overcame, both by his lofty assurance, in which his enemies could see only the arrogance of an over-weening vanity, and by his persistence until his faith had overcome mountains, raise him above the ranks of common men.
—*Editorial. Atlantic Monthly March 1892*

No kingly conqueror, since time began
The long career of ages, hath to man
A scope so ample given for trade's bold range,
Or caused on earth's wide stage such rapid mighty change.
—*Joanna Baillie*

The impression he made on those with whom he came in contact even in the days of his poverty . . . shows that he had great powers of persuasion and was possessed of personal magnetism.
—*Adolph Francis Alphonse Bandelier*

Columbus looked; and still around them spread,
From south to north, th' immeasurable shade;
At last, the central shadows burst away,
And rising regions open'd on the day.
—*Joel Barlow*

What mild seas and blossomed vales
Awaited you? haply a paradise
But not the one which drew your swerveless eyes;
Could you have known what lands were there beyond the main,
You surelier would have turned to gladsomeness from pain.
—*Louis James Block*

A noble form, the looming mast beside,
Columbus, calm, his prescience verified.
—*Richard E. Burton*

It has taken the older world a long time to understand and to appreciate what really happened when Columbus discovered this New World. At that time the curtain rose upon a new and impressive act in the drama of civilization. —*Nicholas Murray Butler*

The sails hung listless on the pictured sea
Where green Sargasso meadows pulsed and dreamed
In liquid atmosphere; the sea birds free,
On silken pinions, sank and rose and gleamed—
A sea of glass and mingling gold it seemed.
—*Hezekiah Butterworth*

In robes of scarlet and princely gold,
On the new world's land they kneel;
In the name of Christ, whom all adore,
They christened the island San Salvador,
For the crown of their own Castile.
—*S. H. M. Byers*

He began in error yet reached a triumph greater than he lived to know.
—*W. J. Cameron*

Mixed motives moved Columbus. There were religion and the inner urge of the explorer and the much-derided profit-motive. Columbus was not modest in computing what his own rewards should be, and, indeed, for what he accomplished, no reward could be too great. But his richest reward was just the power to do his task—and no one ever receives a higher. —*W. J. Cameron*

He leaves in the background of fame all other navigators whose names are written in the priceless annals of discovery.
—*Emilio Castelar*

How a man ever should hope to get thither,
E'en if he knew there was another side!
But to suppose he should come anywhither,
Sailing straight on into chaos untried,
In spite of the motion,
Across the whole ocean,
To stick to the notion
That in some nook or bend
Of a sea without end,
He should find North and South America,
Was a pure madness, indeed, I must say.
—*Arthur Hugh Clough*

Columbus! With proud love, yet reverently,
Pronounce that name—the name of one who heard
A word of life, and, answering that word,
Braved death, unfearing, on the Shadowy Sea.
—*Florence Earle Coates*

Columbus! Other title needs he none.
—*Florence Earle Coates*

The Lord hath blessed me abundantly with a knowledge of marine affairs. Of the science of the stars He has given me that which would suffice; so, also, of geometry and arithmetic. Besides this He has granted me the mind and skill to draw globes and maps, and indicate upon them in their proper places the various cities and rivers and mountains. I have studied all sorts of writings, history, the Chronicles, and some of the other arts, for which our Lord has quickened my intelligence and understanding.

—*Christopher Columbus*

And I purpose to make a chart and to set down therein the lands and waters of the Ocean Sea, with all their positions and bearings, and to compose it into a book, and to illustrate the whole with paintings, showing, as we go, the latitude from the Equator, and also the western longitude.

—*Christopher Columbus*

Eight years I was torn with disputes, and in a word, my proposition was a thing for mockery. —*Christopher Columbus*

Then guided by th' Almighty Hand,
Columbus spread his daring sail;
Ocean received a new command,
And Zephyrs breath'd a gentle gale.

The Western World appear'd to view,
Her friendly arms extended wide;
Then Freedom o'er th' Atlantic flew,
With pure Religion by her side.

—*Commemorative Ode written for the Boston celebration of the Tercentenary of the Discovery of America*

There is no recorded instance of more admirable tenacity of purpose nor of more unflinching devotion to one single idea; none of courage more steadfast in the face of perils of every kind.

—*Frederic R. Coudert*

Yet comes the dawn
Of centuries which myth and mould defy,
Whose rays of promise, brighter than the sun,
Spread far and near when brave Columbus won.

—*W. I. Crandall*

All hail, Columbus, discoverer, dreamer, hero, and apostle! We, here, of every race and country, recognize the horizon which bounded his vision and the infinite scope of his genius. The voice of gratitude and praise for all of the blessings which have been showered upon mankind by his adventure is limited to no language, but is uttered in every tongue. Neither marble nor brass can fitly form his statue. Continents are his monument, and unnumbered millions present and to come, who enjoy in their liberties and their happiness the fruits of his faith, will reverently guard and preserve, from century to century, his name and fame.

—*Chauncey M. Depew*

He was a man whom danger could not daunt,
Nor sophistry perplex, nor pain subdue;
A stoic, reckless of the world's vain taunt.

—*Aubrey De Vere*

Columbus discovered no isle or key so lonely as himself.

—*Emerson*

Every ship that comes to America got its chart from Columbus.

—*Emerson*

Here is that Christopher Columbus, the discoverer of a wonderful world unknown to any age before; whom we may believe to have been born under the benign influence of fortunate stars, to be an incomparable honor to Ligyria, a choice adornment of Italy, a flaming light of our age, and that he might outshine the fame of the heroes of old.

—*Eulogy from a parchment scroll attached to a portrait*

With this humble instrumentality did it please Providence to prepare the theatre for those events by which a new dispensation of liberty was to be communicated to man.

—*Edward Everett*

He was an idealist, a poetic dreamer, a religious fanatic, a man hard for some people to understand. —*John Fiske*

To Columbus we owe the fresh soil in which a nationality of the highest type has begun to be developed. —*John Fiske*

We shall be inclined to pronounce the voyage that led to the way to this New World as the most epoch-making event of all that have occurred since the birth of Christ.

—*John Fiske*

Oh, rest thee, mighty Sailor!
Thou splendid, fearless soul.

—*Annie Johnson Flint*

He cleft far wider seas
Than met his gaze—He never heard the roar
Of waves of wondrous human destinies
Upon that farther shore.

—*Mary Isabella Forsyth*

Ah! what a waste of ocean here begins,
And lonely waves, so black and confortless!

—*Philip Freneau*

This persevering man succeeds at last!
The last gazette has publish'd to the world
That Ferdinand and Isabella grant
Three well rigg'd ships to Christopher Columbus;
And have bestowed the noble titles too
Of Admiral and Vice-Roy—great indeed!

—*Philip Freneau*

And thus she bids me say:
"Columbus, haste away,
"Hasten to Palos, and if you can find
"Three barques, of structure suited to your mind,
"Straight make a purchase in the royal name;
"Equip them for the seas without delay,
"Since long the journey is (we heard you say)
"To that rich country which we wish to claim.—
"Let them be small—for know the crown is poor
"Though basking in the sunshine of renown.
"Long wars have wasted us: the pride of Spain
"Was ne'er before so high, nor purse so mean;
"Time must restore past splendor to our reign."

—Philip Freneau

In three small barques to cross so vast a sea,
Held to be boundless, even in learning's eye,
. . . .
It is a bold attempt!—Yet I must go,
Travelling the surge to its great boundary;
Far, far away beyond the reach of men,
Where never galley spread her milk-white sail
Or weary pilgrim bore the Christian name!

—Philip Freneau

"Yet to the west what lengthen'd seas!
"Are no gay islands found in these,
"No sylvan worlds that Nature meant
"To balance Asia's vast extent?"

—Philip Freneau

He dreads no tempest on the untravell'd deep,
Reason shall steer, and skill disarm the gale.

—Philip Freneau

Great Master Dreamer!

—Charles Buxton Going

For all mankind that unstained scroll unfurled,
Where God might write anew the story of the World.

—Edward Everett Hale

One storm-trained seaman listened to the word;
What no man saw he saw, he heard what no man heard.

—Edward Everett Hale

Columbus had all the spirit of a crusader, and, at the same time, the investigating nature of a modern man of science.

—Edmund Arthur Helps

Whose indomitable spirit changed the face of the earth for us.

—Edmund Arthur Helps

If some of his conclusions were erroneous, they were at least ingenious and splendid; and their error resulted from the clouds which still hung over his peculiar path of enterprise. His own discoveries enlightened the ignorance of the age; guided conjecture to certainty, and dispelled that very darkness with which he had been obliged to struggle.

—Washington Irving

How would his magnanimous spirit have been consoled, amidst the afflictions of age and the cares of penury, the neglect of a fickle public, and the injustice of an ungrateful king, could he have anticipated the splendid empires which were to spread over the beautiful world which he had discovered; and the nations, and tongues, and languages which were to fill its lands with his renown, and revere and bless his name to the latest posterity!

—Washington Irving

I undertake the enterprise for my own crown of Castile, and will pledge my jewels to raise the necessary funds.

—Isabella, Queen of Castile

The true greatness, then, of Columbus lay not in conceiving a totally new idea, but in grasping the practical bearing of one which he shared with others, in having faith to trust it, and in clinging with indomitable persistency to the purpose of realizing it.

—William Henry Johnson

Lo! in the West a pale unsteady light
Shines in the mirk, and darts its silver rays,
A trembling gleam, now here, now pass'd away
Behind the shadowy curtains of the night,
Mocking the ken. Oh happy, blissful beam!

—T. P. Johnston

This was the land, and grief was turn'd to joy;
This was the land, and all their toil was o'er;
This was the land, and where the Master stood
They turn'd in transport of delirious joy,
And laugh'd, and sobb'd, and kneeling clasp'd his knees.

—T. P. Johnston

"All my course
A voice has whisper'd ever in my ear,
'Go on, go on, Columbus, it is thine
To plant new jewels in the ancient crowns
That rule in Europe, and to lift the Cross
For healing of another Christendom.
Go on, and prosper!' "

—T. P. Johnston

Now through two weary moons, the restless keels
Had journey'd onward to the Gates of Eve;
Still fortune shone not, and no hopeful sign
Gladden'd their toil with earnest of success.
Still Ocean hid within his circling arms
The land they sought, and on her thousand shores
Whisper'd unheard, unseen.
Each early Morn
With eager watching eyes they scann'd the verge
Of outmost ocean, and each weary Eve
In sadness turn'd to meditate and mourn.

—T. P. Johnston

He stands out among the beacon lights of history as a man of vision dominated by a definite purpose. —*John George Jones*

He completed the universe, he achieved the physical unity of the globe. —*Lamartine*

"Wait! the Pinta's gun!
Why, look, 'tis dawn, the land is clear: 'tis done!
Two dawns do break at once from Time's full hand—
God's, East—mine, West: good friends, behold my Land!"
—*Sidney Lanier*

He had a figure that was above medium height, a countenance long and imposing, an aquiline nose, clear blue eyes, a light complexion tinged with red, beard and hair blond in youth, but early turned to white. He was rough in character, with little amiability of speech, affable, however, when he wished to be, and passionate when irritated.
—*Bartolomé de Las Casas*

He kept them pointed straight ahead—
Due west they sailed toward shores unknown.
The fearless leader standing deep
In thought, beside the helm—alone.
—*Elias Lieberman*

Would that we had the fortunes of Columbus.
Sailing his caravels a trackless way,
He found a Universe—he sought Cathay.
—*Vachel Lindsay*

A great intuition, amounting almost to genius, was Columbus's.
—*Cesare Lombroso*

"The old sea-fearing men
Came to me now and then,
With their Sagas of the seas;—
. . . .
I could not eat nor sleep,
For thinking of those seas."
—*Longfellow*

On either side, behind, before,
The ocean stretches like a floor.
—*Longfellow*

He now shines as a fixed star in the constellation of the great lights of modern times.
—*John Lord*

The inward assurance that he was right in his calculation gave to his character a blended boldness, arrogance, and dignity.
—*John Lord*

It was the surmounting of moral difficulties which gives to Columbus his true greatness as a man of genius and resources.
—*John Lord*

To prove his position by absolute experiment and hazardous enterprise makes him one of the greatest of human benefactors, whose fame will last through all the generations of men. —*John Lord*

Strength found he in the unsympathizing sun,
And strange stars from beneath the horizon won,
And the dumb ocean pitilessly grave:
High-hearted surely he.
—*James Russell Lowell*

Flawless his heart and tempered to the core
Who, beckoned by the forward-leaning wave,
First left behind him the firm-footed shore,
And, urged by every nerve of sail and oar,
Steered for the Unknown which gods to mortals gave.
—*James Russell Lowell*

"What should we do but sing His praise,
That led us through the watery maze,
Unto an isle so long unknown,
And yet far kinder than our own?"
—*Andrew Marvell*

Behind him lay the great Azores,
Behind the Gates of Hercules;
Before him not the ghost of shores,
Before him only shoreless seas.
—*Joaquin Miller*

He gained a world; he gave that world
Its grandest lesson: "On! sail on!"
—*Joaquin Miller*

In spirit perhaps he also saw
Rich Mexico, the seat of Montezume,
And Cusco in Peru, the richest seat
Of Atabalipa, and yet unspoiled
Guiana, whose great city Geryon's sons
Call El Dorado.
—*Milton*

The world was all before him, where to choose.
And Providence his guide. —*Milton*

Rejoice, Iberis! see thy fame increased!
Another world Columbus from the East
And the mid-ocean summons to thy sway!
—*Bishop of Montepeloso*

Hope swells thy sail;—in spirit I behold
That maiden-world, twin-sister of the old,
By nature nursed beyond the jealous sea,
Denied to ages, but betroth'd to me.
—*James Montgomery*

Then first Columbus, with the mighty hand
Of grasping genius, weigh'd the sea and land.
—*James Montgomery*

Ye sons of freedom, hail the day
That brought a second world to view,
To great Columbus' memory pay
The praise and honor justly due.
—*From Ode composed and sung on the occasion of the 300th Anniversary of New York City*

When the first sea-gulls, fluttering their wings in the wake of the three caravels, soothed the irritation and relieved the despair of the crew who had accompanied the hardy Genoese on his venturesome voyage, and heralded the nearness of land, the circumstance really marked not so much the close of a hazardous expedition that was approaching, as the glory of a great new dawn, limning itself lustrous on the dim and distant future. —*Felix Pacheco*

He was gifted with a brilliant and soaring imagination, that would have stamped him a visionary, but for a balancing penetration of mind and soundness of judgment.
—*H. F. Parker*

I have found new Lands—a World, maybe,
Whose splendor will yet the Old outshine;
And life and death are alike to me,
For earth will honor, and heaven is mine.
—*Edna Dean Proctor*

His bark
The daring mariner shall urge far o'er
The Western wave, a smooth and level plain,
Albeit the earth is fashioned like a wheel.
—*Luigi Pulci*

I am that Christopher that knew no rest,
Urged by one thought, one faith, one hope to be.
—*Mary Eleanor Roberts*

At day-break might the Caravels be seen,
Chasing their shadows o'er the deep serene.
—*Samuel Rogers*

But hope was his—a faith sublime,
That triumphs over place and time;
And here, his mighty labour done,
And his course of glory run,
Awhile as more than man he stood,
So large the debt of gratitude!
—*Samuel Rogers*

Still, as beyond this mortal life impelled
By some mysterious energy, He held
His everlasting course. Still self-possessed,
High on the deck He stood, disdaining rest;
. . . .
Fathomed, with searching hand, the dark profound,
And scattered hope and glad assurance round.
—*Samuel Rogers*

Yet who but He undaunted could explore
A world of waves, a sea without a shore,
Trackless and vast and wild as that revealed
When round the Ark the birds of tempest wheeled;
. . . .
No sign of man! no vestige of his power!
—*Samuel Rogers*

His deed makes him immortal. —*S. Ruge*

This remains to him: the resolution to do the deed; the invincible courage which made him persevere through years of scorn and insult, which made him devote his life to the idea. —*S. Ruge*

A fertile continent thou gavst mankind,
Which only lay in lonely idleness;
Through sufferings terrible, and great distress,
This was accomplished. . . . . . .
Immortal man, the world yet owes to thee
A tribute for thy hardships and thy pain.
—*Albert J. Rupp*

He gave the world another world.
—*George Santayana*

Columbus found a world, and had no chart,
Save one that faith deciphered in the skies.
—*George Santayana*

Steer, bold mariner, on! albeit witlings deride thee,
And the steersman drop idly his hand at the helm.
Ever and ever to the westward! there must the coast be discovered,
If it but lie distinct, luminous lie in thy mind.
Trust to the God that leads thee, and follow the sea that is silent;
Did it not yet exist, now would it rise from the flood.
Nature with Genius stand united in league everlasting;
What is promised by one, surely the other performs.
—*Friedrich von Schiller*

Courage, World-finder! Thou hast need!
In Fate's unfolding scroll
Dark woes and ingrate wrongs I read
That rack the noble soul.
—*Lydia Huntley Sigourney*

Courage, thou Genoese! Old Time
Thy splendid dream shall crown.
—*Lydia Huntley Sigourney*

He accomplished more than anyone else towards making us masters of the world on which we tread, and giving us, instead of yawning abysses and realms of vapour, wide waters for our ships, and lands for the city and the plough. . . He stands in history as the completer of the globe. —*John Sterling*

O immeasurable scope of human genius! O mighty strength of trust in God! O miserable inequality of earthly fortunes! O mysterious complication of mortal power and weakness! how wonderfully are they all displayed in the story of Columbus!
—*John Sterling*

Columbus discovered only the shell of this country.
—*Thomas DeWitt Talmage*

For my purpose holds
To sail beyond the sunset, and the paths
Of all the western stars.

—Alfred Tennyson

"O hundred shores of happy climes,
How swiftly stream'd ye by the bark!
At times the whole sea burn'd, at times
With wakes of fire we tore the dark;
At times a carven craft would shoot
From havens hid in fairy bowers,
With naked limbs, and flowers and fruit,
But we nor paused for fruit nor flowers.

—Alfred Tennyson

Last night a dream—I sail'd
On my first voyage, harass'd by the frights
Of my first crew, their curses and their groans.
The great flame-banner borne by Teneriffe,
The compass, like an old friend false at last
In our most need, appall'd them, and the wind
Still westward, and the weedy seas—at length
The landbird, and the branch with berries on it,
The carven staff—and last the light, the light
On Guanahani! but I changed the name;
San Salvador I call'd it.

—Alfred Tennyson

The slender cocoa's drooping crown of plumes,
The lightning flash of insect and of bird,
The luster of the long convulvuluses
That coiled around the stately stems, and ran
Even to the limit of the land, the glows
And glories of the broad belt of the world,
All these he saw.

—Alfred Tennyson

"Chains for the Admiral of the Ocean! chains
For him who gave a new heaven, a new earth,
As Holy John had prophesied of me,
Gave glory and more empire to the kings
Of Spain than all their battles! chains for him
Who push'd his prows into the setting sun,
And made West East.

—Alfred Tennyson

Columbus dreamed of an unknown shore,
At the rim of a far-flung sky.

—Unknown

The course of his life bears much resemblance to a mediaeval legend. . . He rose from nothing, a vagabond Italian adventurer, to become Grand Admiral of Spain, and Viceroy of a mighty Empire; he paid for seven years of glory and of power by sudden ruin and such humiliation as few men have known and, after a feeble afterglow of fame, he died a lonely death, almost forgotten.

—Jacob Wassermann

If Christopher Columbus is the man who, according to the common historical view, shut the door upon the Middle Ages and inaugurated a new world and a new age, the moment when those three paltry vessels left that Spanish harbour is one of the most epoch-making in the history of humanity.

—Jacob Wassermann

When shall the world forget
The glory and our debt;
Indomitable soul,
Immortal Genoese?

—William Watson

What treasure found he? Chains and pains and sorrow—
Yea, all the wealth those noble seekers find
Whose footfalls mark the music of mankind!
'Twas his to lend a life; 'twas man's to borrow;
'Twas his to make, but not to share, the morrow.

—Theodore Watts-Dunton

Ah Genoese, thy dream! thy dream!
Centuries after thou art laid in thy grave,
The shore thou foundest verifies thy dream!

—Walt Whitman

The age created him and the age left him. There is no more conspicuous example in history of a man showing the path and losing it.

—Justin Winsor

Hardly a name in profane history is more august than his. Hardly another character in the world's record has made so little of its opportunities. His discovery was a blunder; his blunder was a new world; the New World is his monument! *—Justin Winsor*

Was this his face, and these the finding eyes
That plucked a new world from the rolling seas?

—George Edward Woodberry

What faith in man must in our new world beat,
Thinking how once he saw before his face
The west and all the host of stars retreat
Into the silent infinite of space!

—George Edward Woodberry

Three ships and a crew and a great, great soul—
Columbus—had found a world!

—Annette Wynne

CONSERVATION WEEK

Waste is a tax on the whole people.
—Albert W. Atwood

We saw miles of young trees being destroyed by fires started by engine sparks, and left to burn. We saw farms divided by wooden fences that contain enough lumber to build the homes of all Belgium. Everywhere in the country was wasted land. If we had such bounteous wealth of land and other resources as are wasted here, we could transform our people into conditions of prosperity beyond dreams.
—Belgian Commission sent to the United States

The earth belongs to each generation, and it is as criminal to fetter future generations with perpetual franchises, making the multitudes servants to a favored faction of the population, as it would be to impair, unnecessarily, the common store.
—William Jennings Bryan

Before these fields were shorn and tilled
Full to the brim our rivers flowed;
The melody of waters filled
The fresh and boundless woods;
And torrents dashed, and rivulets play'd,
The fountains spouted in the shade.
—William Cullen Bryant

For ages, on the silent forest here,
Thy beams did fall before the red man came
To dwell beneath them; in their shade the deer
Fed, and feared not the arrow's deadly aim.
Nor tree was felled, in all that world of woods,
Save by the beaver's tooth, or winds, or rush of floods.
—William Cullen Bryant

In the green veins of these fair growths of earth
There dwells a nature that receives delight
From all the gentle processes of life
And shrinks from loss of being.
—William Cullen Bryant

A nation's growth from sea to sea
Stirs in his heart who plants a tree.
—H. C. Bunner

Living in the midst of abundance we have the greatest difficulty in seeing that the supply of natural wealth is limited and that the constant increase of population is destined to reduce the American standard of living unless we deal more sanely with our resources.
—W. H. Carothers

His are the mountains and the valleys his,
And the resplendent rivers. His t' enjoy
With a propriety that none can feel,
But who, with filial countenance inspir'd,
Can lift to heaven an unpresumptuous eye,
And smiling say—My Father made them all!
—Cowper

Let no one longer conceive the question of wildlife conservation to be limited to the interest of sportsmen and bird lovers. It is fundamentally economic in its major aspects and is a vital element in our existence, happiness and prosperity. *—Jay N. Darling*

When you restore environment for wild life, you accomplish restoration of all the other important conservation elements: water conservation, soil conservation, forest and vegetable conservation, and every other type of resource. *—Jay N. Darling*

When you defile the pleasant streams
And the wild bird's abiding place,
You massacre a million dreams
And cast your spittle in God's face.
—John Drinkwater

He who tenderly saves a tree,
All in a night of God-sent dream,
He shall list to a hermit thrush
Deep in the forest by mountain stream,
With friendly branches that lead and shade,
All in a woodland that he has made.
—The Dryad's Message

He who wantonly kills a tree,
All in a night of God-sent dream,
He shall travel a desert waste
Of pitiless glare, and never a stream,
Nor a blade of grass, nor an inch of shade—
All in a wilderness he has made.
—The Dryad's Message

The forest is my loyal friend,
Like God it useth me.
—Ralph Waldo Emerson

He who knows what sweets and virtues are in the ground, the waters, the plants, the heavens, and how to come at these enchantments, is the rich and royal man.
—Ralph Waldo Emerson

The animals prey upon each other because it is their nature to do so and because their lives depend upon it. Savages hunt because they must have food. We do not need to hunt, but, because of our higher intelligence, our hunting methods are far more destructive than are those of either animals or savages.
—Harold W. Fairbanks

The most important thing that we can do to bring wild creatures back again is to let them alone. *—Harold W. Fairbanks*

Trouble always follows the destruction of the forests on the headwaters of the streams. *—Harold W. Fairbanks*

We came into possession of a land unspoiled by its primitive inhabitants. It was just as Nature made it. In a few short years we have almost exterminated the Indian. We have swept away a large part of the forests. We have almost destroyed many of the species of animals and birds. We have robbed the soil and injured the flow of the rivers. Some of this loss we could not help, for when many millions of people occupy a land there must be many changes. But for the losses that we have needlessly and carelessly caused we shall sometime be sorry.
—Harold W. Fairbanks

Conservation does not mean the locking up of our resources, nor a hindrance to real progress in any direction. It means only wise, careful use. *—Mary Huston Gregory*

Man has let in the passionate sun
To suck the life-blood of the mountain,
And drink up its fountains one by one;
And out of the immortal freshness made
A thing of barter, and sold in trade
The sons of the mother mountain.
—Millard F. Hudson

We do not so soon forget the magnificence of the deep woods and unbroken prairies, nor the fascination of contact with wild creatures, even though our main enterprise is to turn natural resources to practical use.
—Iowa Twenty-five Year Conservation Plan Report 1933

To be poor through neglect and waste of nature's offerings, through one's own ignorance and laziness; to deprive self and others, through one's own remissness, of comfort and cheer of life, of culture of mind and heart, such as affluence allows, is a sin against human life, a sin against the almighty God.
—John Ireland

You call them thieves and pillagers; but know
They are the winged wardens of your farms,
Who from the cornfields drive the insidious foe,
And from your harvests keep a hundred harms;
Even the blackest of them all, the crow,
Renders good service as your man-at-arms,
Crushing the beetle in his coat of mail,
And crying havoc on the slug and snail.
—Longfellow

Conservation of natural resources also must reach the stage of an economic necessity.
—Frank L. McVey

When we have followed Conservation to its full development, have purified and regulated our rivers, reservoired them against floods, improved their channels, and revetted their banks to prevent erosion, this is what we may expect to see—graceful, curving channels, navigable, beautiful, bordered with grass and trees, or with handsome and smokeless cities, adding to the fascination both of traveling on and of dwelling by them.
—John L. Mathews

Accuse not Nature: she hath done her part;
Do thou but thine.
—Milton

Wherefore did Nature pour her bounties forth
With such a full and unwithdrawing hand,
Covering the earth with odours, fruits, and flocks,
Thronging the seas with spawn innumerable,
But all to please, and sate the curious taste?
—Milton

Our wild-life resources are among our most valuable assets, and there can be no higher public duty than to aid in their preservation.
—Charles Lathrop Pack

[Conservation] recognizes fully the right of the present generation to use what it needs and all it needs of the natural resources now available, but it recognizes equally our obligation so to use what we need that our descendants shall not be deprived of what they need.
—Gifford Pinchot

[Conservation] stands for an equal opportunity for every American citizen to get his fair share of benefit from these resources, both now and hereafter. *—Gifford Pinchot*

We are beginning to realize that the conservation question is a question of right and wrong, as any question must be which may involve the difference between prosperity and poverty, health and sickness, ignorance and education, well-being and misery, to hundreds of thousands of families.
—Gifford Pinchot

The same rules govern a nation that govern a boy or a man. If the boy or the man or the nation spend more than they earn, they do not get on and up. We have wasted and we go on wasting so much, and the number of people in America is increasing so rapidly, that we are fast using up what we have instead of using it wisely.
—Overton W. Price

This nation must make both ends meet by living within its means. That calls for wasting less and producing more—for growing bigger crops, for so handling the forests as to improve them, for commonsense and knowledge and self-restraint in our use, not only of what grows, but of the things which do not grow, like minerals and water. To-day we are not living within our means. Until we do we are harming ourselves, and we are robbing those who will come after us.

—*Overton W. Price*

My squandered forests, hacked and hewed,
Are gone; my rivers fail;
My stricken hillsides, stark and nude,
Stand shivering in the gale.
Down to the sea my teeming soil
In yellow torrents goes;
The guerdon of the farmer's toil
With each year lesser grows.

—*Robert M. Reese*

A nation less bountifully endowed than ours, would have ceased to exist a long time ago. The remarkable thing was that the people of the United States were complacent for so long in the face of exploitation and waste and mismanagement, yes, and even larceny, of the national wealth that belongs to all the people. —*Franklin D. Roosevelt*

The conservation of our natural resources and their proper use constitute the fundamental problem which underlies almost every other problem of our national life.

—*Theodore Roosevelt*

So any nation which in its youth lives only for a day, reaps without sowing, and consumes without husbanding, must expect the penalty of the prodigal, whose labor could with difficulty find him the bare means of life.

—*Theodore Roosevelt*

Therefore, when we build, let us think that we build forever. Let it not be for present delight, nor for present use alone; let it be such work as our descendants will thank us for. —*John Ruskin*

Of all the sinful wasters of man's inheritance on earth, and all are in this regard sinners, the very worst are the people of America. —*Nathaniel Southgate Shaler*

Stop killing and start creating. Stop cutting and start planting. Stop wasting and start saving. Stop hating and start loving. These are the ten commandments of conservation for each of us within his own dooryard and neighborhood, over his own ranch and farm; a sower of seed, a planter of trees, a nourisher of life, where heretofore we have each plucked and burned and slaughtered.

—*Dallas Lore Sharp*

Conservation, while a question of national importance, is at bottom a local issue. . . . . . With government so with conservation; to be for the people, conservation must be by the people. —*George Otis Smith*

As long as the forest shall live,
The streams shall flow onward, still singing
Sweet songs of the woodland, and bringing
The bright, living waters that give
New life to all mortals who thirst.

—*Alexander Blair Thaw*

Yea, the hour of destruction shall come
To the children of men in that day
When the forest shall pass away;
When the low woodland voices are dumb;
And death's devastation and dearth
Shall be spread o'er the face of the earth.

—*Alexander Blair Thaw*

Conservation means "the greatest good to the greatest number—and that for the longest time." —*Charles Richard Van Hise*

I do not hesitate to assert that from the point of view of our descendants this question of the conservation of our natural resources is more important than any political or social question,—indeed more important than all political and social questions upon the solution of which we are now engaged.

—*Charles Richard Van Hise*

The lengthening of human life is ultimately connected with that of the conservation of the natural resources.

—*Charles Richard Van Hise*

What is the purpose of conservation? It is for man. Its purpose is to keep the resources of the world in sufficient abundance so that man may have a happy, fruitful life, free from suffering—a relatively easy physical existence. —*Charles Richard Van Hise*

I am led to reflect how much more delightful to an undebauched mind is the task of making improvements on the earth than all the vainglory which can be acquired from ravaging it by the most uninterrupted career of conquests. —*George Washington*

Gives fools their gold and knaves their power;
Let fortune's bubbles rise and fall;
Who sows a field, or trains a flower,
Or plants a tree, is more than all.
For he who blesses most is blest;
And God and man shall own his worth,
Who toils to leave as his bequest
An added beauty to the earth.

—*Whittier*

Anything that is irreplaceable should be conserved and protected for its fullest use.

—*Ray Lyman Wilbur and William Atherton DuPuy*

Our greatest difficulties in getting the best out of our continent in the future will come from our own actions, from the artificial decisions which we have made or will make regardless of natural conditions.

—*Ray Lyman Wilbur and William Atherton DuPuy*

In the affairs of a great nation we plan and labor not for the present only but for the long future as well. —*Woodrow Wilson*

We are admittedly the richest, most powerful Nation in the world and we took this power of wealth out of the ground. Now, we must invoice our resources and determine how we should proceed from here. For a nation begins but once. —*Hubert Work*

Final Ruin fiercely drives
Her ploughshare o'er creation.

—*Edward Young*

Ah, how unjust to Nature and himself
Is thoughtless, thankless, inconsistent man!

—*Edward Young*

Man makes a death which Nature never made.

—*Edward Young*

EASTER

Immortality is a present possession. You are immortal or you never will be. . . . Live here and now the immortal life; and then if you are mistaken and there is no life after the grave, still you will have been immortal.
—Lyman Abbott

The stars shall fade away, the sun himself
Grow dim with age, and Nature sink in years;
But thou shalt flourish in immortal youth,
Unhurt amid the war of elements,
The wreck of matter, and the crush of worlds.
—Joseph Addison

What though, in solemn silence, all
Move round the dark, terrestrial ball?
What though no real voice nor sound
Amid their radiant orbs be found?
In reason's ear they all rejoice,
And utter forth a glorious voice,
Forever singing as they shine,
"The hand that made us is divine."
—Joseph Addison

The golden gates are lifted up,
The doors are opened wide;
The King of Glory is gone in
Unto His Father's side.
—Mrs. Cecil Frances Alexander

Easter triumph, Easter joy,
Sin alone can this destroy;
From sin's power do Thou set free
Souls new-born, O Lord, in Thee.
—Ambrosian Hymn

The Son of David bowed to die,
For man's transgression stricken;
The Father's arm of power was nigh,
The Son of God to quicken.
Praise Him that He died for men:
Praise Him that He rose again.
—Joseph Anstice

For death,
Now I know, is that first breath
Which our souls draw when we enter
Life, which is of all life center.
—Edwin Arnold

The shell is broken—it lies there;
The pearl, the all, the soul, is here.
—Edwin Arnold

Sweet friends! what the women lave
For its last bed of the grave
Is a hut which I am quitting,
Is a garment no more fitting,
Is a cage, from which at last,
Like a hawk, my soul hath passed.
—Edwin Arnold

The energy of life may be
Kept on after the grave, but not begun;
And he who flagg'd not in the earthly strife,
From strength to strength advancing—only he,
His soul well-knit, and all his battles won,
Mounts, and that hardly, to eternal life.
—Matthew Arnold

Yesterday the twig was brown and bare;
To-day the glint of green is there;
Tomorrow will be leaflets spare;
I know no thing so wondrous fair,
No miracle so strangely rare.
I wonder what will next be there!
—L. H. Bailey

It is the hour to rend thy chains,
The blossom time of souls.
—Katherine Lee Bates

Let those deplore their doom
Whose hope still grovels in this dark sojourn;
But lofty souls can look beyond the tomb,
Can smile at fate, and wonder how they mourn.
Shall Spring to these sad scenes no more return?
Is yonder wave the sun's eternal bed?
Soon shall the orient with new lustre burn,
And Spring shall soon her vital influence shed,
Again attune the grove, again adorn the mead.
—James Beattie

Christ is risen! There is life, therefore, after death! His resurrection is the symbol and pledge of universal resurrection!
—Henry Ward Beecher

Could life so end, half told; its school so fail?
Soul, soul, there is a sequel to thy tale!
—Robert Mowry Bell

Wintry heart, why wear'st the hue
Of sleep and night?
Christ is risen!
—Thomas Blackburn

Oh, and why not then
Lie down to our last sleep, still trusting Him
Who guided us so oft through shadows dim,
Believing somewhere on our sense again
Some lark's sweet note, some golden beam, shall break,
And with glad voices cry, "Awake! awake!"
—Gertrude Bloede

Well pleaseth me the sweet time of Easter
That maketh the leaf and the flower come out.
—Bertran de Born

Thus Nothing dies, or only dies to live,—
Star, stream, sun, flower, the dewdrop, and the gold:
Each goodly thing, instinct with buoyant hope,
Hastes to put on its purer, finer mold.
—Horatius Bonar

There is not room for Death,
Nor atom that his might could render void:
Thou—Thou art Being and Breath,
And what Thou art may never be destroyed.
—Emily Brontë

The great Easter truth is not that we are to live newly after death—that is not the great thing—but that we are to be new here and now by the power of the resurrection; not so much that we are to live forever as that we are to, and may, live nobly now because we are to live forever.
—Phillips Brooks

Let every man and woman count himself immortal. Let him catch the revelation of Jesus in his resurrection. Let him say not merely, "Christ is risen," but "I shall rise."
—Phillips Brooks

When some belovèd voice that was to you
Both sound and sweetness, faileth suddenly,
And silence, against which you dare not cry,
Aches round you like a strong disease and new—
What hope? what help? what music will undo
That silence to your sense? Not friendship's sigh,
Not reason's subtle count; not melody
Of viols, nor of pipes that Faunus blew;
Not songs of poets, nor of nightingales
Whose hearts leap upward through the cypress-trees
To the clear moon; nor yet the spheric laws
Self-chanted, nor the angels' sweet "All hails,"
Met in the smile of God: nay, none of these.
Speak *Thou,* availing Christ!—and fill this pause.
—Elizabeth Barrett Browning

But Easter Day breaks! But
Christ rises! Mercy every way
Is infinite.
—Robert Browning

The year's at the spring
And day's at the morn;
Morning's at seven;
The hillside's dew-pearled;
The lark's on the wing;
The snail's on the thorn;
God's in His heaven—
All's right with the world!
—Robert Browning

Gently, and without grief, the old shall glide
Into the new; the eternal flow of things,
Like a bright river of the fields of heaven,
Shall journey onward in perpetual peace.
—William Cullen Bryant

So live, that when thy summons comes to join
The innumerable caravan that moves
To the pale realms of shade, where each shall take
His chamber in the silent halls of death,
Thou go not, like the quarry-slave at night,
Scourged to his dungeon, but, sustained and soothed
By an unfaltering trust, approach thy grave
Like one who wraps the drapery of his couch
About him, and lies down to pleasant dreams.
—William Cullen Bryant

Is life so hopeless, brother, to thee,
That naught but death can bring victory?
Rise thou above thine own despair,
Forget thyself and thy pressing care;
Let the voice of praise from thy lips arise,
Thine Alleluia mount to the skies;
And on thy heart's glad Easter-Day,
Thy foes, in terror, shall flee away.
—Maria H. Bulfinch

Two things the Easter Light does definitely: it liberates us from the closely cabined and confining thought of life as an hour-glass running down; and it infinitely enhances the present quality of life. *—W. J. Cameron*

The season pricketh every gentle heart,
And maketh him out of his sleep to start.
—Chaucer

Consider these, my soul!
How the blind buds unroll
Touched with one tranquil ray
Of rising day,
Into the full delight
Of lilies white.
—Rose Terry Cooke

Morn's roseate hues have decked the sky;
The Lord has risen with victory;
Let earth be glad, and raise the cry:
Alleluia!
—William Cooke

Lift up your heads, ye sorrowing ones,
And be ye glad of heart,
For Calvary and Easter Day,
Earth's saddest day and gladdest day,
Were just one day apart!
—Susan Coolidge

So also is the resurrection of the dead. It is sown in corruption; it is raised in incorruption: It is sown in dishonour; it is raised in glory: It is sown in weakness; it is raised in power: It is sown a natural body; it is raised a spiritual body.
—I Corinthians 15:42-44

Behold I shew you a mystery; we shall not all sleep, but we shall all be changed, in a moment, in the twinkling of an eye, at the last trump: for the trumpet shall sound, and the dead shall be raised incorruptible, and we shall be changed. For this corruptible must put on incorruption, and this mortal must put on immortality. So when this corruptible shall have put on incorruption, and this mortal shall have put on immortality, then shall be brought to pass the saying that is written, Death is swallowed up in victory. O death, where is thy sting? O grave, where is thy victory? —*I Corinthians 15:51-55*

Let them sleep, let them sleep on,
Till the stormy night be gone,
And the eternal morrow dawn;
Then the curtains will be drawn,
And they wake into a light
Whose day shall never die in night.
—*Richard Crashaw*

O, listen, man!
A voice within us speaks the startling word,
"Man, thou shalt never die!" Celestial voices
Hymn it around our souls: according harps,
By angel fingers touched when the mild stars
Of morning sang together, sound forth still
The song of our great immortality:
Thick clustering orbs, and this our fair domain,
The tall, dark mountains, and the deep-toned seas,
Join in this solemn, universal song.
—*Richard Henry Dana*

Blossoms of Easter, make us, too,
As brave as you and as gay!
—*Mary Carolyn Davies*

What song shall the song of Easter be?
Moses' and Miriam's song by the sea!
"The Lord hath triumphed gloriously."
—*William Croswell Doane*

One short sleep past, we wake eternally,
And Death shall be no more: Death, thou shalt die!
—*John Donne*

Bloom in every meadow, leaves on every bough,
Speak His sorrow ended, hail His triumph now.
—*Venantius H. C. Fortunatus*

Jesus lives! henceforth is death
But the gate of life immortal.
—*C. F. Gellert*

The Lord is risen indeed,
He is here for your love, for your need.
—*Richard Watson Gilder*

Easter spells out beauty, the rare beauty of new life.
—*S. D. Gordon*

Awake, my soul, rise from the dead,
See life's grand light around thee shed.
—*Nicolai Grundtvig*

See, the chains of death are broken;
Earth below and heaven above
Joy in each amazing token
Of His rising, Lord of love.
—*A. T. Gurney*

How calm and beautiful the morn
That gilds the sacred tomb,
Where Christ the Crucified was borne,
And veiled in midnight gloom!
O weep no more the Saviour slain;
The Lord is risen,—He lives again.
—*Thomas Hastings*

With Thee
Oh let me rise
As larks, harmoniously,
And sing this day Thy victories.
—*George Herbert*

Up and away,
Thy Saviour's gone before.
Why dost thou stay,
Dull soul? Behold, the door
Is open, and his Precept bids thee rise,
Whose power hath vanquished all thine enemies.
—*George Herbert*

Rise, heart; Thy Lord is risen. Sing His praise
Without delays,
Who takes thee by the hand, that thou likewise
With Him may'st rise:
That, as His death calcinèd thee to dust,
His life may make thee gold, and much more, just.
—*George Herbert*

To show a heart grief-rent;
To starve thy sin,
Not bin:
And that's to keep thy Lent.
—*Robert Herrick*

"Lord, Lord, let me take heart again,
Let my faith shine white and clear,
Let me awaken with the earth,
And leave my old self here!"
—*Ella Higginson*

The next year stands for the coming time. Then shall the nature which had lain blanched and broken rise in its full stature and native hues in the sunshine. Then shall God's minstrels build their nests in the hearts of a new-born humanity. Then shall beauty—Divinity taking outlines and color—light upon the souls of men as the butterfly, image of the beatified spirit rising from the dust, soars from the shell that held a poor grub, which would never have found wings had not the stone been lifted.
—*Oliver Wendell Holmes*

Build thee more stately mansions, O my soul,
As the swift seasons roll!
Leave thy low-vaulted past!
Let each new temple, nobler than the last,
Shut thee from heaven with a dome more vast,
Till thou at length art free,
Leaving thine outgrown shell by life's unresting sea!

—*Oliver Wendell Holmes*

When wasting age and wearying strife
Have sapped the leaning walls of life,
When darkness gathers over all,
And the last tottering pillars fall,
Take the poor dust thy mercy warms,
And mould it into heavenly forms!

—*Oliver Wendell Holmes*

O ye who still watch in the valley of tears
And wait for the night to go by,
Lift, lift up your eyes, on the mountains appears
The day-spring of God from on high!

—*Frederic L. Hosmer*

For surely in the blind
deep-buried roots
Of all men's souls to-day
A secret quiver shoots.

—*Richard Hovey*

Alas! we think not what we daily see
About our hearths,—angels that are to be,
Or may be if they will, and we prepare
Their souls and ours to meet in happy air,—
A child, a friend, a wife whose soft heart sings
In unison with ours, breeding its future wings.

—*Leigh Hunt*

Life eternal! Heaven rejoices,
Jesus lives who once was dead;
Join, O man, the deathless voices,
Child of God, lift up thy head.

—*William Josiah Irons*

I am the resurrection, and the life: he that believeth in me, though he were dead, yet shall he live: And whosoever liveth and believeth in me, yet shall he live.

—*John 11:25, 26*

Marvel not at this: for the hour is coming, in the which all that are in the graves shall hear his voice, And shall come forth.

—*John 5:28, 29*

The day of resurrection! Earth tell it out abroad;
The Passover of gladness, The Passover of God.
From death to life eternal, from this world to the sky,
Our Christ hath brought us over, with hymns of victory.

—*John of Damascus*

Now the queen of seasons, bright
With the day of splendor,
With the royal feast of feasts,
Comes its joy to render.

—*John of Damascus*

O Day of days! shall hearts set free,
No "minstrel rapture" find for thee?

—*John Keble*

Come, ye saints, look here and wonder,
See the place where Jesus lay;
He has burst His bands asunder;
He has borne our sins away;
Joyful tidings,
Yes, the Lord has risen today.

—*Thomas Kelly*

Arise, O soul, and gird thee up anew,
Though the black camel Death kneel at thy gate.

—*James Benjamin Kenyon*

O teach me to see Death and not to fear,
But rather to take truce!

—*Henry King*

See the land, her Easter keeping,
Rises as her Maker rose.
Seeds, so long in darkness sleeping,
Burst at last from winter snows.
Earth with heaven above rejoices.

—*Charles Kingsley*

Here, while heaven and earth rejoices,
Each his Easter tribute bring—
Work of fingers, chant of voices,
Like the birds who build and sing.

—*Charles Kingsley*

Arise, yes, yes, arise, O thou my dust,
From short repose thou must!
Immortal liveth
The soul the Maker giveth.

—*Friedrich Gottlieb Klopstock*

Where man sees but withered leaves,
God sees sweet flowers growing.

—*Albert Laighton*

I see the rainbow in the sky,
The dew upon the grass;
I see them, and I ask not why
They glimmer or they pass.

With folded arms I linger not
To call them back; 'twere vain:
In this, or in some other spot,
I know they'll shine again.

—*Walter Savage Landor*

Lo, the unfolding mystery!
We shall bloom, some wondrous hour,
As the lily blooms, when she
Dies a bulb, to live a flower!

—*Lucy Larcom*

This is the wonder of the Resurrection—
That things unvalued now reveal their worth.
—*Lucy Larcom*

This is the beauty of our Easter morning;
In Him humanity may now arise
Out of the grave of self, all baseness scorning.
—*Lucy Larcom*

All the powers of darkness vanish;
Christ our Day-Star mounts the skies.
—*Latin*

And He, the wheat-corn, sown in earth,
Has given a glorious harvest birth.
Rejoice, and sing with holy mirth
Alleluia!
—*Latin*

The three sad days are quickly sped;
He rises glorious from the dead;
All glory to our risen Head!
—*Latin*

Celestial spirit that doth roll
The heart's sepulchral stone away,
Be this our resurrection day,
The singing Easter of the soul—
O gentle Master of the Wise,
Teach us to say: "I will arise."
—*Richard Le Gallienne*

'Twas Easter Sunday. The full blossomed trees
Filled all the air with fragrance and with joy.
—*Longfellow*

Once more to new creation
Awake, and death gainsay,
For death is swallowed up of life,
And Christ is risen today!
—*George Newell Lovejoy*

O chime of sweet Saint Charity,
Peal soon that Easter morn
When Christ for all shall risen be,
And in all hearts new-born!
—*James Russell Lowell*

Now upon the first day of the week, very early in the morning, they came unto the sepulchre, bringing the spices which they had prepared, and certain others with them. And they found the stone rolled away from the sepulchre. And they entered in, and found not the body of the Lord Jesus. And it came to pass, as they were much perplexed thereabout, behold, two men stood by them in shining garments: And as they were afraid, and bowed down their faces to the earth, they said unto them, Why seek ye the living among the dead? He is not here but is risen.
—*Luke 24:1-6*

Jesus Christ today is risen,
And o'er death triumphant reigns.
—*Martin Luther*

Our Lord has written the promise of the resurrection, not in books alone, but in every leaf in spring-time. —*Martin Luther*

In the Bonds of death He lay
Who for our offence was slain;
But the Lord is risen today,
Christ hath brought us life again,
Wherefore let us all rejoice,
Singing loud, with cheerful voice,
Hallelujah!
—*Martin Luther*

Jesus Christ is risen today,
Alleluia!
Our triumphant holy day,
Alleluia!
Who did once upon the cross,
Alleluia!
Suffer to redeem our loss.
Alleluia!
—*Lyra Davidica*

The holy spirit of the Spring
Is working silently.
—*George MacDonald*

"We shall sleep," was the sigh of the midnight;
"We shall rise!" is the song of today.
—*Francis L. Mace*

For three days He had travelled with the dead,
And now was risen to go with stiller tread
The old earth ways again,
To stay the heart and build the hope of men.
—*Edwin Markham*

Then suddenly an angel burning white
Came down with earthquake in the breaking light,
And rolled the great stone from the Sepulchre,
Mixing the morning with a scent of myrrh.
And lo, the Dead had risen with the day;
The Man of Mystery had gone His way!
—*Edwin Markham*

There can be no heart so unresponsive as not to be able to feel the transcending glory of the hope with which Easter morning today fills the Christian world. . . It is far more than a day of commemoration, although it is that, too, for the resurrection which it commemorates is the heart and the keystone of the Christian religion.
—*Minneapolis Tribune, March 28, 1937*

The grave is only where we lay
The soul, for its eternal spring!
—*John Richard Moreland*

In vain with stone the cave they barred;
In vain the watch kept ward and guard;
Majestic from the spoilèd tomb,
In pomp of triumph Christ is come.
—*John Mason Neale*

The giving Earth remembers
And only men forget!
—*John G. Neihardt*

Risen, like this resurrection of the year,
This grand ascension of the choral spring.
—*Alfred Noyes*

Why, if the soul can fling the dust aside,
And naked on the air of heaven ride,
Were't not a shame—were't not a shame for him
In this clay carcase crippled to abide?
—*Omar Khayyam*

For I remember it is Easter morn,
And life and love and peace are all new born.
—*Alice Freeman Palmer*

Ye sleeping buds, break
Open your green cerements, and wake
To fragrant blossoming for His sweet sake.
—*Margaret French Patton*

The world recedes; it disappears!
Heav'n opens on my eyes! my ears
With sounds seraphic ring!
Lend, lend your wings! I mount! I fly!
O Grave! where is thy victory?
O Death! where is thy sting?
—*Pope*

The fasts are done; the Aves said;
The moon has filled her horn,
And in the solemn night I watch
Before the Easter morn.
—*Edna Dean Proctor*

But from this earth, this grave, this dust,
My God shall raise me up, I trust.
—*Sir Walter Raleigh*

Spring bursts today,
For Christ is risen and all the earth's at play.
—*Christina G. Rossetti*

For shall we not believe He lives
Through such awakening?
Behold, how God each April gives
The miracle of Spring.
—*Edwin L. Sabin*

Ever the wings of the summer
Are folded under the mould;
Life, that has known no dying,
Is Love's, to have and to hold,
Till, sudden, the burgeoning Easter!
The song! the green and the gold!
—*Margaret E. Sangster*

There is a Resurrection Life
That I must share,
A tomb that I must leave.
—*Henry Park Schauffler*

Angels, roll the rock away;
Death, yield up thy mighty prey:
See, He rises from the tomb,
Glowing with immortal bloom.
Al-le-lu-ia! Al-le-lu-ia!
Christ the Lord is risen today!
—*Thomas Scott*

Didst thou not fall out with a tailor for wearing his new doublet before Easter?
—*Shakespeare*

'Tis something, if at last,
Though only for a flash, a man may see
Clear-eyed the future as he sees the past,
From doubt, or fear, or hope's illusion free.
—*Edward Rowland Sill*

Oh, let us keep the soul embalmed and pure
In living virtue,—that when both must sever,
Although corruption may our frame consume,
The immortal spirit in the skies may bloom!
—*Horace Smith*

God expects from men . . . that their Easter devotions would in some measure come up to their Easter dress.
—*Robert South*

Most glorious Lord of life, that on this day
Didst make Thy triumph over death and sin,
. . . .
This joyous day, dear Lord, with joy begin,
And grant that we, for whom Thou diddest die,
Being with Thy dear blood clean washed from sin,
May live forever in felicity.
—*Edmund Spenser*

For though from out our bourne of Time and Place
The floods may bear me far,
I hope to see my Pilot face to face,
When I have crossed the bar.
—*Alfred Tennyson*

He lifts me to the golden doors;
The flashes come and go;
All heaven bursts her starry floors,
And strows her lights below,
And deepens on and up! the gates
Roll back, and far within
For me the Heavenly Bridegroom waits,
To make me pure of sin.
—*Alfred Tennyson*

Sing, little children, sing!
The lilies white you bring
In the joyous Easter morning for hope are blossoming.
—*Celia Thaxter*

"Rise grateful dust!" I heard Him say:
"For thee have I put death to scorn
On Easter morn."
—*Edith M. Thomas*

Thou art not dead! Thou art the whole
Of life that quickens in the sod.
—Charles Hanson Towne

But heaven and earth, and saints and friends and flowers,
Are keeping Easter Day!
—Unknown

And is not the best of all our hopes—the hope of immortality—always before us? How can we be dull and heavy while we have that new experience to look forward to? It will be the most joyful of all our travels and adventures. *—Henry van Dyke*

Farewell! I goe to sleep; but when
The day-star springs, I'll wake again.
—Henry Vaughan

And I, a child of God, by Christ made free,
Start from Death's slumbers to Eternity!
—Jones Very

"Christ the Lord is risen today,"
Sons of men and angels say:
Raise your joys and triumphs high,
Sing, ye heavens; and earth, reply.
—Charles Wesley

I know I am deathless.
—Walt Whitman

O dearest bloom the seasons know,
Flowers of the resurrection blow,
Our hope and faith restore;
And through the bitterness of death,
And loss and sorrow, breathe a breath
Of life forevermore!
—John Greenleaf Whittier

Oh! keep the morning of His incarnation,
The burning noontide of His bitter passion,
The night of His descending, and the height
Of His ascension—ever in my sight!
That, imitating Him in what I may,
I never follow an inferior way.
—George Wither

Christ is risen, Christ the first-fruits
Of the holy harvest-field,
Which will of its full abundance
At His second coming yield.
—Christopher Wordsworth

O joy! that in our embers
Is something that doth live;
That Nature yet remembers
What was so fugitive!
—William Wordsworth

Shall man alone, for whom all else revives,
No resurrection know? Shall man alone,
Imperial man! be sown in barren ground,
Less privileged than grain, on which he feeds?
—Edward Young

FATHER'S DAY

Blessed—more blessed, I am sure, than we can ever measure—are we who look into the life of such an earthly father for the interpretation of the tender mercies and loving-kindnesses of our heavenly Father. More than all word-teaching has been the teaching of his life, not merely in its lesson of the consecration, the firmness, the fidelity and gentleness of love, but in its suggestion of what must be the tender strength and the infinite condescension of the heavenly Father to His children. It has fashioned and vivified all the religious life and experience of his four sons. If such a life is but a spark, what must the great sun be? —*Lyman Abbott*

I never recall those early conversations with my father, nor a score of others like them, but there comes into my mind a line from Mrs. Browning in which a daughter describes her relations with her father:—

"He wrapt me in his large
Man's doublet, careless did it fit or no."

—*Jane Addams*

The father's merit sets thee up to view,
And shows thee in the fairest point of light,
To make thy virtues, or thy faults, conspicuous. —*Joseph Addison*

For the Lord hath given the father glory as touching the children. . .

The glory of a man is from the honour of his father.

Apocrypha: Ecclesiasticus 1:7

My son, help thy father in his old age; and grieve him not as long as he liveth. And if he fail in understanding, have patience with him; and dishonour him not while thou art in thy full strength. . . He that forsaketh his father is as a blasphemer.

Apocrypha: Ecclesiasticus 1:7

My father's nature turned out no waste product; he had none of that useless stuff in him that lies in heaps near factories. He took his own happiness with him.

—*Margot Asquith*

He that hath wife and children hath given hostages to fortune, for they are impediments to great enterprises, either of virtue or of mischief. . . . Yet it were great reason that those that have children should have greatest care of future times, unto which they know they must transmit their dearest pledges.

—*Francis Bacon*

I know just what my father was to me—
And is unto this day;
And so unto my boy would I as truly be
And in the selfsame way.

—*D. G. Bechers*

Our walks with you were full of things mysterious
Made magic by your twinkle and half-drawl,
Because we could not tell if you were serious.
You rose to some occasions quite imperious.

—*William Rose Benét*

Can a father see his child
Weep, nor be with sorrow filled?

—*William Blake*

The life in our old home was a training for me. While father was always a forceful and dominating personality, and also most sensitive to anything that seemed like unfaithfulness or undutifulness, he was remarkably tolerant of different opinions over the family table. . . .

One beautiful trait of his was that if, in the long run, it turned out that he had been mistaken in his judgment, he would always acknowledge it with a quite delightful frankness. At times he would go unnecessarily out of his way to have it made clear that another had proved right and he had been wrong. That also helped to win for him not only the affection and esteem but the perfect confidence of those he led.

—*Bramwell Booth*

Father, it's your love that safely guides me,
Always it's around me, night and day;
It shelters me, and soothes, but never chides me.

—*Robert Bridges ("Droch")*

Fathers love as well
—Mine did, I know,—but still with heavier brains,
And wills more consciously responsible,
And not as wisely, since less foolishly.

—*Elizabeth Barrett Browning*

The pitying heart that felt for human woe,
The dauntless heart that fear'd no human pride,
The friend of man—to vice alone a foe;
For ev'n his failings lean'd to virtue's side.

—*Robert Burns*

Father was an absolutely honest man, honest not only in packing a crate of grapes, but honest as to his own weaknesses and shortcomings. . . .

He asked little for himself and was generous with what was his, and generous to the faults and shortcomings of others.

—*Julian Burroughs*

Diogenes struck the father when the son swore.

—*Robert Burton*

Yet in my lineaments they trace
Some features of my father's face.
—*Lord Byron*

I'll meet the raging of the skies,
But not an angry father.
—*Thomas Campbell*

He that has his father for judge goes safe to the trial. —*Cervantes*

Character is largely caught, and the father and the home should be the great sources of character infection.
—*Frank H. Cheley*

He believed that being a father is the greatest privilege given to any man, and so took his fatherhood seriously.
—*Frank H. Cheley*

No one can father a boy so well as his own father. —*Frank H. Cheley*

The present problem of the American boy is the problem of the American dad, and no one else on God's green earth can solve that problem. —*Frank H. Cheley*

The father in praising his son extols himself.
—*Chinese*

The widespread observance of this occasion is calculated to establish more intimate relations between fathers and their children, and also to impress upon fathers the full measure of their obligations. —*Calvin Coolidge*

My father is a quiet man
With sober, steady ways.
—*Countee Cullen*

"Father is rather vulgar, my dear. The word Papa, besides, gives a pretty form to the lips. Papa, potatoes, poultry, prunes and prism are all very good words for the lips; especially prunes and prism."
—*Charles Dickens*

My love for my father has never been touched or approached by any other love. I hold him in my heart of hearts as a man apart from all other men, as one apart from all other beings. —*Mamie Dickens*

As to Father, perhaps he should be relieved of all reference to his carking cares when he enters the house, BUT don't you think if all of us cared more intensely for father's success, not as a mode of income but as an expression of his talents, don't you agree that he would cease to be jumping like a toad under a harrow to support us, and would come to feel that as a man and a contributor we were from sheer pride in him holding up his hands?
—*Samuel S. Drury*

Every father ought to say: Wist ye not that I must be about my boy's business?
—*Samuel S. Drury*

"My son, my son" is the joyous or agonized or doting cry of every man that has a boy. Though he stifle his emotion or laugh about it, it is there. Swords pierce fathers' hearts as well as mothers.'
—*Samuel S. Drury*

"What is the greatest grief of fathers?" I asked a friend. Promptly he replied: "Why, seeing our sons inherit all of our weaknesses."
—*Samuel S. Drury*

I am far frae my hame, an' I'm weary aften whiles,
For the longed-for hame-bringing an' my father's welcome smiles.
—*Erastus Ellsworth*

And, ye fathers, provoke not your children to wrath: but bring them up in the nurture and admonition of the Lord.
—*Ephesians 6:4*

The gods visit the sins of the fathers upon the children. *Euripides*

A happy father thou, when sturdy sons
In mellowing age a golden youth renew,
In them thy name through generations runs,
By them achieved, thy early dreams come true.
—*William Dudley Foulke*

He's all my own, and mine the joy
Of finding the very heart of a boy
In daddy.
—*Robert Freeman*

A father maintains ten children better than ten children one father. *German*

As the field, so the crops; as the father, so the sons. *German*

So my dear father met me at the end of the journey, welcoming me home! I have a notion that St. Peter, when I knock at his gate, may forgive my transgressions for the sake of the name I bear.
—*Richard Watson Gilder*

His form, his face, his voice have always been with me; many of the scenes in which he appeared have returned to me continually through all my life. . . . This man had so wound himself into the life of this child that they could not be torn apart without lasting suffering. —*Washington Gladden*

Who rideth so late through the night-wind wild?
It is the father with his child;
He has the little one well in his arm;
He holds him safe, and he folds him warm. —*Goethe*

It is a pious wish of all fathers to see what they have themselves failed to attain, realized in their sons, as if in this way they could live their lives over again, and, at last, make a proper use of their early experience.

—*Goethe*

The right sort of father is always a hero in the eyes of his boy. —*Jesse R. Grant*

Ah, little one! to thee thy father seems
A world of mystery; thy great desire
To be a man—in all things like thy sire.

—*Arthur Vine Hall*

Such virtues as I have—the power to endure, the will to achieve—I must have inherited from my mother; but there is something rash in me with a reach to it, like a pair of wings in a high wind, that descends to me with a splendid sweep from this father.

—*Corra Harris*

If my mother was the heart, he was the soul of our family life. —*William Dean Howells*

The clock is on the stroke of six,
The father's work is done;
Sweep up the hearth, and stir the fire,
And put the kettle on.

. . . .

I know he's coming by this sign,
That baby's almost wild;
See how he laughs, and crows, and stares—
Heaven bless the merry child!
His father's self in face and limb,
And father's heart is strong in him.

—*Mary Howitt*

For father's heart is stout and true
As ever human bosom knew.

—*Mary Howitt*

The fathers have eaten a sour grape, and the children's teeth are set on edge.

—*Jeremiah 31:29*

Look how the father's face
Lives in his issue.

—*Ben Jonson*

He didn't tell me how to live; he lived, and let me watch him do it.

—*Clarence Budington Kelland*

Henry James once defined life as that predicament which precedes death, and certainly nobody owes you a debt of honor or gratitude for getting him into that predicament. But a child does owe his father a debt, if Dad, having gotten him into this peck of trouble, takes off his coat and buckles down to the job of showing his son how best to crash through it.

—*Clarence Budington Kelland*

All we have of freedom—all we use or know—
This our fathers bought for us, long and long ago.

—*Rudyard Kipling*

Would that a father's thought could bring
Prophetic counsel more than wise
To guide thee as a father's love would yearn!

—*Wilbur Larremore*

Father of fathers, make me one,
A fit example for a son.

—*Douglas Malloch*

Here's your responsibility,
The greatest mortal ever had—
Just to be worthy, friend, to be
Some youngster's dad.

—*Douglas Malloch*

No family is quite complete without a father, though a family that has once had a good one never loses him altogether, for he will keep cropping out down to the third and fourth generation, and so on, world without end. —*Edward Sandford Martin*

There's little pleasure in the house
When our gudeman's awa'.

—*W. J. Mickle*

What a joy to be a father! What new emotions crowd the eye with tears, and make the hand tremble! What a benevolence radiates from you toward the nurse—toward the physician—toward everybody! What a holiness and sanctity of love grows upon your old devotion to that wife of your bosom—the mother of your child!

—*Donald G. Mitchell*

"Sentence me," said a father in court at his son's trial for one of the hideous crimes of today. "I have been so busy all his life making money, that I did not know what he was about. I alone am to blame—sentence me." —*Anne Shannon Monroe*

Not love me, eh? She better had!
By Jove, I'll make her love me one day;
For, don't you see, I am her Dad,
And she'll be three weeks old on Sunday!

—*Christopher Morley*

When one becomes a father, then first one becomes a son. Standing by the crib of one's own baby, with that world-old pang of compassion and protectiveness toward this so little creature that has all its course to run, the heart flies back in yearning and gratitude to those who felt just so toward one's self.

—*Christopher Morley*

No one appreciated more than I did the excellent qualities of mind and character which distinguished my father. I always thoroughly respected and honored his perfect integrity, his vigorous and uncommon powers of mind, his remarkable vein of wit and native humour, with which all who knew him were familiar, his large experience, his honourable prudence, his practical sagacity, and his singular tenderness of heart.

—*John Lothrop Motley*

Every morning I would salute my mother and my father. To my mother I said, "You are my God, my way to God," and to my father, "You are the Way, and the End. O my father, teach me to find the Way."
—Dhan Gopal Mukerji

Many an excellent man is tempted to forget that the best offering he can make his children is himself. *—Henry Neumann*

And thou, dearest father, whose life was as hard as thy hard trade, thou hast shown to me what patience and protracted effort can accomplish. It is to thee that I owe perseverance in daily work. Thou hadst the qualities which go to make a useful life, and admiration for great men and great things. To look upward, to learn the utmost, and to seek to rise even higher—such was thy teaching. *—Pasteur*

This fathering is a man's second chance at living. *—Angelo Patri*

The father who would taste the essence of his fatherhood must turn back from the plane of his experience, take with him the fruits of his journey and begin again beside his child, marching step by step over the same old road. *—Angelo Patri*

The graduating class at Yale University voted on this question: "What man in the world do you most admire?" And a majority answered: "My father."
—William Lyon Phelps

It behooves a father to be blameless, if he expects his son to be more blameless than he was himself. *—Plautus*

And still tomorrow's wiser than today.
We think our fathers fools, so wise we grow;
Our wiser sons, no doubt, will think us so.
—Pope

My first debt to my father—and the one for which I think I should be more devoutly thankful than for any other—is the one I owe for having been brought into the world bearing an old and honorable name.

When I say an "honorable" name, in the case of my father, I mean a name that never was touched by any faintest breath of scandal of any kind. . . . I mean a name which stood for love in his family, for recognition of and fidelity to manifest duty, for kindly consideration of his neighbors, for intelligent participation in affairs tending toward the betterment of the neighborhood, of the state, and of the nation. *—Gene Stratton-Porter*

A wise son maketh a glad father.
—Proverbs 10:1

The eye that mocketh at his father, and despiseth to obey his mother, the ravens of the valley shall pick it out, and the young eagles shall eat it. *—Proverbs 30:17*

The just man walketh in his integrity; his children are blessed after him.
—Proverbs 20:7

Father and Mother were Law, Light and Love to us. *—W. S. Rainsford*

There are many kinds of success in life worth having. It is exceedingly interesting and attractive to be a successful business man, a railroad man, a farmer, or a successful lawyer or doctor; or a writer, or a President, or a ranchman, or the colonel of a fighting regiment, or to kill grizzly bears and lion. But for unflagging interest and enjoyment, a household of children, if things go reasonably well, certainly makes all other forms of success and achievement lose their importance by comparison.
—Theodore Roosevelt

Come with me then, my son;
Thine eyes are wide for truth:
And I will give thee memories,
And thou shalt give me youth.
—Sir Ronald Ross

Posterity pays for the sins of their fathers.
—Quintus Curtius Rufus

The fundamental defect of fathers is that they want their children to be a credit to them. *—Betrand Arthur William Russell*

A father's blessing cannot be drowned in water nor consumed by fire. *—Russian*

A father lives after death in his son.
—Sanscrit

Your dad may be the loneliest creature on earth, and hungry for understanding, sympathy, and friendship. Get acquainted with him while he is up and doing; it isn't a pleasant thing to have your conscience lash you—too late—after he is dead.
—W. O. Saunders

For years, as a boy, I had eaten the food and worn the clothes provided by that humble, slaving, threadbare man, without giving a thought to the weary toil he had endured to provide them. I had seen him mend his own shoes and toil for an hour drawing rusty nails out of old boards to get nails to patch up the woodshed or the garden fence, without having once realized that he practiced these economies that I might wear better shoes than he, and have leisure that was never his. *—W. O. Saunders*

It is not flesh and blood but the heart which makes us fathers and sons.
—Johann Schiller

If there be a human tear
From passion's dross refin'd and clear,
. . . .
'Tis that which pious fathers shed
Upon a duteous daughter's head.
—Sir Walter Scott

The father does indeed like to be a person of consideration to his son, to be admired and respected by him, as well as to be a good comrade, but this feeling on his part is not a circumstance compared with the son's desire to look up to him.
—*Editorial. Scribner's Magazine May 1914*

Fathers that wear rags do make their children blind:
But fathers that bear bags shall see their children kind.
—*Shakespeare*

How quickly nature falls into revolt
When gold becomes her object!
For this the foolish over-careful fathers
Have broke their sleep with thoughts, their brains with care,
Their bones with industry.
—*Shakespeare*

If I chance to talk a little wild, forgive me;
I had it from my father.
—*Shakespeare*

He was a man, take him for all in all,
I shall not look upon his like again.
—*Shakespeare*

Methinks a father
Is, at the nuptial of his son, a guest
That best becomes the table.
—*Shakespeare*

"You are old, Father William," the young man cried,—
"The few locks that are left you are gray;
You are hale, Father William,—a hearty old man:
Now tell me the reason, I pray."
"In the days of my youth," Father William replied,
"I remembered that youth would fly fast;
And abused not my health and my vigor at first,
That I never might need them at last."
—*Robert Southey*

'Tis happy for him that his father was before him. —*Jonathan Swift*

This is the duty of a father, to accustom his son to act rightly rather of his own accord than from unnatural fear. —*Terence*

Whom should he bear with if not with his own father? —*Terence*

Then I thought of you,
Your gentle soul,
Your large and quiet kindness;
Ready to caution and console,
And, with an almost blindness
To what was mean and low.
—*Louis Untermeyer*

The child is father of the man.
—*William Wordsworth*

O dearest, dearest boy! my heart
For better lore would seldom yearn,
Could I but teach the hundredth part
Of what from thee I learn.
—*William Wordsworth*

In deep and awful channel runs
This sympathy of Sire and Sons.
—*William Wordsworth*

Father!—to God himself we cannot give
A holier name.
—*William Wordsworth*

FLAG DAY

May never traitor's touch pollute
Those colors of the sky.
—Thomas Bailey Aldrich

Stout hearts have fought for that bright flag,
Strong hands sustained it masthead high.
—American Naval Officer, 1812

Fling out the flag. Let us hope that this splendid banner will give us a higher ideal of national character; an ideal that will exclude the jingo, the bully and the public charlatan, and an ideal that will dedicate the national conscience to a still deeper love of country, to a more reverent regard to its institutions, to a higher civilization and to peace, yea, to eternal peace among the nations of the earth. This flag means that or it means nothing. *—Anon.*

The whole inspiration of our life as a nation flows out from the waving folds of this banner. *—Anon.*

If anyone, then, asks me the meaning of our flag, I say to him—it means just what Concord and Lexington meant; what Bunker Hill meant; which was, in short, the rising up of a valiant young people against an old tyranny to establish the most momentous doctrine that the world had ever known—the right of men to their own selves and to their liberties. *—Henry Ward Beecher*

Our flag means, then, all that our fathers meant in the Revolutionary War; it means all that the Declaration of Independence meant; it means all that the Constitution of our people, organizing for justice, for liberty, and for happiness, meant.
—Henry Ward Beecher

Made by liberty, made for liberty, nourished in its spirit, carried in its service, and never, not once, in all the earth made to stoop to despotism! *—Henry Ward Beecher*

A thoughtful mind, when it sees a nation's flag, sees not the flag only, but the nation itself; and whatever may be its symbols, its insignia, he reads chiefly in the flag the government, the principles, the truths, the history, which belong to the nation.
—Henry Ward Beecher

I pledge allegiance to the flag of the United States and to the Republic for which it stands, one nation, indivisible, with liberty and justice for all. *—Francis M. Bellamy*

Uncover when the flag goes by, boys,
'Tis freedom's starry banner that you greet.
—Charles L. Benjamin and George D. Sutton

Hats off!
Along the street there comes
A blare of bugles, a ruffle of drums,
A flash of color beneath the sky:
Hats off!
The flag is passing by.
—Henry Holcomb Bennett

We follow the flag and independence is ours. We follow the flag and nationality is ours. . .everywhere and always it means larger liberty, noble opportunity, and greater human happiness; for everywhere and always it means the blessings of the greater Republic.
—Albert J. Beveridge

And there, while thread shall hang to thread,
Oh, let that ensign fly!
The noblest constellation set
Against the Northern sky.
—George Henry Boker

Off with your hat as the flag goes by!
And let the heart have its say;
You're man enough for a tear in your eye
That you will not wipe away.
—Henry Cuyler Bunner

Our flag the sceptre all who meet obey.
—Lord Byron

High on the world did our fathers of old,
Under the stars and stripes,
Blazon the name that we now must uphold,
Under the stars and stripes.
—Madison Cawein

Uncover to the flag, for there
The patriot past is typified.
Of those who taught us how to dare
For liberty, and died.
—E. C. Cheverton

We join ourselves to no party that does not carry the flag and keep step to the music of the Union. *—Rufus Choate*

Having learned to stand by the flag, we may also learn to stand by what the flag symbolizes; to stand up for equal rights, universal freedom, for justice to all, for a true republic. *—James F. Clarke*

Fling out, fling out, with cheer and shout,
To all the winds Our Country's Banner!
Be every bar, and every star,
Displayed in full and glorious manner!
—Abraham Coles

The stars of the flag represent a new constellation rising in the West. The idea is taken from the great constellation Lyra, which in the hands of Orpheus, signifies harmony. The blue in the field is taken from the edge of the Covenanters Banner of Scotland, significant of the covenant of the United States against oppression. The stars are disposed in a circle, symboblizing the perpetuity of the Union, the ring signifying eternity. The thirteen stars show the number of the united colonies and denote subordination of the States of the Union as well as equality among themselves. The red, the color which in the Roman days was a symbol of defiance, denotes daring, and the white purity.

—Report of a special committee appointed by the Continental Congress to suggest a design for the flag.

In radiance heavenly fair,
Floats on the peaceful air
That flag that never stooped from victory's pride.

—Francis Marion Crawford

A holy standard, pure and free,
To light the home of peace, or blaze in victory.

—Francis Marion Crawford

Here's to the red of it,
There's not a thread of it,
No, not a shred of it,
In all the spread of it,
From foot to head,
But heroes bled for it,
Faced steel and lead for it,
Precious blood shed for it,
Bathing in red.

—John Daly

Heart of me, soul of me, yours to command,
Flag o' my land! flag o' my land!

—Thomas Augustin Daly

It was adopted by the old Congress while the new-born Republic was struggling into life. . . In the hour of victory we have given it to the winds, as the expression of our thankfulness and joy. In the days of our calamity we have turned to it for support, as the people of God turned in the darkness of the night to the Pillar of Fire, which was conducting them through the perils of the wilderness. *—John Adams Dix*

What is the magic of the flag?
What influence holds
Within its graceful folds,
That, though it be a smoked-grimed rag,
Faded and frayed and tattered,
Strife-eager men will die
To hold it high
Before the cannon belching shotted fire.

—Nathan Haskell Dole

It is the symbol of a majesty,
A vast idea, a concept that appeals
To ignorant and to learned equally,
To every heart that feels.

—Nathan Haskell Dole

When Freedom from her mountain height
Unfurled her standard to the air,
She tore the azure robe of night,
And set the stars of glory there.

—Joseph Rodman Drake

Flag of the free heart's hope and home!
By angel hands to valour given;
Thy stars have lit the welkin dome,
And all thy hues were born in heaven.

—Joseph Rodman Drake

One flag is ours! one fame! one fate!

—S. P. Driver

See the power of national emblems. Some stars, lilies, leopards, a crescent, a lion, an eagle, or other figure which came into credit God knows how, on an old rag of bunting, blowing in the wind on a fort at the ends of the earth, shall make the blood tingle under the rudest or most conventional exterior.

—Emerson

All hail to our glorious ensign! courage to the heart, and strength to the hand, to which, in all time, it shall be entrusted! May it ever wave in honor, in unsullied glory, and patriotic hope! *—Edward Everett*

On whatever spot it is planted, there may freedom have a foothold, humanity a brave champion, and religion an altar! Though stained with blood in a righteous cause, may it never in any cause be stained with shame!

—Edward Everett

Those *Stars* that, veil'd in dark attire,
Long glimmer'd with a feeble fire,
But radiant now ascend.

—Philip Freneau

For where'er our country's banner may be planted,
All other local banners are defied!

—W. S. Gilbert

The starry banner speaks for itself. Its mute eloquence needs no aid to interpret its significance. Fidelity to the Union blazes from its stars, allegiance to the government beneath which we live is wrapped in its folds.

—Edward Everett Hale

When boys and girls salute the flag, they do not merely express their pride that it is a flag honored over the world. They ought to remember that the flag represents the country to which they owe duties in every hour of their lives. All the time they are receiving blessings from that country, and all the time they have duties to that country.

—Edward Everett Hale

Oh, God of our Fathers! God of Peace
And War—to Thee we pray!
Keep Thou this flag thro' every fate
As dauntless as today!
—Ella Higginson

I have seen the glories of art and architecture, and mountain and river; I have seen the sunset on the Jungfrau, and the full moon rise over Mont Blanc: but the fairest vision on which these eyes ever looked was the flag of my country in a foreign land. Beautiful as a flower to those who love it, terrible as a meteor to those who hate it, it is the symbol of the power and glory, and the honor, of fifty millions of Americans. (1878)
—George Frisbie Hoar

During the whole history of America, therefore, our flag has been the flag of a *country,* not the personal standard of a king or of an emperor. It stands, and it has stood for us as the symbol of an abstract idea, not as the sign of the power of any ruler.
—Edward S. Holden

From treason's rent, from murder's stain,
Guard Thou its folds till peace shall reign.
—Oliver Wendell Holmes

What flower is this that greets the morn,
Its hues from Heaven so freshly born?
With burning star and flaming band
It kindles all the sunset land;
Oh tell us what its name may be—
Is this the Flower of Liberty?
It is the banner of the free,
The starry Flower of Liberty!
—Oliver Wendell Holmes

Heaven keep her ever free,
Wide as o'er land and sea
Floats the fair emblem her heroes have won!
—Oliver Wendell Holmes

The red, that fires the southern rose,
With spotless white from northern snows,
And, spangled o'er its azure, see,
The sister stars of Liberty;
Then hail the Banner of the Free,
The starry Flower of Liberty!
—Oliver Wendell Holmes

Its stripes were a holy lesson, its spangles a deathless creed. *—Julia Ward Howe*

There is not a thread in it but scorns self-indulgence, weakness and rapacity.
—Charles Evans Hughes

This flag means more than association and reward. It is the symbol of our national unity, our national endeavor, and our national aspiration. It tells you of the struggle for Independence, of a Union preserved, of Liberty and Union, one and inseparable, of the sacrifices of brave men and women to whom ideals and honor have been dearer than life. *—Charles Evans Hughes*

The simple stone of Betsy Ross
Is covered now with mold and moss,
But still her deathless banner flies,
And keeps the color of the skies.
A nation thrills, a nation bleeds,
A nation follows where it leads.
—Minna Irving

And the star-spangled banner in triumph shall wave
O'er the land of the free and the home of the brave.
—Francis Scott Key

I am whatever you make me, nothing more. I am your belief in yourself, your dream of what a people may become. . . I am the clutch of an idea, and the reasoned purpose of resolution. I am no more than you believe me to be and I am all that you believe I can be. I am whatever you make me, nothing more. *—Franklin Knight Lane*

I swing before your eyes as a bright gleam of color, a symbol of yourself, the pictured suggestion of that big thing which makes this nation. My stars and my stripes are your dream and your labors. They are bright with cheer, brilliant with courage, firm with faith, because you have made them so out of your heart. For you are the makers of the flag and it is well that you glory in the making.
—Franklin Knight Lane

Each red stripe has blazoned forth
Gospels writ in blood;
Every star has sung the birth
Of some deathless good.
—Lucy Larcom

Bid it wave, to shame the wrong;
To inspire mankind
With a larger human love.
—Lucy Larcom

Patriotism is not the mere holding of a great flag unfurled, but making it the goodliest in the world. *—W. J. Linton*

I will never admit that that beloved flag is to me merely the symbol of a land where I can live in rich content and make money.
—Henry Cabot Lodge

Ah, when the wanderer, lonely, friendless,
In foreign harbors shall behold
That flag unrolled,
'Twill be as a friendly hand
Stretched out from his native land,
Filling his heart with memories sad and sweet.
—Longfellow

Take thy banner! May it wave
Proudly o'er the good and brave.
—Longfellow

Wrap round his breast
The flag his breast defended,—
His country's flag,
In battle's front unrolled:
For it he died.
—George Lunt

Our flag has never waved over any community but in blessing.
—William McKinley

Cheers for the sailors that fought on the wave for it,
Cheers for the soldiers that always were brave for it,
Tears for the men that went down to the grave for it,
Here comes the Flag!
—Arthur Macy

Your flag demands your best today,
Not sometime, by and by!
—John Clair Minot

May the God we trust as a nation
Throw the light of His peace and grace
On a flag with its stripes untarnished,
And with every star in place.
—John Clair Minot

A flag for the soldier's bier
Who dies that his land may live.
—William Vaughn Moody

The union of hearts, the union of hands,
And the flag of our Union forever!
—George P. Morris

The one flag—the great flag—the flag for me and you—
Glorified all else beside—the red and white and blue!
—Wilbur D. Nesbit

And the flags were all a-flutter, and the bells were all a-chime. *—Henry Newbolt*

That piece of red, white and blue bunting means five thousand years of struggle upwards. It is the full-grown flower of ages of fighting for liberty. It is the century plant of human hope in bloom.
—Alvin Owsley

Right nobly do you lead the way, Old Flag.
—Hubbard Parker

See how the starry banner floats,
And sparkles in the morning ray.
—James Gates Percival

And did you see the waving flags,
The fluttering flags, the tattered flags,
Red, white, and blue, shot through and through,
Baptized with battle's deadly dew?
—Nora Perry

Invincible banner! the flag of the free,
Oh, where treads the foot that would falter for thee? *Edna Dean Proctor*

And wherever that flag has gone it has been a herald for a better day—it has been the pledge of freedom, of justice, of order, of civilization, and of Christianity. Tyrants only have hated it. *—A. P. Putnam*

Fair is the Flag's renown,
Sacred her scars.
—Wallace Rice

Yes, we'll rally round the flag, boys, we'll rally once again,
Shouting the battle-cry of Freedom,
We'll rally from the hill-side, we'll gather from the plain,
Shouting the battle-cry of Freedom.
—George F. Root

For God and liberty evermore
May that banner stand from shore to shore.
—Margaret E. Sangster

Stood for his country's glory fast,
And nailed her colours to the mast!
—Sir Walter Scott

Banners flout the sky. *—Shakespeare*

She'll wave for us living, or droop o'er us dead—
The flag of our country forever.
—F. L. Stanton

There is the National Flag. He must be cold, indeed, who can look upon its folds rippling in the breeze without pride of country. *—Charles Sumner*

White is for purity; red, for valor; blue for justice. And altogether, bunting, stripes, stars, and colors, blazing in the sky, make the flag of our country, to be cherished by all our hearts, to be upheld by all our hands.
—Charles Sumner

Its highest beauty is in what it symbolizes.
—Charles Sumner

God lives and reigns! He built and lent
The heights for Freedom's battlement,
Where floats her flag in triumph still!
—Will Henry Thompson

Keep, then, the flag of the nation waving before our eyes; in other words, make conspicuous the principles of which it is the emblazonry: fealty to truth, to honor, to liberty and law. *—E. P. Thwing*

Its red for love, and its white for law;
And its blue for the hope that our fathers saw,
Of a larger liberty.
—Unknown

O brave flag, O bright flag, O flag to lead the free!
—Henry van Dyke

Thy sons, in peace or war,
That emblem who behold,
Bless every shining star,
Cheer every streaming fold!
—William Henry Venable

Might his last glance behold the glorious ensign of the Republic still full high advanced, its arms and trophies streaming in all their original lustre. *—Daniel Webster*

O hasten flag of man—O with sure and steady step, passing highest flag of kings,
Walk supreme to the heaven's mighty symbol—run up above them all,
Flag of stars! thick-sprinkled bunting!
—Walt Whitman

"Shoot, if you must, this old gray head,
But spare your country's flag," she said.
—Whittier

Peace and order and beauty draw
Round thy symbol of light and law.
—Whittier

And still we trust the years to be
Shall prove his hope was destiny,
Leaving our flag, with all its added stars,
Unrent by faction and unstained by wars.
—Whittier

We seemed to see our flag unfurled,
Our champion waiting in his place
For the last battle of the world,—
The Armageddon of the race.
—Whittier

Then let the sovereign millions, where
Our banner floats in sun and air,
From the warm palm-lands to Alaska's cold,
Repeat with us the pledge a century old!
—Whittier

By it your fathers stood unmoved and true.
—John Nichols Wilder

Stand by the Flag! Immortal heroes bore it
Through sulphurous smoke, deep moat, and armed defence,
And their imperial shades still hover o'er it,
A guard celestial from Omnipotence.
—John Nichols Wilder

Stand by the Flag, all doubt and treason scorning!
Believe with courage firm, and faith sublime,

That it will float, until the eternal morning
Pales in its glories all the lights of Time!
—John Nichols Wilder

Bright flag at yonder tapering mast,
Fling out your field of azure blue;
Let star and stripe be westward cast,
And point as Freedom's eagle flew!
—N. P. Willis

This is Flag Day, but that only means that it is a day when we are to recall the things which we should do every day of our lives. There are no days of special patriotism.
—Woodrow Wilson

The flag of the United States has not been created by rhetorical sentences in declarations of independence and in bills of rights. It has been created by the experience of a great people, and nothing is written upon it that has not been written by their life. It is the embodiment, not of a sentiment, but of a history. *—Woodrow Wilson*

This flag meant a great enterprise of the human spirit. *—Woodrow Wilson*

We meet to celebrate Flag Day because this flag which we honor and under which we serve is the emblem of our unity, our power, our thought and purpose as a nation. It has no other character than that which we give it from generation to generation. The choice is ours. It floats in majestic silence above the hosts that execute those choices whether in peace or war. And yet, though silent, it speaks to us—speaks to us of the past, of the men and women who went before us and of the records they wrote upon it. We celebrate the day of its birth; and from its birth until now it has witnessed a great history, has floated on high the symbol of great events, of a great plan of life worked out by a great people. *—Woodrow Wilson*

A star for every State, and a State for every star. *—Robert C. Winthrop*

The Colors make the Country whatever be the sky. *—George Edward Woodberry*

HALLOWE'EN

There was not a village in England that had not a ghost in it; the church-yards were all haunted; every large common had a circle of fairies belonging to it; and there was not a shepherd to be met with who had not seen a spirit. —*Joseph Addison*

Then, like the last priest of a vanished nation,
The Shadow drew the cowl about its head,
And with a web-like hand made salutation,
And went back to the Dead.
—*Hervey Allen*

I heard the dogs howl in the moonlight night;
I went to the window to see the sight;
All the Dead that ever I knew
Going one by one and two by two.
—*William Allingham*

Up the airy mountain
Down the rushy glen,
We daren't go a-hunting
For fear of little men;
Wee folk, good folk,
Trooping all together;
Green jacket, red cap,
And white owl's feather!
—*William Allingham*

Turn your boots toward the street,
Leave your garters on your feet,
Put your stockings on your head,
You'll dream of the one you're going to wed.
—*Anon.*

Just at the mirk and midnight hour
The fairy folk will ride.
—*Ballad of Tam Lin*

Bring forth the raisins and the nuts—
Tonight All-Hallows' Spectre struts
Along the moonlit way.
—*John Kendrick Bangs*

There came a shrill and a whistling sound,
Above, beneath, beside, around,
Yet leaf ne'er moved on tree!
—*Richard Harris Barham*

Their figures and forms to describe, language fails—
They'd such very odd heads, and such very odd tails.
—*Richard Harris Barham*

And oh! such awful music! ne'er
Fell sounds so uncanny on mortal ear,
There were the tones of a dying man's groans
Mixed with the rattling of a dead men's bones:
Had you heard the shrieks, and the squeals, and the squeaks,
You'd not have forgotten the sound for weeks.
—*Richard Harris Barham*

As they sat in that old and haunted room,
In each one's hand was a huge birch broom,
On each one's head was a steeple-crown'd hat,
On each one's knee was a coal-black cat;
Each had a kirtle of Lincoln green—
It was, I trow, a fearsome scene.
—*Richard Harris Barham*

Ghosts, like ladies, never speak till spoke to.
—*Richard Harris Barham*

Pixie, kobold, elf, and sprite,
All are on their rounds tonight;
In the wan moon's silver ray,
Thrives their helter-skelter play.
—*Joel Benton*

Come, bairnies, hide in daddy's coat,
Beside the fire so bright—
Perhaps the little fairy folk
Will visit you tonight.
—*Robert Bird*

Horrid apparition, tall and ghastly,
That walks at dead of night, or takes his stand
O'er some new-open'd grave; and (strange to tell!)
Evanishes at crowing of the cock.
—*Robert Blair*

It is a custom at Hallowe'en in Ireland, when the young women would know if their lovers are faithful, to put three nuts upon the bars of the grate, naming the nuts after the lovers. If a nut cracks or jumps, the lover will prove unfaithful; if it begins to blaze or burn, he has a regard for the person making the trial. If the nuts named after the girl and her lover burn together, they will be married. —*John Brand*

And, vow! Tam saw an unco sight!
Warlocks and witches in a dance. . . .
Coffins stood round, like open presses,
That shaw'd the dead in their last dresses;
And, by some devilish cantraip sleight,
Each in its cauld hand held a light.
—*Robert Burns*

The auld guidwife's weel-hoordet nits
Are round an' round divided,
An' monie lads' an' lasses' fates
Are there that night decided.
—*Robert Burns*

Some merry, friendly, countra folks,
Together did convene,
To burn their nits, an' pou their stocks,
An' haud their Hallowe'en,
Fu' blythe that night.
—*Robert Burns*

There sat Auld Nick, in shape o'beast;
A tousie tyke, black, grim, and large,
To gie them music was his charge.
He screw'd the pipes and gart them skirl,
Till roof an' rafters a' did dirl.
—*Robert Burns*

Till presently he hears a squeak,
An' then a grane an' gruntle;
He by his shouther gae a keek,
An' tumbl'd wi' a wintle
Out owre that night.
—*Robert Burns*

Wi' merry sangs, an' friendly cracks,
I wat they did na weary;
An' unco tales, an' funnie jokes,
Their sports were cheap an' cheery.
—*Robert Burns*

Oh, Heaven, it is mysterious, it is awful to consider that we not only carry a future Ghost within us; but are, in very deed, Ghosts! —*Thomas Carlyle*

Fasten the chamber!
Hide the red key;
Cover the portal,
That eyes may not see.
—*Rose Terry Cooke*

Silence and horror
Brood on the walls;
Through every crevice
A little voice calls:
"Quicken, mad footsteps,
On pavement and stair;
Look not behind thee,
The chamber is there!"
—*Rose Terry Cooke*

'Tis the night—the night
Of the grave's delight,
And the warlocks are at their play;
Ye think that without
The wild winds shout,
But no, it is they—it is they.
—*Arthur Cleveland Coxe*

We are spirits clad in veils.
—*Christopher P. Cranch*

No ghost should be allowed to walk
And make such havoc with its talk.
—*Charles Dalmon*

Ireland, too, has a story about the origin of the Jack-o'-lanterns carried on Hallowe'en. It seems that a stingy man named Jack was barred from heaven because of his penuriousness and forbidden to enter hell because of his practical jokes on the devil so he was condemned to walk the earth with his lantern until Judgment Day.
—*George William Douglas*

Tied to the hornet's shardy wings;
Tossed on the pricks of nettle's stings;
Or seven long ages doomed to dwell
With the lazy worm in the walnut-shell;
Or every night to writhe and bleed
Beneath the tread of the centipede;
Or bound in a cobweb dungeon dim,
Your jailer a spider hugh and grim,
Amid the carrion bodies to lie,
Of the worm, and the bug, and the murderous fly.
—*Joseph Rodman Drake*

The leaf-harp sounds our roundelay,
The owlet's eyes our lanterns be;
Thus we sing, and dance, and play,
Round the wild witch-hazel tree.
—*Joseph Rodman Drake*

Ouphe and goblin! imp and sprite!
Elf of eve! and starry Fay!
Ye that love the moon's soft light,
Hither—hither wend your way.
—*Joseph Rodman Drake*

See the Furies arise!
See the snakes that they rear
How they hiss in their hair,
And the sparkles that flash from their eyes!
Behold a ghastly band,
Each a torch in his hand!
—*Dryden*

Auld Daddy Darkness creeps frae his hole,
Black as a blackmoor, blin' as a mole.
—*James Ferguson*

Red serpents, fiery forms, and yelling hags,
Fit company for mad adventurers.
—*Philip Freneau*

Shadowy forms, and ghosts and sleepy things.
—*Philip Freneau*

The staring owl her note has sung;
With gaping snakes my cave is hung;
Of maiden hair my bed is made,
Two winding-sheets above it laid;
With bones of men my shelves are pil'd,
And toads are for my supper boil'd;
Three ghosts attend to fill my cup;
And four to serve my pottage up;
The crow is waiting to say grace:—
Wouldst thou in such a dismal place
The secrets of thy fortune trace?
—*Philip Freneau*

At first cock-crow the ghosts must go
Back to their quiet graves below.
—*Theodosia Garrison*

At even o' Hallowmas no sleep I sought,
But to the field a bag of hemp-seed brought.
I scattered round the seed on every side,
And three times three in trembling accents cried,
"This hemp-seed with my virgin hand I sow,
Who shall my true-love be, the crop shall mow."
—*John Gay*

Two hazel-nuts I threw into the flame,
And to each nut I gave a sweet-heart's name.
This with the loudest bounce me sore amaz'd,
That in a flame of brightest color blaz'd;
As blaz'd the nut, so may thy passion grow,
For 'twas thy nut that did so brightly glow.
—*John Gay*

Last Hallow Eve I sought a walnut-tree,
In hope my true Love's face that I might see;
Three times I called, three times I walked apace;
Then in the tree I saw my true Love's face.
—*John Gay*

I pare this pippin round and round again,
My sweetheart's name to flourish on the plain:
I fling the unbroken paring o'er my head.
A perfect "L" upon the ground is read.
—*John Gay*

See, from the core two kernals brown I take:
This on my cheek for Lubberkin is worn,
And Booby Clod on t'other side is borne;
But Booby Clod soon drops upon the ground,
A certain token that his love's unsound;
While Lubberkin sticks firmly to the last.
Oh! were his lips to mine but joined so fast.
—*John Gay*

For ghosts and for the devil 'tis a law,
Where they stole in, there they must forth. We're free
The first to choose; as to the second, slaves are we.
—*Goethe*

The master of the rats and mice,
Of flies and frogs, of bugs and lice,
Commands thy presence.
—*Goethe*

What goblin of malevolence
Runs through the frozen night
In superhuman flight?
—*Julian Hawthorne*

What fearful thing speeds hither,
Running, running, running
Swifter than cloud or wind?
What omen of nameless ill,
Whence coming, speeding whither,
Running, running, running,
Leaves all save fear behind?
—*Julian Hawthorne*

The hag is astride
This night for a ride,
The devils and she together.
—*Robert Herrick*

Sprites away! elf and fay,
From thicket, lake, and hollow;
The blind bat, look! flits to his nook,
And we must quickly follow.
—*George Hill*

Haste! hither whip them with this end
Of spider's web—anon
The ghost will have fled to his grave-bed
And the bat winked in the sun.
—*George Hill*

A hunter of shadows, himself a shade.
—*Homer*

Thin, airy shoals of visionary ghosts.
—*Homer*

O'er all there hung a shadow and a fear,
A sense of mystery the spirit daunted,
And said as plain as whisper in the ear,
The place is Haunted.
—*Thomas Hood*

Fierce dragons hover in the air,
And serpents crawl along the ground
—*Thomas Hood*

Ha! They are on us, close without!
Shut tight the shelter where we lie;
With hideous din the monster rout,
Dragon and vampire, fill the sky.
—*Victor Hugo*

What gentle ghost, besprent with April dew,
Hails me so solemnly to yonder yew?
—*Ben Jonson*

When larks 'gin sing
Away we fling;
And babes new borne steal as we go,
And elfe in bed
We leave instead,
And wend us laughing, ho, ho, ho!
—*Ben Jonson*

The girls are laughing with the boys and gaming by the fire,
They're wishful, every one of them, to see her heart's desire.
—*Winifred M. Letts*

This horseshoe will I nail upon the threshold;
There, ye night-hags and witches that torment
The neighborhood, ye shall not enter here.
—*Longfellow*

So many ghosts, and forms of fright,
Have started from their graves tonight,
They have driven sleep from mine eyes away;
I will go down to the chapel and pray.
—*Longfellow*

Through the open doors
The harmless phantoms on their errands glide,
With feet that make no sound upon the floors.
—*Longfellow*

The stranger at my fireside cannot see
The forms I see, nor hear the sounds I hear.
—*Longfellow*

Adown the leafy lane we two
Heard fairy pipes play fairy music sweet,
And now and then the tramp of fairy feet,
And screams of laughter 'mong the fairy crew—
The elves and fays that haunt old Corradhu.
—*D. A. MacAleese*

Black spirits and white, red spirits and gray,
Mingle, mingle, mingle, you that mingle may.
—*Thomas Middleton*

Some say no evil thing that walks by night,
In fog or fire, by lake or moorish fen,
Blue meagre hag, or stubborn unlaid ghost
That breaks his magic chains at curfew time,
No goblin, or swart fairy of the mine,
Hath hurtful power o'er true virginity.
—*Milton*

Black it stood as night,
Fierce as ten furies, terrible as hell,
And shook a dreadful dart.
—*Milton*

On a sudden open fly,
With impetuous recoil and jarring sound,
Th' infernal doors, and on their hinges grate
Harsh thunder.
—*Milton*

Hail horrors, hail
Infernal world.
—*Milton*

Of calling shapes, and beck'ning shadows dire,
And airy tongues that syllable men's names.
—*Milton*

For spirits when they please
Can either sex assume, or both.
—*Milton*

The other shape,
If shape it might be call'd that shape had none
Distinguishable in member, joint, or limb;
Or substance might be call'd that shadow seem'd.
—*Milton*

Men say that in this midnight hour,
The disembodièd have power
To wander as it liketh them,
By wizard oak and fairy stream.
—*William Motherwell*

The rosy apple's bobbing
Upon the mimic sea—
'Tis tricksy and elusive,
And glides away from me.
—*Richard Munkittrick*

Strange shadows, stranger shades, are seen—
It is the mystic Hallowe'en.
—*A. F. Murray*

This is the nicht o' Hallowe'en,
When a' the witchie micht be seen;
Some o' them black, some o' them green,
Some o' them like a turkey bean.
—*Old song*

They are neither man nor woman—
They are neither brute nor human,
They are Ghouls!
—*Edgar Allan Poe*

By the grey woods,—by the swamp
Where the toad and the newt encamp,—
By the dismal tarns and pools
Where dwell the Ghouls,—
By each spot the most unholy,—
In each nook most melancholy,—
There the traveller meets, aghast,
Sheeted Memories of the Past—
Shrouded forms that start and sigh
As they pass the wanderer by.
—*Edgar Allan Poe*

But see amid the mimic rout
A crawling shape intrude:
A blood-red thing that writhes from out
The scenic solitude!
—*Edgar Allan Poe*

What beckoning ghost along the moonlight shade
Invites my steps, and points to yonder glade?
—*Alexander Pope*

O, when the moon shines, and the dogs do howl,
Then, then is the cry of the hornèd owl!
—*B. W. Procter*

The Willis are out to-night,
In the ghostly pale moonlight,
With robes and faces white.

Swiftly they circle round,
And make not any sound,
Nor footprint on the ground.
—*David Law Proudfit*

Scampering as if the Devil drove them.
—*Rabelais*

God save us from the skeleton
Who sitteth at the feast!
—*James Jeffrey Roche*

Fierce as the snake, with his eye-balls of fire,
When his scales are all brilliant and glowing with ire.
—*Robert Charles Sands*

It's weel kenn'd she was born on Hallowe'en, and they that are born on Hallowe'en whiles see mair than ither folk.
—*Sir Walter Scott*

I have tied red thread round the bairns' throats, and given ilk ane of them a riding-wand of rowan-tree, forbye sewing up a slip of witch-elm into their doublets; and I wish to know of your reverence if there be onything mair that a lone woman can do in the matter of ghosts and fairies?
—*Sir Walter Scott*

By day they scour earth's cavern'd space,
At midnight's witching hour, ascend.
—*Sir Walter Scott*

He that dare sit on St. Swithin's Chair,
When the Night-Hag wings the troubled air,
Questions three, when he speaks the spell,
He may ask, and she must tell.
—*Sir Walter Scott*

The devil rides upon a fiddlestick.
—*Shakespeare*

'Tis now the very witching time of night,
When churchyards yawn and hell itself breathes out
Contagion to this world.
—*Shakespeare*

Double, double toil and trouble;
Fire burn, and cauldron bubble.
—*Shakespeare*

By the pricking of my thumbs,
Something wicked this way comes.
Open, locks,
Whoever knocks!
—*Shakespeare*

How now, you secret, black, and midnight hags!
—*Shakespeare*

I have supp'd full with horrors.
—*Shakespeare*

Angels and ministers of grace, defend us!
Be thou a spirit of health or goblin damn'd,
Bring with thee airs from heaven or blasts from hell,
Be thy intents wicked or charitable,
Thou comest in such a questionable shape
That I will speak to thee.
—*Shakespeare*

"Fillet of a fenny snake,
. . . .
Eye of newt, and toe of frog,
Wool of bat, and tongue of dog,
Adder's fork, and blindworm's sting,
Lizard's leg, and owlet's wing,
For a charm of powerful trouble—"
—*Shakespeare*

It is an honest ghost, that let me tell you.
—*Shakespeare*

Avaunt! and quit my sight! let the earth hide thee!
Thy bones are marrowless, thy blood is cold;
Thou hast no speculation in those eyes
Which thou dost glare with!
—*Shakespeare*

The graves stood tenantless, and the sheeted dead
Did squeak and gibber in the Roman streets.
—*Shakespeare*

Peace, break thee off; look, where it comes again!
—*Shakespeare*

Now it is the time of night,
That the graves, all gaping wide,
Every one lets forth his sprite,
In the church-way paths to glide.
—*Shakespeare*

Now the wasted brands do glow,
Whilst the scritch owl, scritching loud,
Puts the wretch that lies in woe,
In remembrance of a shroud.
—*Shakespeare*

Hence, horrible shadow! Unreal mockery, hence!
—*Shakespeare*

What are these
So wither'd, and so wild in their attire,
That look not like the inhabitants o' the earth,
And yet are on 't?
—*Shakespeare*

This is the foul fiend Flibbertigibbet. He begins at curfew, and walks till the first cock. He . . . squints the eye and makes the hare-lip.
—*Shakespeare*

Aroint thee, witch, aroint thee!
—*Shakespeare*

Hark! Hark to the wind! 'Tis the night, they say,
When all souls come back from the far away—
The dead, forgotten this many a day!
—*Virna Sheard*

Still the pale spirit, singing through the night,
Came to this window, looking from the dark
Into the room; then passing to the door
Where crouched the whining dog, afraid to bark,
Tapped gently without answer, pressed the latch,
Pushed softly open, and then tapped once more.
—*Mrs. Clement Shorter*
(*Dora Sigerson*)

Whass dat creepin' up de road,
Quiet like a ferret,
Hoppin' sof'ly as a toad?
Maybe hit's a sperrit!
—*Carlyle Smith*

From his brimstone bed at break of day
A-walking the Devil is gone,
To look at his little snug farm of the world,
And see how his stock went on. . . . .
His coat was red and his breeches were blue,
And there was a hole where his tail came through.
—*Robert Southey*

In the white moonlight, where the willow waves,
He halfway gallops among the graves—
A tiny ghost in the gloom and gleam,
Content to dwell where the dead men dream.
—*Frank L. Stanton*

For the graveyard rabbit, though sceptics scoff,
Charmeth the witch and the wizard off!
—*Frank L. Stanton*

I stamp upon the ground, and adders rouse,
Sharp-eyed, with poisonous fangs; beneath the leaves
They couch, or under rocks, and roots of trees
Felled by the winds; through briery undergrowth
They slide with hissing tongues.
—Richard Henry Stoddard

And bats sail there athwart the silver light,
Flapping their wings; by day in hollow trees
They hide, and slink into the gloom of dens.
We live, my mother Sycorax and I,
In caves with bloated toads and crested snakes.
—Richard Henry Stoddard

Then the witches, laughing scornfully, ride to Blocksberg, upon the mountain-top, on their broomsticks, the same broomsticks with which at other times their witchcraft is whipped out of them,—then the whole wild company skims along the forest way,—and then the wild desires awaken in our hearts which life has not fulfilled. *—Hermann Sudermann*

While the wolves that late did howl
Slink to dens and coverts foul,
Guarded by the demon owl,
Who, last night, with mocking croon,
Wheeled athwart the chilly moon,
And with eyes that blankly glared,
On my direful torment stared.
—Bayard Taylor

A footstep, a low throbbing in the walls,
A noise of falling weights that never fell,
Weird whispers, bells that rang without a hand,
Door-handles turn'd when none was at the door,
And bolted doors that open'd of themselves.
—Alfred Tennyson

I saw the toad and scaly snake
From tangled covert start.
—Mary Ashley Townsend

Black cats, swooping bats, and impish goblins green,
Combine with witches riding brooms
To challenge Hallowe'en.
—Unknown

Peeping in the windows, tapping on the doors,
Creeping, crawling, chilly things,
Scurrying over floors.
—Unknown

You wouldn't believe
On All Hallow Eve
What lots of fun we can make,
With apples to bob,
And nuts on the hob,
And a ring-and-thimble cake.
—Carolyn Wells

Arrah, Barney, it's raly too bad
Bedad,
To see you there lookin' so sad,
My lad.
It's now Halloweve,
An' you sit there an' grieve,
On account of your sittin' alone,
Like a stone,—
Poor, dismal pilgarlic Maglone!
—Robert A. Wilson

I look for ghosts; but none will force
Their way to me: 'tis falsely said
That there was ever intercourse
Between the living and the dead.
—William Wordsworth

HEALTH WEEK

Health and cheerfulness mutually beget each other. —*Addison*

Physic is, for the most part, only a substitute for temperance and exercise.
—*Joseph Addison*

Give me a healthy body, Lord,
And sense to keep it at its best.
—*Anon.*

Health and good estate of body are above all gold, and a strong body above infinite wealth. —*Apocrypha: Ecclesiasticus 40:15*

How sufficient to a well-mannered man is a very little, and he doth not breathe hard upon his bed. Healthy sleep cometh of moderate eating; he riseth early and his wits are with him; the pain of wakefulness, and colic, and griping, are with an insatiable man.
—*Apocrypha: Ecclesiasticus 2:24*

Because of surfeiting many have perished; but he that taketh heed shall prolong his life.
—*Apocrypha: Ecclesiasticus 3:13*

He who has health, has hope; and he who has hope, has everything.
—*Arabian Proverb*

Without health, life is not life; life is lifeless.
—*Ariphon the Sicyonian*

Know, then, whatever cheerful and serene
Supports the mind supports the body too.
—*John Armstrong*

Cleanness of body was ever deemed to proceed from a due reverence to God.
—*Francis Bacon*

A healthy body is the guest-chamber of the soul; a sick, its prison. —*Francis Bacon*

If you fly physic in health altogether, it will be too strange for your body when you shall need it: if you make it too familiar, it will work no extraordinary effect when sickness cometh. —*Francis Bacon*

There is a wisdom in this beyond the rules of physic. A man's own observation, what he finds good of and what he finds hurt of, is the best physic to preserve health.
Francis Bacon

Good old Doctor Cheerful Thinking!
He's the chap when hearts are sinking,
And with tears your eyes are blinking.
—*John Kendrick Bangs*

What fools indeed we mortals are
To lavish care upon a Car,
With ne'er a bit of time to see
About our own machinery!
—*John Kendrick Bangs*

A good digestion is as truly obligatory as a good conscience; pure blood is as truly a part of manhood as a pure faith; a vigorous brain is as necessary to useful living as a vigorous will, which it often helps to make vigorous; and a well-ordered skin is the first condition of that cleanliness which is next to godliness.
—*Henry Ward Beecher*

Half the spiritual difficulties that men and women suffer arise from a morbid state of health. —*Henry Ward Beecher*

I think you might dispense with half your doctors if you would only consult Dr. Sun more. —*Henry Ward Beecher*

Mirth is God's medicine. Everybody ought to bathe in it. —*Henry Ward Beecher*

Health is the greatest of all possessions; a hale cobbler is better than a sick king.
—*Bickerstaff*

Health is like munny, we never have a true idea of its value until we lose it.
—*Josh Billings*

Good health is the secret of physical and mental power. Occasionally we hear of a genius who achieved great work despite the handicap of ill health and suffering; but the strong, vigorous, clear-eyed person has the best chance in life's battles.
—*Harvey A. Blodgett*

Do honor to your bodies. Reverence your physical natures, not simply for themselves. Only as ends they are not worthy of it, but because in health and strength lies the true basis of noble thought and glorious devotion. A man thinks well and loves well and prays well, because of the rich running of his blood.
—*Phillips Brooks*

Rest of body and mind, education in regard to what is safe and what is dangerous, good food and fresh air are the medicines that restore health. —*Dr. Lawrason Brown*

Men that look no further than their outsides, think health an appurtenance unto life, and quarrel with their constitutions for being sick; but I that have examined the parts of man, and know upon what tender filaments that fabric hangs, do wonder that we are not always so; and considering the thousand doors that lead to death, do thank my God that we can die but once. —*Sir Thomas Browne*

I think it frets the saints in heaven to see
How many desolate creatures on the earth
Have learnt the simple dues of fellowship
And social comfort, in a hospital.
—Elizabeth Barrett Browning

My good friends, while I do most earnestly recommend you to take care of your health and safety, as things most precious to us, I would not have that care degenerate into an effeminate and over-curious attention, which is always disgraceful to a man's self, and often troublesome to others.
—Edmund Burke

[Diseases] crucify the soul of man, attenuate our bodies, dry them, wither them, shrivel them up like old apples, make them as so many anatomies. *—Robert Burton*

Restore a man to his health, his purse lies open to thee. *—Robert Burton*

Who lives medically, lives miserably.
—Robert Burton

Take it by and large, it is perhaps less important how many years we live than how many years we live in sound health.
—Nicholas Murray Butler

Despair of all recovery spoils longevity.
—Lord Byron

There is no kind of achievement you could make in the world that is equal to perfect health. What to it are nuggets and millions?
—Thomas Carlyle

The bow cannot possibly always stand bent, nor can human nature or human frailty subsist without some lawful recreation.
—Cervantes

Physical ills are the taxes laid upon this wretched life; some are taxed higher, and some lower, but all pay something.
—Lord Chesterfield

The surest road to health, say what they will,
Is never to suppose we shall be ill.
Most of those evils we poor mortals know
From doctors and imagination flow.
—Charles Churchill

In nothing do men more nearly approach the gods than in giving health to men.
—Cicero

A man too busy to take care of his health is like a mechanic too busy to take care of his tools. *—Cicero*

On the bathing-tub of King T'ang the following words were engraved: "If you would one day renovate yourself, do so from day to day. Yea, let there be daily renovation."
—Confucian Analects

Every day, in every way, I am getting better and better. *—Emil Coué*

Some men employ their health, an ugly trick,
In making known how oft they have been sick.
—Cowper

There are all manner of cures from mud baths and Perkins's Patent Porous Plaster up to Thought Vibrations, but the greatest of all is the Mirth Cure. *—Dr. Frank Crane*

Our national habit of shutting ourselves up with a hot stove for the winter and never opening a window, brings on more premature deaths than whiskey ever did.
—Samuel Crowther

Happiness lies, first of all, in health.
—George William Curtis

As for food, half of my friends have dug their graves with their teeth.
—Chauncey M. Depew

The health of the people is really the foundation upon which all their happiness and all their powers as a state depend.
—Benjamin Disraeli

Better to hunt in fields for health unbought
Than fee the doctor for a nauseous draught.
—John Dryden

Oh to be strong! Each morn to feel
A fresh delight to wake to life.
To spring with bounding pulse to meet
Whate'er of work, or joy or strife
Day brings to me. Each night to sleep
The dreamless sleep that health can give.
—John Dryden

The wise for cure on exercise depend;
God never made his work for man to mend.
—John Dryden

Though I have patches on me pantaloons,
I've ne'er a wan on me intestines.
—Finley Peter Dunne

And he that will his health deny
Down among the dead men let him lie.
—Edward Dyer

Yet this is health: To have a body functioning so perfectly that when its few simple needs are met it never calls attention to its own existence. . . If the machine is going to work over a long period of time at maximum efficiency, it must receive intelligent care.
—Bertha Stuart Dyment

Why shouldst thou die before thy time?
—Ecclesiastes 7:17

A sound mind in a sound body; if the former be the glory of the latter, the latter is indispensable to the former.
—Tryon Edwards

The best part of health is fine disposition. It is more essential than talent, even in the works of talent. Nothing will supply the want of sunshine to peaches, and, to make knowledge valuable, you must have the cheerfulness of wisdom. —*Emerson*

Sickness is poor-spirited, and cannot serve anyone; it must husband its resources to live. But health or fulness answers its own ends, and has to spare, runs over, and inundates the neighborhoods and creeks of other men's necessities. —*Emerson*

Give me health and a day, and I will make the pomp of emperors ridiculous.
—*Emerson*

Get health. No labor, effort nor exercise that can gain it must be grudged.
—*Emerson*

Ruddy Health the loftiest Muse.
Live in the sunshine, swim the sea,
Drink the wild air's salubrity.
—*Emerson*

Hail! Auspicious Health! Thou propitious power
Whose blessings mortals next to life implore;
With so much luster your bright looks endear
That cottages are palaces when you appear.
Mankind, as you vouchsafe to smile or frown,
Finds ease in chains or anguish in a crown.
—*Esarth*

Fighting trim is a term used in the navy for the immediate readiness of a battle-ship for battle. Applied to a boy or girl, it means a condition of health that means immediate readiness to fight disease or accident.
—*William Byron Forbush*

Anybody can be sick who takes the attitude of being a victim. An athlete of will is almost never sick, and when he is he gets well easily. —*William Byron Forbush*

Be sober and temperate and you will be healthy. —*Benjamin Franklin*

The best of all medicines are rest and fasting.
—*Benjamin Franklin*

Early to bed and early to rise,
Makes a man healthy, wealthy, and wise.
—*Benjamin Franklin*

Many dishes, many diseases. Many medicines, few cures. —*Benjamin Franklin*

Tolerate no uncleanliness in body, clothes or habitation. —*Benjamin Franklin*

Civilization begins with soap.
—*Galveston Times.*

Nor love, nor honour, wealth nor pow'r,
Can give the heart a cheerful hour
When health is lost. —*John Gay*

Healthy and cheerful he wakes from his repose,
Breasts the keen air and carols as he goes.
—*Oliver Goldsmith*

His best companions, innocence and health.
—*Oliver Goldsmith*

We are not sent into this world to be miserable. —*J. Mortimer Granville*

The old Romans held that in a sound body dwelt a sound mind. We can go further and admit that the actions of a soul itself are influenced by the health of the body, for it is only the soul's machine, and it is the soul's only machine on this planet.
—*Wilfred T. Grenfell*

Keep well. No single factor is so basal to vividness of life and work as is good health. I do not mean merely the absence of disease or disability, but that freshness that comes with good digestion, good sleep, and outdoor air. —*Luther Halsey Gulick*

The mental attitude of defeat, of discouragement, lowers the resisting power of the individual. It predisposes him to disease. The whole tone of his system is let down. His body becomes a fertile seeding-ground for infection. —*Luther Halsey Gulick*

To live at a low level is to deaden every faculty for high thought and high feeling—it makes drudgery not only of work but also of life. —*Luther Halsey Gulick*

A wise physician is a John Baptist, who recognizes that his only mission is to prepare the way for a greater than himself—Nature.
—*A. S. Hardy*

Obey the conservative laws of your body, and a sound and healthy constitution is your reward. —*J. R. Hayes*

Sickness comes on horseback, but goes away on foot. —*W. C. Hazlitt*

To carry out the rich emotional and intellectual life of humanity, we need a good tool, a good body, a strong and beautiful and well trained organism, and this is gained only through cultivation. —*O. H. Henderson*

Against diseases here the strongest fence
Is the defensive virtue, abstinence.
—*Robert Herrick*

Health is the first good lent to men;
A gentle disposition then.
—*Robert Herrick*

When the artless doctor sees
No one hope, but of his fees,
And his skill runs on the lees,
Sweet Spirit, comfort me!
When his potion and his pill,
His, or none, or little skill,
Meet for nothing, but to kill,
Sweet Spirit, comfort me!
—*Robert Herrick*

All the physical universe takes the side of health and activity, wooing us forth into Nature, imploring us hourly, and in unsuspected ways, to receive her blessed breath into body and soul, and share in her eternal youth.
—*Thomas Wentworth Higginson*

Few things are more important to a community than the health of its women. If strong is the frame of a mother, says a proverb, the son will give laws to the people. And in nations where all men give laws, all men need mothers of strong frames.
—*Thomas Wentworth Higginson*

Your child's mind is not an earthen jar, to be filled by pouring into it; it is a delicate plant, to be wisely and healthfully reared.
—*Thomas Wentworth Higginson*

If men are to be reformed they must be well fed. —*Martin L. Holbrook*

I firmly believe that if the whole *materia medica* could be sunk to the bottom of the sea, it would be all the better for mankind and all the worse for the fishes.
—*Oliver Wendell Holmes*

Happy the man, and he alone,
Who, master of himself, can say,
This day, at least, hath been mine own,
For I have cleanly lived today.
—*Horace*

Health to enjoy the blessings sent
From Heaven; a mind unclouded, strong.
—*Horace*

If all be well with belly, feet, and sides,
A king's estate no greater good provides.
—*Horace*

After these two, Dr. Diet and Dr. Quiet, Dr. Merriman is requisite to preserve health.
—*James Howell*

If you have health, you probably will be happy, and if you have health and happiness, you have all the wealth you need, even if it is not all you want. —*Elbert Hubbard*

"The word 'heaven' means harmony." . . . Health is the key to this heaven, in this and in all conceivable worlds. . . . Disease is war with the laws of our being, and all war, as a great general has said, is hell.
—*Lewis G. Janes*

For I will restore health unto thee, and I will heal thee of thy wounds, saith the Lord.
—*Jeremiah 30:17*

Beloved, I wish above all things that thou mayest prosper and be in health, even as thy soul prospereth.
—*III John 2*

Health is, indeed, so necessary to all the duties as well as pleasures of life, that the crime of squandering it is equal to the folly.
—*Samuel Johnson*

Remember, men need laughter sometimes more than food.
—*Anna Fellows Johnston*

O, health! health! the blessing of the rich! the riches of the poor! who can buy thee at too dear a rate, since there is no enjoying this world without thee? —*Ben Jonson*

Our prayers should be for a sound mind in a healthy body. —*Juvenal*

He whose blood is red, whose muscles are hard, whose sleep is sound, whose digestion is good, whose posture is erect, whose nerves are steady has a good bank account in life.
—*Calvin P. Kendall*

Dyspepsia is the remorse of a guilty stomach.
—*A. Kerr*

Sickness is the most calamitous of the hazards of life. —*John A. Lapp*

He keeps watch over a good castle who guards well his constitution.
—*Latin Proverb*

The building of a perfect body crowned by a perfect brain, is at once the greatest earthly problem and grandest hope of the race.
—*Dio Lewis*

The clean city may not be a health resort, but it has a tendency in that direction.
—*Life*

If by gaining knowledge we destroy our health, we labour for a thing that will be useless in our hands. —*John Locke*

A sound mind in a sound body, is a short but full description of a happy state in this world. He that has these two, has little more to wish for; and he that wants either of them, will be little the better for anything else. —*John Locke*

If the mind, that rules the body, ever so far forgets itself as to trample on its slave, the slave is never generous enough to forgive the injury, but will rise and smite the oppressor. —*Longfellow*

Joy and Temperance and Repose
Slam the door on the doctor's nose.
—*Longfellow*

Refuse to be ill. Never tell people you are ill; never own it to yourself. Illness is one of those things which a man should resist on principle at the onset. —*Bulwer-Lytton*

We live longer than our forefathers; but we suffer more from a thousand artificial anxieties and cares. They fatigued only the muscles, we exhaust the finer strength of the nerves. —*Bulwer-Lytton*

"May you wear it with health," is an old Macedonian saying offered with anything new, and wishing the receiver joy of it.
—*Macedonian Folklore*

Vigorous health is worth anything it costs.
—*Orison Swett Marden*

It is a great thing to have that bounding health, that excess of vitality, which makes us feel like conquerors, equal to any emergency, which makes us the easy masters of conditions which would discourage weaklings.
—*Orison Swett Marden*

Life is not merely to be alive, but to be well.
—*Martial*

The doctor is sure that my health is poor, he says that I waste away; so bring me a can of the shredded bran, and a bale of the toasted hay. —*Walt Mason*

The only night air that is injurious is last night's.
—*Editorial. Michigan (State) Bulletin*

If thou well observe
The rule of *Not too much,* by tem'prance taught
In what thou eat'st and drink'st, seeking from thence
Due nourishment, not gluttonous delight,
Till many years over thy head return,
So may'st thou live, till, like ripe fruit, thou drop
Into they mother's lap, or be with ease
Gather'd, not harshly pluck'd, for death mature.
—*Milton*

Govern well thy appetite, lest Sin
Surprise thee, and her black attendant, Death.
—*Milton*

All means that conduce to health can neither be too painful nor too dear to me.
—*Montaigne*

Our work is not to train a soul by itself alone, nor a body by itself alone, but to train a man; and in man soul and body can never be divided. —*Montaigne*

A good, real, unrestrained, hearty laugh is a sort of glorified internal massage, performed rapidly and automatically. It manipulates and revitalizes corners and unexplored crannies of the system that are unresponsive to most other exercise methods.
—*Editorial. New York Tribune*

Water, air, and cleanliness are the chief articles in my pharmacopoeia. —*Napoleon I*

Beauty without is born of health within.
—*M. V. O'Shea*

Learn to accept in silence the minor aggravations, cultivate the gift of taciturnity, and consume your own smoke with an extra draft of hard work, so that those about you may not be annoyed with the dust and soot of your complaints.
—*William Osler*

As long as the Romans were the most athletic nation of Europe, they were also the most virtuous. —*Dr. T. L. Oswald*

The optimist has a better chance for health than the pessimist. —*Floyd W. Parsons*

Early rising and much bathing are profitable to keep a man in health, and to increase his riches and wisdom. —*Plato*

A physician, after he had felt the pulse of Pausanias, and considered his constitution, saying, "He ails nothing," "It is because, sir," he replied, "I use none of your physic."
—*Plutarch*

Reason's whole pleasure, all joys of sense,
Lie in these words, health, peace, competence.
—*Alexander Pope*

Health is fashionable now; it will soon be contagious. —*Katherine Pritchett*

To lengthen your life, shorten your meals.
—*Proverb*

A merry heart doeth good like a medicine; but a broken spirit drieth the bones.
—*Proverbs 17:22*

Good health and good sense are two of life's greatest blessings. —*Publilius Syrus*

There is such a thing as physical morality and the preservation of health should be considered a sacred duty. —*W. L. Pyle*

Without health life is not life; it is only a state of languor and suffering—an image of death. —*Rabelais*

Preserving the health by too strict a regimen is a wearisome malady.
—*François, Duc de la Rochefoucauld*

I made my health what it is. I determined to be strong and well, and did everything to make myself so. —*Theodore Roosevelt*

There is one point in which all men might be born free and equal. That is in regard to health. If a child has clean blood, a good brain, and a mother who knows how to care for herself and for him, he is equal to any other child on the face of the earth.
—*Theodore Roosevelt*

Death's servant, sickness.
—*Francis Rous*

Temperance and labor are the two true physicians of man.
—*Jean Jacques Rousseau*

Inactivity, supineness, and effeminacy have ruined more constitutions than were ever destroyed by excessive labors. Moderate exercise and toil, so far from prejudicing, strengthen and consolidate the body.
—*Dr. Richard Rush*

Blessed is the healthy nature; it is coherent and sweetly cooperative. —*John Ruskin*

Cheerfulness is as natural to the heart of a man in strong health as color to his cheek; and whenever there is habitual gloom there must be either bad air, unwholesome food, improperly severe labor or erring habits of life. —*John Ruskin*

Better than grandeur, better than gold,
Than rank and title a thousand fold
Is a healthy body, mind at ease,
And simple pleasures that always please.
Abram Joseph Ryan

Health is a gift of God or a product of common sense. —*Saturday Evening Post*

And if dear life
Has some, though limited and doubtful, worth,
Then health has clear and unambiguous worth.
—*Leopold Schaeffer*

E'en from the body's purity the soul derives a secret, sympathetic aid.
—*Leopold Schaeffer*

Not holy is the soul alone; the body,
That too is holy if the whole man is.
—*Leopold Schaeffer*

Give him air, he'll straight be well.
—*Shakespeare*

My lord leans wondrously to discontent;
His comfortable temper has forsook him;
He is much out of health.
—*Shakespeare*

Nature does require
Her time of preservation, which perforce
I her frail son amongst my brethren mortal
Must give my attendance to.
—*Shakespeare*

Throw physic to the dogs; I'll none of it.
—*Shakespeare*

The ingredients of health and long life, are great temperance, open air, easy labor, and little care. —*Sir Philip Sidney*

Youth will never live to age unless they keep themselves in health with exercise, and in heart with joyfulness.
—*Sir Philip Sidney*

It is only the constant exertion and working of our sensitive, intellectual, moral, and physical machinery that keeps us from rusting, and so becoming useless. —*Charles Simmons*

Sickness is the vengeance of nature for the violation of her laws. —*Charles Simmons*

To re-create strength, rest. To re-create mind, repose. —*Charles Simmons*

It is pleasant to grow old with health and a good friend. —*Socrates*

My mind to me an empire is,
While grace affordeth health.
—*Robert Southwell*

The fact is, that all breaches of the laws of health are *physical sins.*
—*Herbert Spencer*

People who are always taking care of their health are like misers who are hoarding a treasure which they have never spirit enough to enjoy. —*Laurence Sterne*

My state of health none care to learn;
My life is here no soul's concern.
—*Jonathan Swift*

Health is the soul that animates all enjoyments of life, which fade, and are tasteless, if not dead, without it.
—*Sir William Temple*

Who would not be covetous, and with reason, if health could be purchased with gold? Who not ambitious, if it were at the command of power, or restored by honour?
—*Sir William Temple*

Ring out old shapes of foul disease.
—*Alfred Tennyson*

Ah! what avail the largest gifts of Heaven
When drooping health and spirits go amiss?
How tasteless then whatever can be given!
Health is the vital principle of bliss,
And exercise of health.
—*James Thomson*

Let health my nerves and finer fibres brace.
—*James Thomson*

Every man is the builder of a Temple called his body, nor can he get off by hammering marble instead.
—*Henry D. Thoreau*

Some seek for wealth, I seek for health,
For that is wealth for me.
—*Thomas Tusser*

The morality of clean blood ought to be one of the first lessons taught us by our pastors and teachers. —*John Tyndale*

The physical is the substratum of the spiritual; and this fact ought to give to the food we eat, and the air we breathe, a transcendent significance. —*John Tyndale*

Give me a healthy body, Lord, and sense to keep it at its best. —*Unknown*

If doctors fail you, let these three be your doctors: a cheerful mind, rest, and moderate diet. —*Unknown*

The greatest wealth is health. —*Virgil*

Regimen is better than physic. . . What medicine can procure digestion? Exercise. What will recruit strength? Sleep. What will alleviate incurable evils? Patience. —*Voltaire*

It is sometimes as dangerous to be run into by a microbe as by a trolley car. —*Dr. J. J. Walsh*

Look to your health; and if you have it, praise God, and value it next to a good conscience. —*Izaak Walton*

Health is perpetual youth—that is, a state of positive health. —*E. L. Ward*

Ah, what is fame and what is wealth,
Matched with the rich renown of health?
—*Amos R. Wells*

Cleanliness is indeed next to godliness. —*John Wesley*

Health is a large word. It embraces not the body only, but the mind and spirit as well; . . . and not today's pain or pleasure alone, but the whole being and outlook of a man. —*James H. West*

If anything is sacred the human body is sacred,
And the glory and sweet of a man is the token of manhood untainted,
And in man or woman a clean, strong, firm-fibred body is more beautiful than the most beautiful face.
—*Walt Whitman*

To *cure* is the voice of the past, to *prevent* the divine whisper of today.
—*Kate Douglas Wiggin*

Say you are well, or all is well with you,
And God shall hear your words and make them true.
—*Ella Wheeler Wilcox*

Talk Health! The dreary never ending tale
Of mortal maladies is worn and stale.
You cannot charm or interest or please,
By harping on that minor chord—disease.
—*Ella Wheeler Wilcox*

LABOR DAY

The least work is a great work because it is a necessary part of a great work, as the day laborer with his spade at Panama is necessary to the completion of the great world waterway between two oceans. *—Lyman Abbott*

Dr. Henry Sloane Coffin has given a new interpretation to the direction: "Let not thy left hand know what thy right hand doeth." Why not? Because the left hand should be so busy doing its own work that it has no time to be watching its fellow. *—Lyman Abbott.*

A nation is made great, not by its fruitful acres, but by the men who cultivate them; not by its great forests, but by the men who use them; not by its mines, but by the men who work in them; not by its railways, but by the men who build and run them. America was a great land when Columbus discovered it; Americans have made it a great nation.
—Lyman Abbott

It is work which gives flavor to life.
—Amiel

To do what you can
As well as you can,
Is a mighty good plan
For 'most any man.
—Anon.

And I knew in that moment of waiting,
While his look pierced my very soul through,
I was judged not so much by my doing
As by what I had striven to do.
—Anon.

In the handywork of their craft is their prayer. *—Apocrypha: Ecclesiasticus 3:15*

The life of one that laboureth and is contented,
Shall be made sweet.
—Apocrypha: Ecclesiasticus 4:2

Be not over wise in doing thy work. And glorify not thyself in the time of thy distress: better is he that laboureth, and aboundeth in all things, than he that glorifieth himself and lacketh bread.
—Apocrypha: Ecclesiasticus 1:42

Whatsoever thou takest in hand, remember the end, and thou shalt never do amiss.
—Apocrypha: Ecclesiasticus 7:36

And brightest is their glory's sheen,
For greatest hath their labor been.
—Matthew Arnold

It is in fact the quality of a man's work that should determine his place in the hierarchy that every civilized society requires.
—Irving Babbitt

The only true freedom is the freedom to work. *—Irving Babbitt*

Before labor in any sense can be called a curse, the economy of nature must be changed, or the universe be called a curse. All that have being labor, and by labor all was made that exists. *—Herbert Howe Bancroft*

Cheap labor is no more degrading than dear labor. No labor is degrading. It all contributes to the well-being of mankind and the advancement of civilization directly or indirectly. *—Herbert Howe Bancroft*

Hunger is not the worst feature of unemployment; idleness is.
—William E. Barrett

The truth is that Work is the magic which transforms us from dull beings into people worth while. *—Bruce Barton*

I believe that God made us to work. I believe that He meant that we should earn our living by the sweat of our brows. And I believe that He made us to love our work so much that we might play at it; find real and profound pleasure in it; and so labor on until, tired out, we might sleep like little children at the end of each day.
—David Belasco

Now I have noticed four very marked qualities in all the great workers and doers of my acquaintance. They are never in a hurry; they are never late; they are calm and quiet persons; and they always have time to spare for any job that may turn up unexpectedly. *—Arnold Bennett*

To youth I have but three words of counsel—
Work, work, work.
—Otto von Bismarck

When we look upon our daily tasks as playing a part, however humble, in the great commonwealth, as our contribution to the world, they are lighted up with a new light.
—Hugh Black

We may not be master of our daily work, but we are at least master of the spirit in which we do it. *—Hugh Black*

Men trust to what they call their genius, and many a gifted artist has never come to his kingdom because he has never learned to toil. *—Hugh Black*

The languor of idleness is worse than the worst weariness of toil. *—Hugh Black*

Truthfulness in work is as much demanded as truthfulness in speech. *—Hugh Black*

Free men freely work:
Whoever fears God, fears to sit at ease.
—Elizabeth Barrett Browning

Get leave to work
In this world, 'tis the best you get at all; . . . .
Get work; get work;
Be sure 'tis better than what you work to get.
—Elizabeth Barrett Browning

Man's work is to labour and leaven—
As best he may—earth here with heaven;
'Tis work for work's sake that he's needing.
—Robert Browning

Antonio Stradivari has an eye
That winces at false work and loves the true.
—Robert Browning

A country fellow at the pleugh,
His acres tilled, he's right eneugh;
A country girl at her wheel,
Her dizzen's dune, she's unco weel;
But gentlemen, and ladies warst,
Wi' ev'n-doon want o' wark are curst.
—Robert Burns

Hardly a life anywhere so befouled or stagnant, but it would clear and renew itself, if the currents were set going by the proper kind and amount of honest work.
—John Burroughs

A horse in a stable that never travels, a hawk in a mew that seldom flies, are both subject to diseases, which left to themselves are most free from any such incumbrances. An idle dog will be mangy, and how can an idle person think to escape? *—Robert Burton*

If we find the job where we can be of use, we are hitched to the star of the world, and move with it. *—Richard C. Cabot*

Work cure is the best of all psychotherapy, in my opinion. . . As well might we expect a patient to recover without food as to recover without work. . . . The sound man needs work to keep him sound, but the nervous invalid has an even greater need of work to draw him out of his isolation, to stop the miseries of doubt and self-scrutiny, to win back self-respect and the support of fellowship. *—Richard C. Cabot*

We do not expect people to pay us for our best. We look to the approval of conscience, to the light of our ideal seen more clearly when our work is good, or to the judgment of God. *—Richard C. Cabot*

They must hunger in frost that will not work in heat. *—William Camden*

Blessed is he who has found his work; let him ask no other blessedness.
—Carlyle

There is a perennial nobleness, and even sacredness, in work. Were he never so benighted, forgetful of his high calling, there is always hope in a man that actually and earnestly works: in idleness alone is there perpetual despair. *—Carlyle*

Properly speaking, all true work is religion; and whatsoever religion is not work may go and dwell among the Brahmins, Antinomians, Spinning Dervishes, or where it will; with me it shall have no harbor.
—Carlyle

Work is the grand cure of all maladies and miseries that beset mankind—honest work which you intend getting done. *—Carlyle*

Genuine Work alone, what thou workest faithfully, that is eternal, as the Almighty Founder and World-Builder himself.
—Carlyle

The *best* worship, however, is stout working.
—Carlyle

Work, and your house shall be duly fed:
Work, and rest shall be won;
I hold that a man had better be dead
Than alive when his work is done.
—Alice Cary

Every man is the son of his own works.
—Miguel de Cervantes

Labor is dicovered to be the great conqueror, enriching and building up nations more surely than the proudest battles.
—William Ellery Channing

Strength shall he have, the toiler, strength and grace. *—John Vance Cheney*

A truly American sentiment recognizes the dignity of labor and the fact that honor lies in honest toil. *—Grover Cleveland*

Work, for the night is coming:
Work through the sunny noon;
Fill brightest hours with labor,
Rest comes sure and soon;
Give every flying minute
Something to keep in store;
Work, for the night is coming,
When man works no more.
—Anna L. Coghill

All growth depends upon activity. Life is manifest only by action. There is no development physically or intellectually without effort, and effort means work. Work is not a curse, it is the prerogative of intelligence, the only means to manhood, and the measure of civilization. Savages do not work. The growth of a sentiment that despises work is an appeal from civilization to barbarism.
—Calvin Coolidge

Work thou for pleasure.
Paint or sing or carve
The thing thou lovest,
Though the body starve.
—*Kenyon Cox*

He who loves work gains all the favor of the gods. —*Dr. Frank Crane*

The habit of rewarding all work with pay is destructive of the right attitude toward work. Labor brings a reward in accomplishment—and that reward should be felt above all others. —*Clara B. Dean*

Honest labour bears a lovely face.
—*Thomas Dekker*

I have never believed it possible that any natural or improved ability can claim immunity from the companionship of the steady, plain, hard-working qualities, and hope to gain its end. —*Charles Dickens*

Unless a man undertakes more than he possibly can do he will never do all that he can.
—*Henry Drummond*

You said to me, "Be sure, my boy, there is something else in life besides pleasure, love, sport, dancing, and all the wild dreams of youth. There is *work*: learn to work—learn, that is, to be happy." —*Alexander Dumas*

Whatsoever thy hand findeth to do, do it with thy might.
—*Ecclesiastes 9:10*

Many years ago, in reply to a question put to me, I said, "If I were to suggest a general rule for happiness, I would say, 'Work a little harder; work a little longer; work!'"
—*Frederick H. Ecker*

There is no substitute for hard work.
—*Thomas A. Edison*

As a cure for worrying, work is better than whiskey. —*Thomas A. Edison*

It is a good rule to endeavor hour by hour and week after week to learn to work hard. It is not well to take four minutes to do what you can accomplish in three. It is not well to take four years to do what you can perfectly accomplish in three. It is well to learn to work intensely.
—*Charles William Eliot*

The high prize of life, the crowning fortune of a man, is to be born with a bias to some pursuit, which finds him in employment and happiness. —*Emerson*

"Work", says Nature to man, "in every hour, paid or unpaid; see only that thou work, and thou canst not escape the reward: whether thy work be fine or coarse, planting corn or writing epics, so only it be honest work, done to thine own approbation, it shall earn a reward to the senses as well as to the thought: no matter how often defeated, you are born to victory. The reward of a thing well done is to have done it." —*Emerson*

I have found beauty in the dust of life,
In men who work in grime of shop and field.
—*Paul Engle*

The gods send us all good things for hard work. —*Epicharmus*

To generous souls, every task is noble.
—*Euripides*

But it is my firm belief that the main source of happiness in life is work. Whatsoever that work may be, I have found that the best gift life can give us is that we have something to set our hand to, something in which to be busy, in which we may be productive. —*Kirsten Flagstad*

By the work one knows the workman.
—*Jean de la Fontaine*

"You make pretty good hammers here," said a visitor to a workman in a factory. "No, sir," came the swift answer. "We make the best hammers that can be made." There is a man who . . . has made a common task into a fine art. —*Harry Emerson Fosdick*

A ploughman on his legs is higher than a gentleman on his knees.
—*Benjamin Franklin*

Handle your tools without mittens.
—*Benjamin Franklin*

Plough deep while sluggards sleep.
—*Benjamin Franklin*

Here I am, compelled by an inevitable necessity to make our bread this summer. Why not consider it a pleasant occupation and make it so by trying to see what perfect bread I can make. It seemed like an inspiration, and the whole of life grew brighter. . . . And this truth, old as creation, seems just now to have become fully mine, that I need not be the shirking slave of toil, but its regal master, making whatever I do yield its best fruits. —*Mrs. James A. Garfield*

In the sweat of thy face shalt thou eat bread, till thou return unto the ground.
—*Genesis 3:19*

The finest eloquence is that which gets things done; the worst is that which delays them. —*David Lloyd George*

The man who turns the soil
Need not have an earthly mind;
The digger 'mid the coal
Need not be in spirit blind:
The mind can shed a light
On each worthy labor done.
—*German*

Properly speaking, such work is never finished; one must declare it so when, according to time and circumstances, one has done one's best. *—Goethe*

Society is doing a great deal for the workingman, for the lower classes; but it seems to me, sometimes, as if it formed associations to obtain for them toys, and then formed other associations to teach them to play with them. *—John B. Gough*

From toil he wins his spirits light,
From busy dav the peaceful night;
Rich, from the very want of wealth,
In Heaven's best treasures, peace and health.
—Thomas Gray

The need to work is not a penal sentence: it is the decree of a father who makes all creation tributary to our needs.
—B. Groethuysen

The big work of the world is being done by the enthusiasts. *—Luther H. Gulick*

When pleasures are intoxicating, work steadies; when pain is paralyzing, work strengthens; when life is empty, work fills it with that deeper companionship with ourselves which is most enlightening and developing. *—Editorial. Harper's Weekly April 27, 1912*

Joy to the Toiler!—him that tills
The fields with Plenty crowned;
Him with the woodman's axe that thrills
The wilderness profound.
—Benjamin Hathaway

Commonplace statesmen and commonplace persons of all kinds live by delay, believe in it, hope in it, pray to it; but great men work as those who know that the night is coming in which no man can work.
—Sir Arthur Helps

Who sweeps a room as for Thy laws
Makes that and th' action fine.
—George Herbert

Be useful where thou livest.
—George Herbert

Have a lust for thine own work, and thou shalt be safe. *—St. Hermas*

We estimate the life of a generation by what it does; and the results of its work stand out in advance of its successor, to show it what it can do, and to show it what it must do, to reach a finer consummation.
—Josiah Gilbert Holland

Nature furnishes material, and work fashions it. . . . Man's record upon this wide world is the record of work, and of work alone. Work explores the secrets of the universe, and brings back those contributions which make up the sum of human knowledge.
—Josiah Gilbert Holland

He who hath builded the house hath more honor than the house.
—Josiah Gilbert Holland

The human race presents no aspect more interesting than that which it wears in its apron and shirt-sleeves. . . . There is nothing more wonderful than that labyrinthine network of human interests, spread finely over a continent and more broadly enveloping a world, out from whose indistinguishable intersections run the daily efforts of the earth's thronging millions.
—Josiah Gilbert Holland

No alms I ask, give me my task:
Here are the arm, the leg,
The strength, the sinews of a Man,
To work, and not to beg.
—Thomas Hood

A spade! a rake! a hoe!
A pickaxe, or a bill!
A hook to reap, or a scythe to mow,
A flail, or what ye will,
And here's a ready hand
To ply the needful tool.
—Thomas Hood

He who would reach the desired goal must, while a boy, suffer and labor much and bear both heat and cold. *—Horace*

Any man who has a job has a chance.
—Elbert Hubbard

No healthy civilization can ever be reared on a foundation of devitalised work.
—William Ralph Inge

Every child should be taught that useful work is worship and that intelligent labor is the highest form of prayer.
—Robert G. Ingersoll

Keep doing some kind of work, that the devil may always find you employed.
St. Jerome

I must work the work of him that sent me, while it is day: the night cometh, when no no man can work. *—John 9:4*

Through labour to rest, through combat to victory. *—Thomas à Kempis*

For God weigheth more with how much love a man worketh than how much he doeth. He doeth much that loveth much.
—Thomas ā Kempis

In work we meet the paradox that by giving we enrich ourselves. *—Basil King*

Thank God every morning when you get up, that you have something to do that day which must be done, whether you like it or not. Being forced to work and forced to do your best will breed in you temperance and self-control, diligence and strength of will, cheerfulness and content, and a hundred virtues which the idle never know.

—*Charles Kingsley*

By my own work, before the night,
Great Overseer, I make my prayer.

—*Rudyard Kipling*

And only the Master shall praise us, and only the Master shall blame;
And no one shall work for money, and no one shall work for fame;
But each for the joy of the working, and each, in his separate star,
Shall draw the Thing as he sees It, for the God of Things as They are!

—*Rudyard Kipling*

We seem as a nation to be suffering from a mania for play. The huge development of pleasure-chasing automobiles merely symbolizes our universal restless eagerness to be running after something, anything, that we can classify as diversion. Under pressure from tormenting constitutents our legislatures are piling up holidays. And the cry of labor everywhere is "Cut down hours; cut down hours," until it seems as if brief, tired minutes were all that would be left for work. The obvious deduction is that work is always something to be got rid of, as if it were a curse. Yet life is work.

—*Editorial. Labor Digest June 1922*

The lady bearer of this says she has two sons who want to work. Set them at it if possible. Wanting to work is so rare a merit that it should be encouraged.

—*Abraham Lincoln*

Toiling,—rejoicing,—sorrowing,
Onward through life he goes;
Each morning sees some task begin,
Each evening sees it close;
Something attempted, something done,
Has earned a night's repose.

—*Longfellow*

Let us, then, be up and doing,
With a heart for any fate;
Still achieving, still pursuing,
Learn to labour and to wait.

—*Longfellow*

No man is born into the world whose work
Is not born with him. There is always work,
And tools to work withal, for those who will;
And blessed are the horny hands of toil.

—*James Russell Lowell*

The idle man does not know what it is to enjoy rest, for he has not earned it.

—*Sir John Lubbock*

It is hardly an exaggeration to say that honest work is never thrown away. If we do not find the imaginary treasure, at any rate we enrich the vineyard.

—*Sir John Lubbock*

All great workers who have achieved the very highest results and have stamped their performances with individuality and distinction, have been men of a mighty passion; they have been enchanted by the thing they were doing; and their devotion to it, their absorption in it, have betrayed the marks of a great affection.

—*Hamilton Wright Mabie*

God gives the earth as a mine, and man must work it; as a field, and man must till it; as a reservoir of force, and man must make connection with it; as the rough material out of which order, sympathy, utility, beauty, culture may be wrought, and men must unfold these higher uses by intelligence, skill, toil, and character.

—*Hamilton Wright Mabie*

A man can never be idle with safety and advantage until he has been so trained by work that he makes his freedom from times and tasks more fruitful than his toil has been.

—*Hamilton Wright Mabie*

But blessèd that child of humanity, happiest man among men,
Who, with hammer or chisel or pencil, with rudder or ploughshare or pen,
Laboreth ever and ever with hope through the morning of life.

—*Denis Florence MacCarthy*

But all work is art in so far as it is the embodiment of faculty, and thus promotes the self-esteem of the doer.

—*Henri de Man*

In the morning, when thou art sluggish at rousing thee, let this thought be present; "I am rising to a man's work."

—*Marcus Aurelius*

If we have found our niche, if we are doing the thing we were made to do, we shall find no other happiness, no other satisfaction quite equal to that which we get out of our day's work.

—*Orison Swett Marden*

The tools were his first teachers, sternly kind.
The plow, the scythe, the maul, the echoing axe,
Taught him their homely wisdom and their peace.

—*Edwin Markham*

"This is the plan:
More work; by work we build the man!"

—*Edwin Markham*

Thou hast made them equal unto us, which have borne the burden and heat of the day.

—*Matthew 20:12*

It seems to me that the first requisite for any intellectual success is the vigor and the persistence of the effort. Nothing is easy; everything can become easy.
—*Andre Maurois*

God be thank'd that the dead have left still
Good undone for the living to do—
Still some aim for the heart and the will
And the soul of a man to pursue.
—*Owen Meredith*

The field, the wheel, the desk have called once more,
And we have stopped to pick the slender threads
By which we weave the patterns of our pride.
—*Scudder Middleton*

Let us go forth and resolutely dare with sweat of brow to toil our little day.
—*Milton*

Say that the man is ploughing if you will,
But I say more: Upon the quiet breast
Of earth his hand indites an epic tale.
—*Edith Mirick*

Toiler, canst thou dream,
At the seam, at the plow?
Higher heritage than kings
Hast thou.
—*Lulu W. Mitchell*

Work!
Thank God for the might of it,
The ardor, the urge, the delight of it. . .
—*Angela Morgan*

So much to do that is not e'en begun,
So much to hope for that we cannot see,
So much to win, so many things to be.
—*William Morris*

If a whistle calls you to or from work, you'll never do much. —*Dr. Harry Myers*

The best servants of the world are those who do not spare themselves in either youth or age, but who are so wisely strenuous that they carry their strength into maturity, and prolong their maturity while strength remains. The will to work is the will to live, and the loss of either will is the loss of the other.
—*Editorial. New York Times Feb. 17, 1924*

Rise and continue the task begun yesterday! Rise in pride and delight to take up again your interrupted work! —*Franc-Nohain*

With what content and merriment
Their days are spent, whose minds are bent
To follow the useful plough.
—*Old Song*

Labor is life! 'Tis the still water faileth;
Idleness ever despaireth, bewaileth;
Keep the watch wound, for the dark rust assaileth.
—*Frances S. Osgood*

All men and women who are doing any kind of work ought to be unsparingly honest with themselves. . . . It is mere justice to others to see in the harvest one gathers the seed one has sown.
—*Editorial. Outlook, Sept. 24, 1904*

While strength and years permit, endure labor; soon bent old age will come with silent foot. —*Ovid*

Only those whose energies are in full play know the great moral truth that work is touched with the fire of the divine creative activity. —*Jules Payot*

She looketh well to the ways of her household, and eateth not the bread of idleness.
—*Proverbs 31:27*

He also that is slothful in his work is brother to him that is a great waster.
—*Proverbs 18:9*

Establish thou the work of our hands upon us: yea, the work of our hands establish thou it. —*Psalms 90:17*

But as for me, one thing I ask:
Grace to perform my daily task.
—*Max Isaac Reich*

If you have great talents industry will improve them; if you have but moderate abilities industry will supply their deficiency. Nothing is denied to well-directed labor; nothing is to be obtained without it.
—*Sir Joshua Reynolds*

The men who with ax in the forest and pick in the mountains and plow on the prairies pushed to completion the dominion of our people over the American wilderness have given the definite shape to our nation.
—*Theodore Roosevelt*

Surely the willfully idle need arouse in the breast of a healthy man no emotion stronger than that of contempt.
—*Theodore Roosevelt*

It is not by finding new and easy ways to accomplish any work that it has ever yet been accomplished in this world; it is by holding hard to the handles of the plow and driving the furrow through. —*Elihu Root*

If I am to be loyal, my cause must from moment to moment fascinate me, awaken my muscular vigor, stir me with some eagerness for work, even if this be painful work.
—*Josiah Royce*

There is a working class—strong and happy—among both rich and poor: there is an idle class—weak, wicked, and miserable—among both rich and poor. —*John Ruskin*

Observe, then, all wise work is mainly threefold in character. It is honest, useful, and cheerful. —*John Ruskin*

When other friends would solace bring, in vain,
Thank God for work!
—Edwin L. Sabin

Love work! *—Samea*

God gave the seed—
The bread we need,
Man's labor must provide it.
—Charles Sangster

The substance of the law of labor is: Work and you will reach a higher mental development; cease work and you will degenerate. The law applies to individuals, to communities, to nations, and to civilizations.
—Dean Herman Schneider

It can be shown by history that a people who will not work will fall to swift decay.
—Dean Herman Schneider

Hard work is the best investment a man can make. *—Charles M. Schwab*

I have always felt that the surest way to qualify for the job just ahead is to work a little harder than anyone else on the job one is holding down. . . . If you must be a glutton, be a glutton for work. *—Charles M. Schwab*

When the deep cunning architect
Had the great minster planned,
They worked in faith for twice
two hundred years
And reared the building grand.
—Duncan Campbell Scott

The man who is greatly interested in his work and who finds delight in overcoming the difficulties of his calling is not likely to become so tired as the man for whom work is a burden. *—Walter Dill Scott*

My nature is subdu'd
To what it works in, like the dyer's hand.
—Shakespeare

A piece of work
So bravely done, so rich, that it did strive
In workmanship and value.
—Shakespeare

To business that we love, we rise betime,
And go to't with delight.
—Shakespeare

A day's work is a day's work, neither more nor less, and the man who does it needs a day's sustenance, a night's repose, and due leisure, whether he be painter or ploughman. *—George Bernard Shaw*

The real source of almost all our crimes, if the trouble is taken to trace them to a common origin, will be found to be in idleness.
—Walter Gaston Shotwell

The Savior was a carpenter;
The Roman's nails crashed through
Fine, manly hands that callouses
Of homely labor knew.
—Sarah Elizabeth Sprouse

The man who labors with his hands will be a bigger man and a better citizen if he can find time to devote to the development of his mind; and the man whose time is given chiefly to intellectual pursuits will gain by getting out into the open, or even into a shop, and putting his hands and muscles to work. *—Alfred E. Stearns*

Shall you complain who feed the world?
Who clothe the world?
Who house the world?
Shall you complain who are the world,
Of what the world may do?
—Charlotte Perkins Stetson

All who have meant good work with their whole hearts, have done good work, although they may die before they have the time to sign it. . . And even if death catch people, like an open pitfall, and in mid-career, laying out vast projects, and planning monstrous foundations, flushed with hope . . . . is there not something brave and spirited in such a termination? and does not life go down with a better grace, foaming in full body over a precipice, than miserably straggling to an end in sandy deltas?
—Robert Louis Stevenson

Not thine to complete the work, yet neither art thou free to lay it down.
—The Talmud

Good for the body is the work of the body, good for the soul the work of the soul, and good for either the work of the other.
—Henry David Thoreau

Labor is part of a total life which it affects, and by which it is affected. . . Every false economic prophet who hides essential facts misleads labor. *—Edward L. Thorndike*

Every country resounds to the lament that the work-fever does not burn in the younger generation, the post-war generation. If this is really true and if this condition lasts and becomes more marked, then the foundations of contemporary civilization have begun to crack. *—Adriano Tilgher*

Heaven is blessed with perfect rest but the blessing of earth is toil.
—Henry van Dyke

Let me but do my work from day to day
In field or forest, at the desk or loom,
In roaring market-place or tranquil room;
Let me but find it in my heart to say,
When vagrant wishes beckon me astray,
"This is my work; my blessing, not my doom;
Of all who live, I am the one by whom
This work can best be done in the right way."

—*Henry van Dyke*

Under the reign of Saturn, the earth produced of itself what was needful so that men in their torpor were becoming as thick-witted as dumb beasts. But Jove made life hard, pierced the hearts of men with cares to stir them from their idleness, and by the sting of necessity, forced them to invent the various arts. —*Virgil*

Yes, I am positive that one of the great curatives of our evils, our maladies, social, moral, and intellectual, would be a return to the soil, a rehabilitation of the work of the fields. —*Charles Wagner*

But when dread Sloth, the Mother of Doom, steals in,
And reigns where Labour's glory was to serve,
Then is the day of crumbling not far off.

—*William Watson*

Labour in this country is independent and proud. It has not to ask the patronage of capital, but capital solicits the aid of labor.

—*Daniel Webster*

There is no trade or employment but the young man following it may become a hero.

—*Walt Whitman*

Man is immortal till his work is done.

—*Dr. James Williams*

We are not put in this world to sit still and know; we are put into it to act.

—*Woodrow Wilson*

I saw her singing at her work,
And o'er the sickle bending.

—*William Wordsworth*

LINCOLN'S BIRTHDAY

No one can look into St. Gaudens' face of Lincoln in Chicago, with its plainness and commonness and yet with its sublimity and gentleness, and fail to see those ideas shining there revealing the real glory of that great common man, and teaching through that melancholy world-face, the whole splendid rise of man to soul and mind and will.
—*Edwin Anderson Alderman*

A spirit mastering fate by faith and love
And imaging right's lordship o'er the world.
—*Lyman Whitney Allen*

His life of labor, thought and burden-bearing
Brought forth his kingly qualities of soul.
—*A. S. Ames*

Not in vain has Lincoln lived, for he has helped to make this republic an example of justice, with no caste but the caste of humanity.
—*George Bancroft*

I swear you to an emulation of his justice, his moderation and his mercy.
—*Henry Ward Beecher*

O Illinois, we took him from your midst, an untried man from among the people! Behold, we return him a mighty conqueror! Not thine, but the Nation's; not ours, but the world's! Give him place, ye prairies! In the midst of this great continent his dust shall rest, a sacred treasure to myriads who shall pilgrim to that shrine to kindle anew their zeal and patriotism. —*Henry Ward Beecher*

He mastered principles that gripped the age;
He saw beneath the coating of all form
The monster slavery, our heritage
From out the past, a curse presaging storm.
—*G. W. Bell*

Some opulent force of genius, soul, and race,
Some deep life-current from far centuries
Flowed to his mind, and lighted his sad eyes,
And gave his name, among great names, high place.
—*Joel Benton*

It is not by the grandeur of his powers that he has most appealed to me, rather by those softer, humbler, homelier traits that bring him down to a closer and more affectionate view.
—*Frank S. Black*

Lincoln loved the truth for truth's sake. He would not argue from a false premise; or be deceived himself, or deceive others, by a false conclusion. He did not seek to say merely the thing which was best for that day's debate, but the thing which would stand the test of time and square itself with eternal iustice.
—*James G. Blaine*

Into his heart's great jar Truth's brother poured
Strong love for men and freedom. . .
—*Charles Granger Blanden*

No king this man, by grace of God's intent;
No, something better, freeman,—President!
—*George Henry Boker*

In him was vindicated the greatness of real goodness and the goodness of real greatness.
—*Phillips Brooks*

May God make us worthy of the memory of Abraham Lincoln! —*Phillips Brooks*

The shepherd of the people! that old name that the best rulers ever craved. What ruler ever won it like this dead President of ours? He fed us with counsel when we were in doubt, with inspiration when we faltered, with caution when we would be rash, with calm, trustful cheerfulness through many an hour when our hearts were dark. He fed hungry souls all over the country with sympathy and consolation.
—*Phillips Brooks*

Abraham Lincoln is one of America's immortals. He grows in the affections of the people with each passing year.
—*William Jennings Bryan*

No debt he owed to wealth or birth;
By force of solid, honest worth
He climbed the topmost height of fame,
And wrote thereon a spotless name.
—*John H. Bryant*

Oh, slow to smite and swift to spare,
Gentle and merciful and just!
Who, in the fear of God, didst bear
The sword of power, a nation's trust!
—*William Cullen Bryant*

Thus, mid the wreck of thrones, shall live
Unmarred, undimmed, our hero's fame,
And years succeeding years shall give
Increase of honors to his name.
—*William Cullen Bryant*

He showed what fame may be won and what services be rendered by a plain son of the people unaided by any gifts of fortune.
—*James Bryce*

He was one of those who expand and ennoble the old traditions, and hand them on, bright with fresh lustre, to the generations that follow.
—*James Bryce*

And so I say he is not dead; not he!
He was too much a part of us to die.
—*Dana Burnet*

The speeches and inaugurals and letters and sayings of Abraham Lincoln make him the most quotable of our public men, and his writings, in at least three instances, by sheer beauty and truth, have attained to immortality.
—*W. J. Cameron*

Who can be what he was to the people,—
What he was to the State?
—*Phoebe Cary*

He had done justice; he had loved mercy; he had walked humbly with his God.
—*Lord Charnwood*

No political theory stands out from his words or actions; but they show a most unusual sense of the possible dignity of common men and common things.
—*Lord Charnwood*

Ay, Earth's he is; not hers alone—
Blood of our blood, bone of our bone.
—*John Vance Cheney*

Our pastoral captain, skilled to crook
The spear into the pruning hook,
The simple, kindly man,
Lincoln, American.
—*John Vance Cheney*

We need him now—his rugged faith that held
Fast to the rock of Truth through all the days
Of moil and strife. . .
—*Thomas Curtis Clark*

He lost himself in the larger self
Of his country and all mankind.
—*Samuel Valentine Cole*

In his freedom from passion and bitterness; in his acute sense of justice; in his courageous faith in the right, and his inextinguishable hatred of wrong; in his warm and heartfelt sympathy and mercy; in his coolness of judgment; in his unquestioned rectitude of intention—in a word, in his ability to lift himself for his country's sake above all mere partisanship, in all the marked traits of his character combined, he has had no parallel since Washington, and while our republic endures he will live with him in the grateful hearts of his grateful countrymen.
—*Schuyler Colfax*

He led with wisdom, for he knew
The common heart. —*W. F. Collins*

O Uncommon Commoner! may your name
Forever lead like a living flame!
Unschooled scholar! how did you learn
The wisdom a lifetime may not earn?
—*Edmund Vance Cooke*

Under the providence of God he was, next to Washington, the greatest instrument for the preservation of the Union and the integrity of our country; and this was brought about chiefly through his strict and faithful adherence to the Constitution of his country.
—*Peter Cooper*

Ambition did not warp, power corrupt, nor glory dazzle him. —*Warren H. Cudworth*

He knew human nature; he knew what chord to strike, and he was never afraid to strike it when the time had arrived.
—*Charles A. Dana*

His honest, homely wisdom outweighed
learning;
He stood for service to his fellow man.
—*William Morris Davis*

He is an example and an inspiration to youth unparalleled in history.
—*Edward Deems*

Great Nature's forces, unrestrained and free,
Produced, by chance, this giant of mankind,
And challenged man to solve his mystery.
—*Rembrandt W. B. Ditmars*

Spontaneous! Inspired! The perfect flower
Of chance, he was by liberal Nature sent
To lead men nobly with unconscious power,
And justify the law of accident.
—*Rembrandt W. B. Ditmars*

Fling forth the banner, then,
On Lincoln's natal day!
Recall this simple-hearted Prince of men.
—*Nathan Haskell Dole*

Hail, Lincoln! As the swift years lengthen
Still more majestic grows thy fame.
—*Nathan Haskell Dole*

Lincoln is the honestest man I ever knew.
—*Stephen A. Douglas*

A great man, tender of heart, strong of nerve, of boundless patience and broadest sympathy, with no motive apart from his country. —*Frederick Douglass*

Earth learned of thee what Heav'n already
knew,
And wrote thee down among her treasured
few!
—*Paul Laurence Dunbar*

There was divine compassion in the man;
A God-like love and pity for his race.
—*J. A. Edgerton*

He offered no shining qualities at the first encounter; he did not offend by superiority; he had a face and manner that disarmed suspicion, which inspired confidence, which confirmed good-will.
—*Ralph Waldo Emerson*

His heart was as great as the world, but there was no room in it to hold the memory of a wrong. —*Ralph Waldo Emerson*

In homely strength he towers almost divine.
—*Horace Spencer Fiske*

He was one of the few great rulers whose wisdom increased with his power, and whose spirit grew gentler and tenderer as his triumphs were multiplied.

—*James A. Garfield*

I doubt if history affords any example of a life so early, so deeply and so permanently influenced by a single political truth, as was Abraham Lincoln's by the central doctrine of the Declaration—the liberty and equality of men.

—*James A. Garfield*

He is one of those giant figures, of whom there are very few in history, who lose their nationality in death.

—*David Lloyd George*

If you look at his portraits they always give you an indelible impression of his great height. So does his life. Height of purpose, height of ideal, height of character, height of intelligence. —*David Lloyd George*

Humble birth did not retard his genius, nor high place corrupt his soul.

—*Cass Gilbert*

Lincoln's career was no matter of chance. His life moved from cause to effect with unswerving logic. There was nothing of the reckless adventurer about him; he was not the shrewd intriguer or the dashing soldier of a more complex or a more romantic age. His course was guided by a compass that did not waver. His policy was the epitome of plain common sense. But with what a vision he saw the truth, with what fervor he followed it. —*Cass Gilbert*

A power was his beyond the touch of art
Or armed strength—his pure and mighty heart.

Richard Watson Gilder

Shade of our greatest, O look down to-day!
Richard Watson Gilder

The qualities that endear him to mankind are those which endure, because they are spiritual and permanent.

—*Albert F. Gilmore*

Let us build with reverent hands to the type of this simple, but sublime life, in which all types are honored. —*Henry W. Grady*

He proved to be the man of all others for the struggle through which the nation had to pass to place itself among the greatest in the family of nations.

—*Ulysses S. Grant*

To know him personally was to love and respect him for his great qualities of heart and head, and for his patience and patriotism.
—*Ulysses S. Grant*

Oh, man of storms! Patient and kingly soul!
Oh, wise physician of a wasted land!
—*Hermann Hagedorn*

A martyr to the cause of man,
His blood is freedom's eucharist,
And in the world's great hero list
His name shall lead the van.
—*Charles G. Halpin*

A colossal figure among the hero-statesmen of all the ages.
—*Warren G. Harding*

God knew the man His sovereign grace had sealed;
God touched the man, and Lincoln stood revealed!
—*Jane L. Hardy*

A statesman of the school of sound common sense, and a philanthropist of the most practical type, a patriot without a superior—his monument is a country preserved.
—*C. S. Harrington*

Lincoln had faith in time, and time has justified his faith. —*Benjamin Harrison*

This nation long as time shall run
Will glory in this South-born son,
Who wrote with gifted pen
A prophecy of that fair day
When God shall write henceforth for aye:
I'll free the souls of men.
—*Thomas H. Herndon*

He was a patriot who was ever willing to make personal sacrifices for his patriotism.
—*Abram S. Hewitt*

He embodied the national conscience.
—*Frederick Trevor Hill*

He was the one leader of public opinion that invariably stated all disrupting problems which confronted him in the terms of the nation, concentrated his attention on its welfare and let that dominate every other issue.
—*Frederick Trevor Hill*

Abraham Lincoln is not dead. Emancipated from the thraldom of time, he has stepped beyond the trammels of birth, and race, and state. He lives in an epic all his own; in ever widening spiritual leadership; in the splendor of realized ideals; in inspiration to good citizenship and in multiplying memorials in literature and art, in progress and reform, in patriotism and philanthropy, in education and humanitarianism.
—*John Wesley Hill*

A government of, by and for the people!—
The only fit memorial for him.
—*Leigh Mitchell Hodges*

The qualities which caused him to be acclaimed the leader, he possessed when he was teaching school, and splitting rails, and reading law in a judge's musty office. From the beginning he was a man among men who always upheld the right, advocated justice for the oppressed, and a square deal for all.
—*Frank Dorrance Hopley*

Slow to threaten, strong to move,
Swift to render good for ill!
—*Julia Ward Howe*

What a grand thing it is that we have the inheritance of the memory of a man who had everything that we could aspire to in intellectual attainments, who was endowed with a strength of moral purpose, who was perfectly sincere in the interest of the people, and who gave his life-work and eventually his life itself in order that our Union with its opportunities might survive.
—*Charles Evans Hughes*

He raised his hands, not to strike, but in benediction. Lincoln was the grandest figure of the fiercest civil war. He is the gentlest memory of our world.
—*Robert G. Ingersoll*

Lincoln was not a type. He stands alone—no ancestors, no fellows, no successors.
—*Robert G. Ingersoll*

O prairie poet, prophet, children's friend!
Great-brained, great-willed, great-hearted man
and true.
—*Charlotte Brewster Jordan*

Time's healing touch but more
Endeared that tender, all-compassionate heart.
—*Charlotte Brewster Jordan*

Nor all America can claim him now:
Forevermore he is Mankind's and
God's.
—*Reginald Wright Kauffman*

Rest to the uncrowned king who, toiling,
brought
His bleeding country through that dreadful
reign;
Who, living, earn'd a world's revering thought,
And, dying, leaves his name without a
stain.
—*Robert Leighton*

Would I might rouse the Lincoln in you all.
—*Vachel Lindsay*

That nation has not lived in vain which has given the world Washington and Lincoln, the best great men and the greatest good men whom history can show.
—*Henry Cabot Lodge*

We can pause today in the hurry of daily life and contemplate that great, lonely, tragic figure; that imagination with its touch of the poet; that keen, strong mind, with its humor and its pathos; that splendid common-sense and pure character, and then learn from the life which the possessor of all these qualities lived, and from the deeds which he did, lessons which may not be without value to each of us in our own lives.
—*Henry Cabot Lodge*

His heart and his brain were utterly foreign to all vindictiveness or personal bitterness. He declared himself hotly and strongly against wrong causes, but never against men.
—*London Spectator*

Nature, they say, doth dote,
And cannot make a man
Save on some worn-out plan
Repeating us by rote:
For him her Old World moulds aside she
threw
And, choosing sweet clay from the breast
Of the unexhausted West,
With stuff untainted shaped a hero new.
James Russell Lowell

Wise, steadfast in the strength of God, and
true.
—*James Russell Lowell*

Our children shall behold his fame,
The kindly earnest, brave, foreseeing man,
Sagacious, patient, dreading praise, not blame,
New birth of our new soil, the first American.
—*James Russell Lowell*

This statesman was no conqueror, but his superiority consisted in his moral conquest; this President vanquished no foreign people, and his superiority lay in his self-constraint; this excellent judge of human nature cast a spell over nobody, yet is more fascinating than the shining victors of history.
—*Emil Ludwig*

To him was given the duty and responsibility of making that great classic of liberty, the Declaration of Independence, no longer an empty promise, but a glorious fulfillment.
—*William McKinley*

A blend of mirth and sadness, smiles and
tears;
A quaint knight-errant of the pioneers;
A homely hero, born of star and sod;
A Peasant-Prince; a Masterpiece of God.
—*Walter Malone*

He held his place—
Held the long purpose like a growing tree—
Held on through blame and faltered not at
praise.
—*Edwin Markham*

Here was a man to hold against the world,
A man to match the mountains and the sea.
—*Edwin Markham*

One fire was on his spirit, one resolve—
To send the keen axe to the root of wrong,
Clearing a free way to the feet of God,
The eyes of conscience testing every stroke.
—*Edwin Markham*

This man will stand out, in the traditions of his country and the world, as an incarnation of the people, and of modern democracy itself. —*Henri Martin*

His grave a nation's heart shall be,
His monument a people free!
—*Caroline Atherton Mason*

Sad eyes that were wearied and blighted by visions and sieges of wars, now watch o'er a country united, from the luminous slopes of the stars. —*Walt Mason*

Lincoln was an idealist, even if he was also a practical politician, and opportunist, knowing where he wanted to go, but never crossing a bridge before he came to it.
—*Brander Matthews*

The purity of his patriotism inspired him with the wisdom of a statesman and the courage of a martyr. —*Stanley Matthews*

A man steps forth between the swinging tides
To teach the world anew that right abides
Where freedom, love, and faith in man abound.
—*Edmond S. Meany*

In his morals, Truth was his star; Honesty the vital air of his living. In his religion, he was faithful as a giant; Providence was his stay; he walked with God.
—*Luther Laflin Mills*

No leader ever more completely combined in his personality the grace of gentleness with rugged determination.
—*Luther Laflin Mills*

Most was he like to Luther, gay and great,
Solemn and mirthful, strong of heart and limb.
Tender and simple too; he was so near
To all things human that he cast out fear.
—*S. Weir Mitchell*

His wisdom, courage, devotion to duty, and simplicity of character seem to me to embody in a very striking way all that is most noble in the American character and American destiny. —*John Lothrop Motley*

And now we see him, whom men called uncouth,
Grown wondrous fair beneath the hand of Time.
—*Wilbur D. Nesbit*

His was a soul above all scorn,
His was a heart above all hate.
—*Wilbur D. Nesbit*

All the symbols of this world's admiration are his. He is embalmed in song; recorded in history; eulogized in panegyric; cast in bronze; sculptured in marble; painted on canvas; enshrined in the hearts of his countrymen, and lives in the memories of mankind.
—*John P. Newman*

His mission was as large as his country, vast as humanity, enduring as time. . . . He has this threefold greatness,—great in life, great in death, great in the history of the world. —*John Philip Newman*

His wisdom, his accurate perceptions, his vigor of intellect, his humor, and his unselfish patriotism are known to all.
—*Cyrus Northrup*

Abraham Lincoln needs no marble shaft to perpetuate his name; his *words* are the most enduring monument, and will forever live in the hearts of the people.
—*Osborn H. Oldroyd*

A faith like Lincoln's would transform the world! —*James Oppenheim*

Riding the storm-column in the lightning-stroke,
Calm at the peak, while down below worlds rage,
And Earth goes out in blood and battle-smoke,
And leaves him with the sun—an epoch and an age!
—*James Oppenheim*

Behold this hero, gaunt and border born,
A man with every shred of soul and heart
Of our new soil a part.
—*Fred Lewis Pattee*

One of many of a mighty Land,
Made by God's providence the Anointed One.
—*John James Piatt*

No man e'er held so much of power so meek.
—*John James Piatt*

Lincoln, the boy, was tender; Lincoln, the youth, was sympathetic and Lincoln, the man, was merciful. —*Mrs. H. Clay Preston*

The saddest among kings of earth,
Bowed with a galling crown, this man
Met rancor with a cryptic mirth,
Laconic—and Olympian.
—*Edwin Arlington Robinson*

Abraham Lincoln—the spirit incarnate of those who won victory in the Civil War—was the true representative of this people, not only for his own generation, but for all time, because he was a man among men.
—*Theodore Roosevelt*

He had no friends among the great and powerful of his time. An equal among equals in the crude simplicity of scattered communities on the borders of the wilderness, he rose above the common level by force of his own qualities. —*Elihu Root*

Never for an instant did the thought of personal advantage compete with the interests of the public cause. —*Elihu Root*

God and Nature together shaped him to lead in the van,
In the stress of her wildest weather when the Nation needed a Man.
—*Margaret E. Sangster*

A man of destiny, with character made and molded by Divine power to save a nation from perdition. —*William H. Seward*

Lincoln's work stands and grows. It has never had to be revised. Upon the foundation of his finished task this America—North and South, black and white—has built.
—*Allanson Shaw*

There is in him—his breadth and wide tolerance of spirit, his iron firmness and utter gentleness—that which responds to the best in humanity, that supremely satisfies, though it baffles the analyst. —*Allanson Shaw*

Abraham Lincoln cannot be compared with any other man. He stands alone. More and more, as time goes on, does his work impress itself upon the world. His genius was fitted exactly to the circumstances under which he lived and labored. He is the conspicuous example of the truth that an all-wise Providence provides the man for the emergency.
—*James S. Sherman*

Thou hast not left thy people quite alone,
Out of thy beautiful life there comes a tone
Of power, of love, of trust, a prophecy,
Whose fair fulfilment all the earth shall be,
And all the future tell.
—*Edward Rowland Sill*

Mute though his lips be, yet they still speak. Hushed is his voice, but its echoes of liberty are ringing through the world, and the sons of bondage listen with joy.
—*Matthew Simpson*

He was a common man expanded into giant proportions; well acquainted with the people, he placed his hand on the beating pulse of the nation, judged of its disease and was ready with a remedy. —*Joshua Speed*

Now he belongs to the ages.
—*Edwin M. Stanton*

Look on this cast, and know the hand
That bore a nation in its hold;
From this mute witness understand
What Lincoln was—how large of mould.
—*E. C. Stedman*

A type that nature wills to plan
But once in all a people's years.
—*E. C. Stedman*

His chief object, the ideal to which his whole soul was devoted, was the preservation of the Union. —*Alexander H. Stephens*

Hold, warriors, councillors, kings! All now give place
To this dear benefactor of the race.
—*Richard Henry Stoddard*

One of the people!
—*Richard Henry Stoddard*

This man whose homely face you look upon,
Was one of nature's masterful, great men.
—*Richard Henry Stoddard*

What trust, what love, thy towering spirit led
Thro' dark, tremendous days! What sanity
Girded thy sadness, Lincoln!
—*M. Woolsey Stryker*

In Lincoln there was always some quality which fastened him to the people and taught them to keep time to the music of his heart. —*David Swing*

It seems to me, as I study the life of Lincoln, that in his development and the position to which he attained there is more inspiration for heroism and usefulness to the country than in the life of any other one man in history. —*William Howard Taft*

His voice all elegies anticipated;
For, whatsoe'er the strain,
We hear that one refrain:
"We consecrate ourselves to them, the Consecrated!"
—*Bayard Taylor*

So he went forth to battle on the side
That he felt clear was Liberty's and Right's.
—*Tom Taylor*

Giant of frame, of soul superbly human,
Best measure of true greatness measures him.
—*Maurice Thompson*

His love shone as impartial as the sun.
—*Maurice Thompson*

Meseems I feel his presence. Is he dead?
Death is a word. He lives and grander grows.
—*Maurice Thompson*

To the conquerors and the conquered, to the white man and the black, to the master and the slave, Abraham Lincoln was God's providence. —*John M. Thurston*

He stands in history a little child in his humility, a king in power.
—*Albion W. Tourgée*

What he endured, no less than what he did,
Has reared his monument, and crowned him saint.
—*J. T. Trowbridge*

A more than king, yet in whose veins there ran
The red blood of the people.
—*Henry Tyrrell*

He learned to rule his spirit, and he grew
Like the young oak with yearning for the sky.
—*Leonard Charles Van Noppen*

His was the genius of common sense; of common sense in action; of common sense in thought; of common sense enriched by experience and unhindered by fear.
—*Henry Watterson*

A thousand years hence no story, no tragedy, no epic poem will be filled with greater wonder, or be followed by mankind with deeper feeling than that which tells of his life and death. —*Henry Watterson*

There is no name in all our country's story
So loved as his today:
No name which so unites the things of glory
With life's plain, common way.
—*Robert Whitaker*

The story of Lincoln, perfect in its unities, appealing to the imagination like some old tragedy, has been told over and over, and will be told over and over again. . . We see him become the wise leader of that old cause, the sad, gentle captain of a mighty war, the liberator of a whole race, and not only the savior of a republic, but the creator of a nation; and then, in the very hour of triumph, —the tragedy for which destiny plainly marked him. Rightly told, the story is the epic of America. —*Brand Whitlock*

His was the nation's sacrifice,
And ours the priceless gain.
—*John Greenleaf Whittier*

His place is among the great men of the earth. To them he belongs by right of his immense power of hard work, his unfaltering pursuit of what seemed to him right, and above all by that childlike directness and simplicity of vision which none but the greatest carry beyond their earliest years.
—*Basil Williams*

It was a very lonely spirit that looked out from underneath those shaggy brows and comprehended men without fully communing with them, as if in spite of all its genial efforts at comradeship, it dwelt apart, saw its visions of duty where no man looked on.
—*Woodrow Wilson*

It is as if Nature had made a typical American, and then had added with liberal hand the royal quality of genius, to show us what the type could be. —*Woodrow Wilson*

Lincoln was a very normal man with very normal gifts, but all upon a great scale, all knit together in loose and natural form, like the great frame in which he moved and dwelt.
—*Woodrow Wilson*

The important thing today is not what we say of Lincoln but what Lincoln would say of us if he were here in this hour and could note the drift and tendency in American life and American politics.
—*Stephen Samuel Wise*

Rightly was it said of Lincoln that his was a character such as only freedom knows how to make. If our democracy become polluted by the taint of caste, it will produce no Abraham Lincolns. —*Stephen Samuel Wise*

We cherish no higher hope for the land we love than that the servants of the Republic in all time may rise to the stature of Abraham Lincoln. —*Stephen Samuel Wise*

Spirit of Lincoln! Summon all thy loyal;
Nerve them to follow where thy feet have trod.
—*Ida Vose Woodbury*

MEMORIAL DAY

We took up arms, not to revenge ourselves,
But free the commonwealth.

—*Addison*

Break not his sweet repose—
Thou whom chance brings to this
sequestered ground,
The sacred yard his ashes close,
But go thy way in silence.

—*John Albee*

Decoration Day is the most beautiful of our national holidays. . . The grim cannon have turned into palm branches, and the shell and shrapnel into peach blossoms.

—*Thomas Bailey Aldrich*

Never forget,
Dying for us, they died for you.
This hallowed dust should knit us closer yet.

—*Thomas Bailey Aldrich*

With the tears a Land hath shed
Their graves should ever be green.

—*Thomas Bailey Aldrich*

With reverent mien and softened, solemn
tread we move
Among the grass-roofed homes of those who
gave their best—
Their lives—because a vision fair their eyes
beheld.

Arthur Newton Alkire

They fought for freedom, not for fame, yet honor claims them as her own.

—*Charles Elmer Allison*

It is a day of memories, a day when we meet in the hallowed past and hold communion with our holy dead. A day when we recall the glorious aspirations which thrilled men's souls in that heroic time, when to love one's country was to lay down one's life; a day filled with that same spirit of freedom, patriotism, and devotion which breathed into the common dust of ordinary humanity the sublime inspiration of heroic deeds.

—*Anon.*

These were honored in their generations, and were the glory of their times.

—*Apocrypha: Ecclesiasticus 44:7*

Leaving his death for an example of a noble
courage. —*Apocrypha: 2 Maccabees 6:31*

They fought for liberty and right; they died,
Unselfishly, in Freedom's cause.

—*George Hurlbut Barbour*

God shed His grace on thee
And crown thy good with brotherhood
From sea to shining sea!

—*Katherine Lee Bates*

They hover as a cloud of witnesses above this Nation. —*Henry Ward Beecher*

Are they dead that yet speak louder than we can speak, and a more universal language? Are they dead that yet act? Are they dead that yet move upon society and inspire the people with nobler motives and more heroic patriotism? —*Henry Ward Beecher*

As man may, he fought his fight,
Proved his truth by his endeavor.

—*George Henry Boker*

Fold him in his country's stars.
Roll the drum and fire the volley!
What to him are all our wars,
What but death bemocking folly?

—*George Henry Boker*

Farewell, high-hearted friends, for God is
dead
If such as you can die and fare not well—
If when you fall your gallant spirit fail.

—*John LeGay Brereton*

Their own souls rose and cried
Alarum when they heard the sudden wail
Of stricken freedom and along the gale
Saw her eternal banner quivering wide.

—*John LeGay Brereton*

Blow out, you bugles, over the rich Dead!
There's none of these so lonely and poor
of old,
But, dying, has made us rarer gifts than
gold.

—*Rupert Brooke*

Bring the Flag and set it there,
Let it proudly wave in air
O'er the grassy hillock where
The sleeping heroes stay.

—*Abbie Farwell Brown*

Who kept the faith and fought the fight;
The glory theirs, the duty ours.

—*Wallace Bruce*

With emotions of pride and of sorrow,
Bring roses and lilies to-day.

—*Wallace Bruce*

Ah! never shall the land forget
How gushed the life-blood of her brave—

—*William Cullen Bryant*

'Twas ours to lay no garlands fair
Upon the graves "unknown":
Kind Nature sets her gentians there,
And fall the sear leaves lone.

—*Hezekiah Butterworth*

Perform, then, one act of remembrance before this Day passes—*Remember* there is an army of defense and advance that never dies and never surrenders, but is increasingly recruited from the eternal sources of the American spirit and from the generations of American youth. —*W. J. Cameron*

What hallows ground where heroes sleep?
'Tis not the sculptured piles you heap!
—*Thomas Campbell*

Is't death to fall for Freedom's right?
He's dead alone who lacks her light!
—*Thomas Campbell*

Few, few shall part where many meet!
The snow shall be their winding-sheet
And every turf beneath their feet
Shall be a soldier's sepulchre.
—*Thomas Campbell*

Cover them over with beautiful flowers,
Deck them with garlands, those brothers of ours,
Lying so silent by night and by day
Sleeping the years of their manhood away.
Give them the meed they have won in the past;
Give them the honors their future forcast;
Give them the chaplets they won in the strife;
Give them the laurels they lost with their life.
—*Will Carleton*

They wait the great hereafter when the last assembly comes.
—*Guy Wetmore Carryl*

These martyrs of patriotism gave their lives for an idea. —*Schuyler Colfax*

How sleep the brave, who sink to rest,
By all their country's wishes blest!
When Spring, with dewy fingers cold,
Returns to deck their hallow'd mould,
She there shall dress a sweeter sod
Than Fancy's feet have ever trod.
By fairy hands their knell is rung,
There Honour comes, a pilgrim gray,
To bless the turf that wraps their clay;
And Freedom shall awhile repair,
To dwell, a weeping hermit, there.
—*William Collins*

Sterner soldiers the world saw never,
Marching lightly, that summer hour,
To death and failure and fame forever.
—*Helen Gray Cone*

Equal in death our gallant heroes sleep
In Southern trench, home grave, and ocean deep;
Equal in glory, fadeless as the light
The stars send down upon them through the night.
Louis Bradford Couch

They fell, but o'er their glorious grave
Floats free the banner of the cause they died to save.
—*Francis Marion Crawford*

Because you perished—must men say
Your deeds were naught, and so profane
Your lives with that cold burden? Nay,
The deeds you wrought are not in vain.
—*Austin Dobson*

Heroes of old, I humbly lay
The laurel on your graves again.
—*Austin Dobson*

So, with the singing of paeans and chorals,
And with the flag flashing high in the sun,
Place on the graves of our heroes the laurels
Which their unfaltering valor has won!
—*Paul Laurence Dunbar*

Spirit, that made those heroes dare
To die, and leave their children free,
Bid Time and Nature gently spare
The shaft we raise to them and thee.
—*Emerson*

But the freedom that they fought for, and the country grand they wrought for,
Is their monument to-day, and for aye.
—*Thomas Dunn English*

Asleep are the ranks of the dead:
Under the sod and the dew,
Waiting the judgment-day;
Under the one, the Blue,
Under the other, the Gray.
—*Francis Miles Finch*

They saw their injured country's woe;
The flaming town, the wasted field;
Then rushed to meet the insulting foe;
They took the spear,— but left the shield.
—*Philip Freneau*

But fame is theirs—and future days
On pillar'd brass shall tell their praise;
Shall tell—when cold neglect is dead—
"These for their country fought and bled."
—*Philip Freneau*

For love of country they accepted death, and thus resolved all doubts, and made immortal their patriotism and virtue.
—*James A. Garfield*

A handful of old men?—Nay, my heart, look well again;
The spirit of America today is marching by!
—*Theodosia Garrison*

Better than honor and glory, and History's iron pen,
Was the thought of duty done and the love of his fellow-men.
—*Richard Watson Gilder*

Knights of the spirit; warriors in the cause
Of justice absolute 'twixt man and man.
—*Richard Watson Gilder*

Glorious and meet
To honor thus the dead.
—*Richard Watson Gilder*

But to the hero, when his sword
Has won the battle for the free,
Thy voice sounds like a prophet's word;
And in its hollow tones are heard
The thanks of millions yet to be.

—Fitz-Greene Halleck

I have never been able to think of the day as one of mourning; I have never quite been able to feel that half-masted flags were appropriate on Decoration Day. I have rather felt that the flag should be at the peak, because those whose dying we commemorate rejoiced in seeing it where their valor placed it. We honor them in a joyous, thankful, triumphant commemoration of what they did. . . The glory of their achievement has set them in an imperishable roll of honor.

—Benjamin Harrison

So moved they calmly to the field,
Thence never to return.

—Felicia Dorothea Hemans

Though they smile in vain for what once was ours,
They are love's last gift; bring ye flowers, pale flowers!

—Felicia Dorothea Hemans

We are not many—we who pressed
Beside the brave who fell that day.

—Charles Fenno Hoffman

Born free, thus we resolve to live:
By Heaven, we will be free!

—James Barron Hope

Our cheer goes back to them, the valiant dead!
Laurels and roses on their graves to-day,
Lilies and laurels over them we lay,
And violets o'er each unforgotten head.

—Richard Hovey

So let our buried heroes live.
In hands that freely guard and give,
In minds that, watchful, entertain
Great thoughts of Justice and her reign.

—Julia Ward Howe

Still may we utter solemn praise
Of those whose prowess filled their days
With thoughts and deeds of high renown,
Which now our floral offerings crown.

—Julia Ward Howe

The Flag still floats unblotted with defeat!
But ah the blood that keeps its ripples red,
The starry lives that keep its field alight.

—Rupert Hughes

Well have ye sought for freedom—nobly done
Your martial task—the meed immortal won—
And Time's last records shall your triumphs tell.

—David Humphreys

These heroes are dead. They died for liberty—they died for us. They are at rest. They sleep in the land they made free, under the flag they rendered stainless, under the solemn pines, the sad hemlocks, the tearful willows, and the embracing vines. They sleep beneath the shadows of the clouds, careless alike of sunshine or of storm, each in the windowless Palace of Rest. Earth may run red with other wars—they are at peace. In the midst of battle, in the roar of conflict, they found the serenity of death. I have one sentiment for soldiers living and dead: cheers for the living; tears for the dead.

—Robert G. Ingersoll

All, all are gone; but still lives on
The fame of those who died;
All true men, like you, men.

—John Kells Ingram

Our battle-fields, safe in the keeping
Of Nature's kind, fostering care,
Are blooming,—our heroes are sleeping,—
And peace broods perennial there.

—John H. Jewett

It was good to die on the firing-line if you died to set men free.

—Reginald Wright Kauffman

Remember, Freedom is our price, since men must die that men be free;
That is thy pledge, by peace or war, to those who sleep upon the ground
Their blood had bought from shore to shore, until the last reveille sound.

—Reginald Wright Kauffman

Life hangs as nothing in the scale against dear Liberty! *—Lucy Larcom*

Over them now—year following year—
Over their graves the pine-cones fall,
And the whippoorwill chants his spectre-call;
But they stir not again; they raise no cheer:
They have ceased. But their glory shall never cease,
Nor their light be quenched in the light of peace.

—George Parsons Lathrop

No more upon his sorrowing heart shall beat
Dull tramp of troops or sullen roar of guns.

—Mary Sinton Leitch

Four score and seven years ago our fathers brought forth on this continent a new nation, conceived in liberty, and dedicated to the proposition that all men are created equal. Now we are engaged in a great civil war, testing whether that nation, or any nation so conceived and so dedicated, can long endure. We are met on a great battlefield of that war. We have come to dedicate a portion of that field, as a final resting-place for those who here gave their lives that that nation might live. It is altogether fitting and proper that we should do this; but, in a larger sense, we cannot dedicate—we cannot consecrate—we cannot hallow—this ground. The brave men, living and dead, who struggled here, have consecrated it, far above our poor power to add or detract. The world will little note, nor long remember what we say here, but it can never forget what they did here. It is for us, the living, rather, to be dedicated here to the unfinished work which they who fought here have thus far so nobly advanced. It is rather for us to be here dedicated to the great task remaining before us— that from these honored dead we take increased devotion to that cause for which they gave the last full measure of devotion—that we here highly resolve that these dead shall not have died in vain—that this nation, under God, shall have a new birth of freedom—and that government of the people, by the people, for the people, shall not perish from the earth.

—*Abraham Lincoln*

Let no vandalism of avarice or neglect, no ravages of time, testify to the present or to the coming generations, that we have forgotten, as a people, the cost of a free and undivided Republic. —*John A. Logan*

They are dead; but they live in each Patriot's breast,
And their names are engraven on honor's bright crest.

—*Longfellow*

The warriors that fought for their country, and bled,
Have sunk to their rest; the damp earth is their bed;
No stone tells the place where their ashes repose,
Nor points out the spot from the graves of their foes.

—*Longfellow*

Your silent tents of green
We deck with fragrant flowers;
Yours has the suffering been,
The memory shall be ours.

—*Longfellow*

Virtue treads paths that end not in the grave;
No ban of endless night exiles the brave.

—*James Russell Lowell*

His country asked his life,
His life he gave!

—*George Lunt*

Fold them, O thou stainless flag that they died to save.

—*John S. McGroarty*

Their bones are on the northern hill,
And on the southern plain,
By brook and river, lake and rill,
And by the roaring main.
The land is holy where they fought,
And holy where they fell;
For by their blood that land was bought,
The land they loved so well.
Then glory to that valiant band,
The honored saviours of the land!

—*Isaac McLellan*

If the graves which America decorates today are more than a memory they speak not of the glory, but of the futility of war.

—*Editorial. Minneapolis Tribune, May 30, 1936*

Alas, how can we help but mourn
When hero bosoms yield their breath!
A century itself may bear
But once the flower of such a death.

—*S. Weir Mitchell*

Dark falls the tear of him that mourneth
Lost joy, or hope that ne'er returneth:
But brightly flows the tear
Wept o'er a hero's bier.

—*Thomas Moore*

Peace to each manly soul that sleepeth;
Rest to each faithful eye that weepeth;
Long may the fair and brave
Sigh o'er the hero's grave!

—*Thomas Moore*

And we remember only this,—
They bravely fought—they bravely died.

—*Henry D. Muir*

The muffled drum's sad roll has beat
The soldier's last tattoo;
No more on life's parade shall meet
That brave and fallen few.

—*Theodore O'Hara*

Rest on, embalmed and sainted dead,
Dear as the blood ye gave;
No impious footstep here shall tread
The herbage of your grave.

—*Theodore O'Hara*

Nor shall your story be forgot,
While Fame her record keeps,
Or Honor points the hallowed spot
Where Valor proudly sleeps.

—*Theodore O'Hara*

Bright honor be theirs who for honor were fearless,
Who charged for their flag to the grim cannon's mouth.

—*John Boyle O'Reilly*

Room for a soldier! lay him in the clover;
He loved the fields, and they shall be his cover.
—*Thomas William Parsons*

On thy grave the rain shall fall from the eyes of a mighty nation!
—*Thomas William Parsons*

Green sods are all their monuments; and yet it tells
A nobler history than pillared piles,
Or the eternal pyramids.
—*James Gates Percival*

Alas! how many lie
Beneath a Southern sky,
Who never heard the fearful fight was done,
And all they fought for, won!
—*Henry Peterson*

Here sleeps their dust: 'tis holy ground.
—*John Pierpont*

We are the richer for valor displayed alike by those who fought so valiantly for the right, and by those who, no less valiantly, fought for what they deemed the right.
—*Theodore Roosevelt*

No lofty pile nor sculptured bust
Can herald their degree.
—*Charles Sangster*

The hero dead cannot expire:
The dead still play their part.
—*Charles Sangster*

The brave die never, though they sleep in dust:
Their courage nerves a thousand living men.
—*Minot J. Savage*

Their place is now
With those who wear, green-set about the brow,
The deathless immortelles.
—*Clinton Scollard*

A weary road these men have trod,
O house them in the home of God!
—*Frederick George Scott*

O fading honours of the dead!
O high ambition, lowly laid!
—*Sir Walter Scott*

Soldier, rest! thy warfare o'er
Sleep the sleep that knows not breaking;
Dream of battled fields no more,
Days of danger, nights of waking.
—*Sir Walter Scott*

'Twas a victory—yes; but it cost us dear:
For that company's roll, when called at night,
Of a hundred men who went into the fight,
Numbered but twenty that answered "*Here!*"
—*Nathaniel Graham Shepherd*

Sleep, soldiers! still in honored rest
Your truth and valor wearing.
—*Bayard Taylor*

For all the land, within its clasping seas,
Is poorer now in bravery and beauty,
Such wealth of manly loves and energies
Was given to teach us all the freeman's sacred duty!
—*Bayard Taylor*

What splendor shall match their deeds?
—*Celia Thaxter*

"Dead upon the field of glory,"
Hero fit for song and story.
—*John Randolph Thompson*

The brave went down! Without disgrace
They leaped to Ruin's red embrace;
They only heard Fame's thunders wake,
And saw the dazzling sunburst break
In smiles on Glory's bloody face!
—*Will Henry Thompson*

A mighty mother turns in tears
The pages of her battle years,
Lamenting all her fallen sons!
—*Will Henry Thompson*

Stoop, angels, hither from the skies!
There is no holier spot of ground
Than where defeated valor lies,
By mourning beauty crowned!
—*Henry Timrod*

Count not the cost of honor to the dead!
The tribute that a mighty nation pays
To those who loved her well in former days
Means more than gratitude for glories fled.
—*Henry van Dyke*

Who serves his country well has no need of ancestors.
—*François M. A. Voltaire*

We come, not to mourn our dead soldiers, but to praise them.
—*Francis A. Walker*

But when your troubled country call'd you forth,
Your flaming courage, and your matchless worth,
To fierce contention gave a prosp'rous end.
—*Edmund Waller*

Gather the fairest flowers of May,
Heap them up on the graves of clay,
Gladden the graves of the noble dead.
—*Cy Warman*

This day the friends of the soldiers keep,
And they will keep it through all the years.
—*Cy Warman*

Although no sculptured marble should rise to their memory, nor engraved stone bear record of their deeds, yet will their remembrance be as lasting as the land they honored.

—*Daniel Webster*

They went where duty seemed to call,
They scarcely asked the reason why;
They only knew they could but die,
And death was not the worst of all!

—*Whittier*

Slowly and sadly we laid him down
From the field of his fame fresh and gory;
We carved not a line, and we raised not a stone—
But we left him alone with his glory.

—*Charles Wolfe*

Their silent wounds have speech
More eloquent than men;
Their tones can deeper reach
Than human voice or pen.

—*William Woodman*

MOTHER'S DAY

And high above all memories
I hold the beauty of her mind.
—Frederick Hentz Adams

All that I am my mother made me.
—John Quincy Adams

Where there is a mother in the house, matters speed well. *—Amos Bronson Alcott*

The Spartan spirit that made life so grand,
Mating poor daily needs
With high, heroic deeds,
That wrested happiness from Fate's hard hand.
—Louisa M. Alcott

Her heart is like her garden,
Old-fashioned, quaint and sweet,
With here a wealth of blossoms,
And there a still retreat.
—Alice E. Allen

Before a day was over,
Home comes the rover,
For mother's kiss,—sweeter this
Than any other thing!
—William Allingham

When by my bed I saw my mother kneel,
And with her blessing took her nightly kiss;
Whatever time destroys, he cannot this;—
E'en now that nameless kiss I feel.
—Washington Allston

The formative period for building character for eternity is in the nursery. The mother is queen of that realm and sways a scepter more potent than that of kings or priests.
—Anon.

The mother in her office holds the key
Of the soul; and she it is who stamps the coin
Of character.
—Anon.

The mother's love—there's none so pure,
So constant and so kind;
No human passion doth endure
Like this within the mind.
—Anon.

The purest thing I know in all earth's holding
Is mother love, her precious child enfolding;
Yet when the mother's footstep feeble groweth,
As sweet the child love then which round her floweth.
—Anon.

"To one whose love for me shall last
When lighter passions long have passed,
So holy 'tis, and true."
Anon.

The crying need of the world is mental mothers. Primitive, physical, passionate mothers we have in abundance. But the mothers we need, the mothers who are to stimulate mentally the town, family, and church are all too rare.
—Frank R. Arnold

For when you looked into my mother's eyes you knew, as if He had told you, why God sent her into the world—it was to open the minds of all who looked, to beautiful thoughts. *—James M. Barrie*

Heaven help all mothers if they be not really dears. *—James M. Barrie*

A mother has, perhaps, the hardest earthly lot; and yet no mother worthy of the name ever gave herself thoroughly for her child who did not feel that, after all, she reaped what she had sown.
—Henry Ward Beecher

The mother's heart is the child's school-room.
—Henry Ward Beecher

Nothing can compare in beauty, and wonder, and admirableness, and divinity itself, to the silent work in obscure dwellings of faithful women bringing their children to honour and virtue and piety.
—Henry Ward Beecher

When God thought of MOTHER, He must have laughed with satisfaction, and framed it quickly,—so rich, so deep, so divine, so full of soul, power, and beauty, was the conception. *—Henry Ward Beecher*

O mother mine! God grant I ne'er forget,
Whatever be my grief, or what my joy,
The unmeasured, inextinguishable debt
I owe thy love.
—George W. Bethune

Can a mother sit and hear
An infant groan, an infant fear?
No, no! never can it be!
Never, never can it be!
—William Blake

My mother's hands are cool and fair,
They can do anything.
Delicate mercies hide them there
Like flowers in the spring.
—Anna Hempstead Branch

A man outwearied with the world's mad race
His mother seeks again.
—Irving Browne

So mothers have God's license to be missed.
—Elizabeth Barrett Browning

A woman lives
Not bettered, quickened toward the truth and good
Through being a mother?—then she's none.
—Elizabeth Barrett Browning

Women know
The way to rear up children (to be just)
They know a simple, merry, tender knack
Of tying sashes, fitting baby-shoes,
And stringing pretty words that make no sense,
And kissing full sense into empty words;
Which things are corals to cut life upon,
Although such trifles.
—Elizabeth Barrett Browning

All-Gracious! grant to those who bear
A mother's charge, the strength and light
To guide the feet that own their care
In ways of Love and Truth and Right.
—William Cullen Bryant

Lord who ordainest for mankind
Benignant toils and tender cares,
We thank Thee for the ties that bind
The mother to the child she bears.
—William Cullen Bryant

Oh, mother's love is glorifying!
—Thomas Burbidge

And now so well I know her that I know
The graciousness of her will always grow
Like daybreak in my spirit, and will be
Through all my life a radiant mystery
Since love like hers ever exceeds the sweep
Of mortal plummet, sound we ne'er so deep.
—Amelia Josephine Burr

The song of the mothers! in infancy our lullaby; in youth our high clear call to straightness of life; in age our oftenest rehearsed refrain. *—W. J. Cameron*

My dear mother with the truthfulness of a mother's heart, ministered to all my woes, outward and inward, and even against hope kept prophesying good. *—Thomas Carlyle*

Who is it that loves me and will love me forever with an affection which no chance, no misery, no crime of mine can do away?—It is you, my mother. *—Thomas Carlyle*

Give me the life of the boy whose mother is nurse, seamstress, washerwoman, cook, teacher, angel, and saint, all in one, and whose father is guide, examplar, and friend. No servants to come between. These are the boys who are born to the best fortune.
—Andrew Carnegie

A lady, the loveliest ever the sun
Looked down upon you must paint for me.
Oh, if I only could make you see
The dear blue eyes, the tender smile,
The sovereign sweetness, the gentle grace,
The woman's soul, and the angel's face
That are beaming on me all the while,
I need not speak these foolish words.
Yet one word tells you all I would say,—
She is my mother.
—Alice Cary

The harshness and general painfulness of life in old times must have been much relieved by certain simple and affectionate customs which modern people have learned to dispense with. Amongst these was a practice of going to see parents, and especially the female one, on the mid Sunday of Lent, taking for them some little present, such as a cake or a trinket. A youth engaged in this amiable act of duty was said to go *a-mothering,* and thence the day itself came to be called Mothering Sunday.
—Chambers Book of Days

No language can express the power and beauty and heroism and majesty of a mother's love. It shrinks not where man cowers, and grows stronger where man faints, and over the wastes of worldly fortune sends the radiance of quenchless fidelity like a star in heaven. *—E. H. Chapin*

Unless the sons fair men and honest prove,
The virtuous mother will dishonored be.
—Chinese

A mother is a mother still,
The holiest thing alive.
—Samuel Taylor Coleridge

So for the Mother's sake the Child was dear,
And dearer was the Mother for the Child.
—Samuel Taylor Coleridge

There is a religion in all deep love, but the love of a mother is the veil of a softer light between the heart and the heavenly Father.
—Samuel Taylor Coleridge

I miss thee, my Mother! Thy image is still
The deepest impressed on my heart.
—Eliza Cook

I look into my inmost mind,
And here her inspiration find.
—Josephine Rice Creelman

God made mothers before He made ministers: the progress of Christ's kingdom depends more upon the influence of faithful, wise and pious mothers than upon any other human agency. *—T. L. Cuyler*

I think it must somewhere be written, that the virtues of mothers shall be visited on their children, as well as the sins of the fathers. *—Charles Dickens*

No mother who stands upon low ground herself can hope to place her children upon a loftier plane. They may reach it, but it will not be through her. —*Julia C. A. Dorr*

Alike for me and you its rays aye glow—
Maternal love, by day and night the same.
—*Georg Ebers*

In the man whose childhood has known caresses there lies a fibre of memory which can be touched to noble issues.
—*George Eliot*

Mighty is the force of motherhood! It transforms all things by its vital heat.
—*George Eliot*

The mother's yearning, that completest type of life within another life which is the essence of human love, feels the presence of the cherished child, even in the base degraded man. —*George Eliot*

Woman in the home has not yet lost her dignity, in spite of Mother's Day, with its offensive implication that our love needs an annual nudging, like our enthusiasm for the battle of Bunker Hill. —*John Erskine*

He is a poor son whose sonship does not make him desire to serve all men's mothers.
—*Harry Emerson Fosdick*

Oh, take me to my kind old mudder!
Dere let me live and die.
—*Stephen Collins Foster*

Mother, there is a love
Men give to wives and children, lovers, friends;
There is a love which some men give to God.
Ah! between this, I think, and that last love,
Last and too-late-discovered love of God,
There shines—and nearer to the love of God—
The love a man gives only to his mother,
Whose travail of dear thought has never end
Until the End.
—*John Freeman*

We must therefore cultivate mothers.
—*Friedrich Wilhelm August Froebel*

Where yet was ever found a mother
Who'd give her booby for another?
—*John Gay*

A mother's love, the best love; God's love, the highest love. —*German*

"Like mother, like son" is a saying so true
The world will judge largely the "mother" by you.
—*Margaret Johnston Grafflin*

How sweet are the thoughts that fill my heart
Today, dear mother of mine!
Memories that stand in the mist of the years,
Fadeless, enduring forever;
The comfort of your arms—my first cradle;
The solace of your voice—my first music;
The caress of your hands—my first shelter;
The touch of your lips—my first message of love.
How lovely you stand today pictured in my heart,
And enshrined in the sanctuary of my soul!
—*Philip E. Gregory*

Easier is it to rule a band of savages than to be the successful autocrat of thy little kingdom. —*John Habberton*

Oh, wondrous power! how little understood,
Entrusted to the mother's mind alone,
To fashion genius, form the soul for good,
Inspire a West, or train a Washington.
—*Mrs. Sarah Josepha Hale*

There was a beautiful ideal in your mind;
I saw it; *that* was my mother!
—*Sophia Hawthorne*

Yet, dearest mother, such the gentle worth
Of thy benignant presence, angel-mild,
It ever hath my proudest moods beguiled,
And given to softer, humbler feelings birth.
—*Heinrich Heine*

There is none,
In all this cold and hollow world, no fount
Of deep, strong, deathless love, save that within
A mother's heart.
—*Felicia Hemans*

What household thoughts around thee as their shrine,
Cling reverently!
—*Felicia Hemans*

One good mother is worth a hundred schoolmasters. —*George Herbert*

What are Raphael's Madonnas but the shadow of a mother's love, fixed in permanent outline forever?
—*Thomas Wentworth Higginson*

The real religion of the world comes from women much more than from men—from mothers most of all, who carry the key of our souls in their bosoms.
—*Oliver Wendell Holmes*

Youth fades; love droops; the leaves of friendship fall;
A mother's secret hope outlives them all.
—*Oliver Wendell Holmes*

Thy mother's lot, my dear,
She doth it naught accuse:
Her lot to bear, to nurse, to rear,
To love—and then to lose.
—*Jean Ingelow*

A Mother's Love endures through all; in good repute, in bad repute, in the face of the world's condemnation, a mother still loves on.
—*Washington Irving*

The tie which links mother and child is of such pure and immaculate strength as to be never violated, except by those whose feelings are withered by vitiated society. Holy, simple, and beautiful in its construction, it is the emblem of all we can imagine of fidelity and truth. . . In all our trials, amid all our afflictions, she is still by our side; if we sin, she reproves more in sorrow than in anger; nor can she tear us from her bosom, nor forget we are her child.
—*Washington Irving*

Motherhood is priced
Of God, at price no man may dare
To lessen or misunderstand.
—*Helen Hunt Jackson*

God could not be everywhere, and therefore He made mothers. —*Jewish saying*

Then spake the woman whose the living child was unto the king, for her bowels yearned upon her son, and she said, O my lord, give her the living child, and in no wise slay it. But the other said, Let it be neither mine nor thine; but divide it.
Then the king answered and said, Give her the living child, and in no wise slay it: she is the mother thereof.
—*I Kings 3:26,27*

If I were hanged on the highest hill,
Mother o' mine, O mother o' mine!
I know whose love would follow me still,
Mother o' mine, O mother o' mine!
—*Rudyard Kipling*

Her soul was so luminous, so highly colored, and so warm, that she left a shadow or a chill on nothing. —*Lamartine*

She is the sweet rallying-point of affection, obedience, and a thousand tendernesses.
—*Lamartine*

Mother's love grows by giving.
—*Charles Lamb*

Children are what the mothers are.
—*Walter Savage Landor*

If the whole world were put into one scale, and my mother in the other, the whole world would kick the beam.
—*Lord Langdale* (*Henry Bickersteth*)

I love the cradle songs the mothers sing
In lonely places when the twilight drops,
The slow endearing melodies that bring
Sleep to the weeping lids.
—*Francis Ledwidge*

All that I am or hope to be I owe to my mother. —*Abraham Lincoln*

No man is poor who has had a godly mother.
—*Abraham Lincoln*

Even He that died for us upon the cross, in the last hour, in the unutterable agony of death, was mindful of His Mother, as if to teach us that this holy love should be our last worldly thought, the last point of earth from which the soul should take its flight for heaven.
—*Longfellow*

For mè, a line from my mother is more efficacious than all the homilies preached in Lent. —*Longfellow*

There was a place in childhood, that I remember well,
And there a voice of sweetest tone, bright fairy tales did tell,
And gentle words, and fond embrace, were given with joy to me,
When I was in that happy place upon my mother's knee.
—*Samuel Lover*

Many make the household but only one the home. —*James Russell Lowell*

A woman's love
Is mighty, but a mother's heart is weak,
And by its weakness overcomes.
—*James Russell Lowell*

Men are what their mothers make them.
—*Bulwer-Lytton*

Nature's loving proxy, the watchful mother.
—*Bulwer-Lytton*

Happy is the child to whom the love of a mother is a noble stimulus.
—*Hamilton Wright Mabie*

The mother loves her child most divinely, not when she surrounds him with comfort and anticipates his wants, but when she resolutely holds him to the highest standards and is content with nothing less than his best.
—*Hamilton Wright Mabie*

I feel again the mother-kiss,
I see again the glad surprise
That lightened up the tranquil eyes.
—*William Gordon McCabe*

For my love make no woman weep
For my love hold no woman cheap.
—*Irene Rutherford McLeod*

And home will sweeten in the coming days,
When widening love shall warm these human ways;
When every mother, pressing to her face,
Her child, shall clasp all children of the race.
—*Edwin Markham*

"Good father," "good child" is a fairly reliable rule, though "good mother," "good child" is a somewhat surer one.
—*Edward Sandford Martin*

If you want to be particularly sagacious, look not at the mother but at the children.
—*E. S. Martin*

My hands are too tired to hold a torch on high, but they can light a candle in a nursery.
—*Ellis Meredith*

It is the general rule, that all superior men inherit the elements of their superiority from their mothers. —*Jules Michelet*

Mothers *are* and are not made.
—*George Middleton*

The bravest battle that ever was fought;
Shall I tell you where and when?
On the maps of the world you will find it not;
It was fought by the mothers of men.
—*Joaquin Miller*

This heart, my own dear mother, bends,
With love's true instinct, back to thee!
—*Thomas Moore*

There is a harmony and beauty in the life of mother and son that brims the mind's cup of satisfaction. —*Christopher Morley*

All that is purest and best in man is but the echo of a mother's benediction.
—*Frederick W. Morton*

France needs nothing so much to promote her regeneration as good mothers.
—*Napoleon I*

The future destiny of the child is always the work of the mother. —*Napoleon I*

Your faith, beyond the silence and the night,
Your love still close and watching through the years.
—*Kathleen Norris*

In me hast thou not learned some signs to trace
Of that dear soul who calleth me her son?
Such as I was that in thy countenance
Found favour, from her it was gathered most.
—*Gilbert Parker*

Because I feel, that in the Heavens above,
The angels, whispering to one another,
Can find, among their burning terms of love,
None so devotional as that of "Mother,"
Therefore by that dear name I long have called you.
—*Edgar Allan Poe*

Strength and dignity are her clothing;
And she laugheth at the time to come.
She openeth her mouth with wisdom;
And the law of kindness is on her tongue.
She looketh well to the ways of her household,
And eateth not the bread of idleness;
Her children rise up and call her blessed,
Her husband also and he praises her, saying,
Many daughters have done virtuously,
But thou excelleth them all.
—*Proverbs 31:25-29*

She faced the world with level blue eyes, filled with the love of love, the hate of tyranny and wrong, the glad recognition of whatever beauty—and there was all too little of it—came within her vision. —*Herbert Quick*

Unhappy is the man for whom his own mother has not made all other mothers venerable. —*Jean Paul Richter*

Into the woman's keeping is committed the destiny of the generations to come after us. —*Theodore Roosevelt*

I love old mothers—mothers with white hair,
And kindly eyes, and lips grown softly sweet
With murmured blessings over sleeping babes.
—*Charles S. Ross*

Blessed Dear and Heart's Delight,
Companion, Friend and Mother mine,
Round whom my fears and love entwine.
—*Christina G. Rossetti*

To my first Love, my Mother, on whose knee
I learnt love-lore that is not troublesome;
Whose service is my special dignity,
And she my lodestar while I go and come.
—*Christina G. Rossetti*

The idea of motherhood covers and sanctifies all human relations.
—*G. W. E. Russell*

A mother's love and a mother's prayers may indeed follow their object round the world; but the personal intercourse and daily contact between mother and son have a sacramental virtue in guarding and shaping a boy's course such as nothing else on earth can supply. —*G. W. E. Russell*

My mother took for her motto in the training of her children the saying of some distinguished man: "Fill the measure with wheat and there will be no room for the chaff." —*Maria Sanford*

Thou art thy mother's glass, and she in thee
Calls back the lovely April of her prime.
—*Shakespeare*

Observe how soon, and to what a degree, a mother's influence begins to operate!
mind. —*Lydia Huntley Sigourney*

Say to mothers, what a holy charge is theirs; with what a kingly power their love might rule the fountains of the new-born mind. —*Lydia Huntley Sigourney*

If you would reform the world from its errors and vices, begin by enlisting the mothers.
—*Charles Simmons*

For the mother is and must be, whether she knows it or not, the greatest, strongest and most lasting teacher her children have.
—*Hannah Whitall Smith*

If there be aught
Surpassing human deed or word, or thought,
It is a mother's love.
—*Marchioness de Spadara*

An ounce of mother is worth a pound of clergy. —*Spanish Proverb*

She seemed an angel to our infant eyes!
—*E. C. Stedman*

He hungered; and she gave
What most His heart did crave,
A Mother's love.
—*John Banister Tabb*

The dignity, the grandeur, the tenderness, the everlasting and divine significance of motherhood. —*T. DeWitt Talmage*

Mother—that was the bank where we deposited all our hurts and worries.
—*T. DeWitt Talmage*

Who ran to help me when I fell,
And would some pretty story tell,
Or kiss the place to make it well?
My Mother.
—*Ann Taylor*

His mother's kindness is a debt,
He never, never will forget.
—*Jane Taylor*

Oh, good mama, to take such care,
And no kind pains and trouble spare,
To feed and nurse you when you were
A baby.
—*Jane and Ann Taylor*

Happy he
With such a mother! faith in womankind
Beats with his blood, and trust in all things high
Comes easy to him; and tho' he trip and fall,
He shall not blind his soul with clay.
—*Alfred Tennyson*

My mother was as mild as any saint,
And nearly canonized by all she knew,
So gracious was her tact and tenderness.
—*Alfred Tennyson*

Mother is the name for God in the lips and hearts of little children.
—*William Makepeace Thackeray*

Sit in the seat of thy mother,
And walk in thy mother's footsteps.
—*Johann Gottfried von Herder*

Mother love . . . hath this unlikeness to any other love: Tender to the object, it can be infinitely tyrannical to itself, and thence all its power of self-sacrifice. —*Lew Wallace*

For the hand that rocks the cradle
Is the hand that rules the world.
—*William Ross Wallace*

My mother was the most beautiful woman I ever saw. . . All I am I owe to my mother.
—*George Washington*

The mothers of brave men must themselves be brave. —*Mary Ball Washington*

To her, the ideal woman, practical, spiritual, of all of earth, life, love, to me the best.
—*Walt Whitman*

My mother's chastening love I own.
—*John Greenleaf Whittier*

All women become like their mothers. That is their tragedy. No man does. That is his.
—*Oscar Wilde*

I thank God for my mother as for no other gift of His bestowing. —*Frances Willard*

One lamp—thy mother's love—amid the stars
Shall lift its pure flame changeless, and before
The throne of God, burn through eternity—
Holy—as it was lit and lent thee here.
—*Nathaniel Parker Willis*

Mother! whose virgin bosom was uncrost
With the least shade of thought to sin allied.
—*William Wordsworth*

Sure I love the dear silver that shines in your hair,
And the brow that's all furrowed, and wrinkled with care.
I kiss the dear fingers, so toil-worn for me,
Oh, God bless you and keep you, Mother Machree.
—*Rida Johnson Young*

MUSIC WEEK

Music can noble hints impart,
Engender fury, kindle love,
With unsuspected eloquence can move,
And manage all the man with secret art.
—*Joseph Addison*

Music, the greatest good that mortals know,
And all of heaven we have below.
—*Joseph Addison*

Angel of Music! when our finest speech
Is all too coarse to give the heart relief,
The inmost fountains lie within thy reach,
Soother of every joy and every grief.
—*William Allingham*

Where words fail, music speaks.
—*Hans Christian Andersen*

For doth not song to the whole world belong?
Is it not given wherever tears can fall,
Wherever hearts can melt, or blushes glow,
Or mirth or sadness mingle as they flow—
A heritage for all?
—*Anon.*

One of the noblest objects of music is the spread of religion and the elevation of the human soul. —*Philip Emanuel Bach*

Generally, music feedeth the disposition of spirit which it findeth. —*Francis Bacon*

Rugged the breast that music cannot tame.
—*J. C. Bampfylde*

Music cleanses the understanding; inspires it, and lifts it into a realm which it would not reach if it were left to itself.
—*Henry Ward Beecher*

Music alone ushers man into the portal of an intellectual world, ready to encompass him, but which he may never encompass.
—*Beethoven*

Music is the mediator between the spiritual and the sensual life. —*Beethoven*

Its language is a language which the soul alone understands, but which the soul can never translate. —*Arnold Bennett*

It calls in my spirits, composes my thoughts, delights my ear, recreates my mind, and so not only fits me for after business, but fills my heart, at the present, with pure and useful thoughts; so that when the music sounds the sweetliest in my ears, truth commonly flows the clearest into my mind.
—*William Beveridge*

There is music wherever there is harmony, order, or proportion; and thus far we may maintain the music of the spheres.
—*Sir Thomas Browne*

Consider it well: each tone of our scale in itself is naught;
It is everywhere in the world,—loud, soft, and all is said:
Give it to me to use!
—*Robert Browning*

There is no truer truth obtainable
By Man than comes of music.
—*Robert Browning*

Music is fundamental—one of the great sources of life, health, strength and happiness.
—*Luther Burbank*

Divine Musicke, besides that excellent power it hath to expell many other diseases, is a soveraigne against Despair and Melancholy, and will drive away the Divell himself. —*Robert Burton*

There's music in the sighing of a reed;
There's music in the gushing of a rill;
There's music in all things, if men had ears:
Their earth is but an echo of the spheres.
—*Lord Byron*

Nobody dreams of music in hell, and nobody conceives of heaven without it.
S. Parkes Cadman

All deep things are song. It seems somehow the very central essence of us, song; as if all the rest were but wrappages and hulls!
—*Thomas Carlyle*

Music is a kind of inarticulate, unfathomable speech, which leads us to the edge of the infinite, and impels us for a moment to gaze into that! —*Thomas Carlyle*

I am a devoted lover of music. I give organs to churches, or help churches to get organs, because I am willing to be responsible for everything the organs say, although I could not be responsible for all that is said from the pulpit. —*Andrew Carnegie*

Music is the child of prayer, the companion of religion. —*Chateaubriand*

The songs of musicians are able to change the feelings and conditions of a state.
—*Cicero*

The best sort of music is what it should be—sacred; the next best, the military, has fallen to the lot of the devil.
—*Samuel Taylor Coleridge*

Swans sing before they die;—'twere no bad thing,
Should certain persons die before they sing.
—Samuel Taylor Coleridge

Indeed Musick, when rightly ordered, cannot be prefer'd too much. It composes the Passions, affords a strong Pleasure, and excites a Nobleness of Thought.
—Jeremy Collier

O Music! sphere-descended maid,
Friend of Pleasure, Wisdom's aid!
—William Collins

Wouldst thou know if a people be well governed, if its laws be good or bad? Examine the music it practices. *—Confucius*

Music has charms to soothe a savage breast,
To soften rocks, or bend a knotted oak.
I've read that things inanimate have moved,
And, as with living souls, have been inform'd,
By magic numbers and persuasive sound.
—William Congreve

Music is the art directly representative of democracy. If the best music is brought to the people there need be no fear about their ability to appreciate it. *—Calvin Coolidge*

Water and air He for the Tenor chose,
Earth made the Bass, the Treble Flame arose,
To th' active Moon a quick brisk stroke He gave,
To Saturn's string a touch more soft and grave.

The motions straight, and round, and swift, and slow,
And short and long, were mixt and woven so,
Did in such artful Figures smoothly fall,
As made this decent measur'd Dance of all.
And this is Musick.
—Abraham Cowley

There is in souls a sympathy with sounds;
And as the mind is pitch'd the ear is pleased
With melting airs, or martial, brisk or grave;
Some chord in unison with what we hear
Is touch'd within us, and the heart replies.
—William Cowper

I am no prophet, but had I the prophesying gift, I think I would risk a safe word about music. I would say that if you can bring music into the streets, into courtyards, into museums, into railway stations, into every place where crowds go and pass, you again and again rout scepticism, drunkenness and ill-health. *—Gordon Craig*

With every child listening daily to the gems of good music, preference for the beautiful in music will follow as dawn follows night. *Hollis Dann*

When music sounds, gone is the earth I know,
And all her lovely things even lovelier grow.
—Walter de la Mare

Were it not for music, we might in these days say, the Beautiful is dead.
—Benjamin Disraeli

With pipe and flute the rustic Pan
Of old made music sweet for man.
—Austin Dobson

But oh! what art can teach,
What human voice can reach
The sacred organ's praise?
—John Dryden

From harmony, from heavenly harmony,
This universal frame began.
—John Dryden

Thus, long ago,
Ere heaving bellows learned to blow,
While organs yet were mute,
Timotheus, to his breathing flute
And sounding lyre,
Could swell the soul to rage, or kindle soft desire.
—John Dryden

For a well rounded life one must have music.
—George Eastman

This world may consist of musical notes as well as of mathematical rules.
—Albert Einstein

My idea is that there is music in the air, music all around us; the world is full of it, and you simply take as much as you require.
—Sir Edward Elgar

Music . . . is the best mind-trainer on the list.
—Charles W. Eliot

'Tis God gives skill,
But not without men's hands: He could not make
Antonio Stradivari's violins
Without Antonio.
—George Eliot

There is no feeling, except the extremes of fear and grief, that does not find relief in music. *—George Eliot*

I think sometimes could I only have music on my own terms, could I live in a great city, and know where I could go whenever I wished the ablution and inundation of musical waves, that were a bath and a medicine.
—Ralph Waldo Emerson

Be filled with the Spirit; speaking to yourselves in psalms and hymns and spiritual songs, singing and making melody in your heart to the Lord.
—Ephesians 5:18,19

Song brings of itself a cheerfulness that wakes the heart of joy. *—Euripides*

O music! thou surely art worship.
—Frederick William Faber

Thou art fugitive splendors made vocal.
—Frederick William Faber

Music is nothing else but wild sounds civilized into time and tune. *—Thomas Fuller*

This day I heard such music that I thought,
Hath human speech the power thus to be wrought
Into such melody?
—Richard Watson Gilder

A song will outlive all sermons in the memory. *—H. Giles*

Music is one of the most forcible instruments for training, for arousing, for governing the mind and spirit of man.
—William Ewart Gladstone

The object of music is to soften men down without injuring them, and to make them favorable to their surroundings, without lowering them. *—Glück*

The effect of good music is not caused by its novelty. On the contrary, it strikes us more the more we are familiar with it.
—Goethe

It raises and ennobles whatever it expresses.
—Goethe

Music is the common tie between races and nationalities, and recognizes no caste.
—Jacques L. Gottlieb

Where through the long-drawn aisle and fretted vault
The pealing anthem swells the note of praise.
—Thomas Gray

Music is a friend of labor for it lightens the task by refreshing the nerves and spirit of the worker. *—William Green*

As the same block of marble is converted by one sculptor into the most exquisite forms, by another into a clumsy botch, so the musical scale, by different manipulation, becomes now an Overture of Beethoven, and now one of Verdi. *—Eduard Hanslick*

Though *all* arts, without exception, have the power to act on our feelings, yet the mode in which *music* displays it is, undoubtedly, peculiar to this art alone.
—Eduard Hanslick

What can one say of the highest music except that, like death, it is the great leveller; it gathers us all to its tender keeping—and we rest. *—Beatrice Harraden*

Sing! that your song may gladden.
—F. R. Havergal

Music will some day become a powerful and acknowledged therapeutic.
—H. R. Haweis

Charm me asleep, and melt me so
With thy delicious numbers,
That, being ravished, hence I go
Away in easy slumbers.
—Robert Herrick

Rare is the voice it selfe; but when we sing
To th' lute or violl, then 'tis ravishing.
—Robert Herrick

Music is a strange bird singing the songs of another shore. *—J. G. Holland*

Alas for those that never sing,
But die with all their music in them!
—Oliver Wendell Holmes

Take a music bath once or twice a week for a few seasons. You will find it is to the soul what a water bath is to the body.
—Oliver Wendell Holmes

O sweet and healing balm of troubles.
—Horace

Music is a making manifest to our dull ears the divine harmony of the universe, and, through music, we read the universal.
—Elbert Hubbard

Music expresses that which cannot be said, and which cannot be suppressed.
—Victor Hugo

Flageolets one by one, and flutes blowing more fast,
And hautboys and clarionets, acrid of reed,
And the violin, smoothlier sustaining the speed
As the rich tempest gathered, and buz-ringing moons
Of tambours, and deep basses, and giant bassoons,
And the golden trombone, that darteth its tongue
Like a bee of the gods; nor was wanting the gong.

. . . .

Then lo! was performed by immense will and pleasure,
And orchestras rose to an exquisite measure.
—Leigh Hunt

Music is the medicine of the breaking heart.
—Leigh Hunt

Music expresses feeling and thought, without language; it was below and before speech, and it is above and beyond all words.
—Robert G. Ingersoll

Delicious sounds! Those little bright-eyed things
That float about the air on azure wings.
—John Keats

Let me have music dying, and I seek no more delight. *—John Keats*

Angel melodies
Burst through the dull dark and
the mad air quivered
Unutterable music.
—Charles Kingsley

Music has been called the speech of angels; I will go further, and call it the speech of God Himself. *—Charles Kingsley*

Music is the literature of the heart; it commences where speech ends.
—Alphonse de Lamartine

The piano is the musical charm of our social life. *—A. E. Lancaster*

The habitual use of vocal music by a family is an almost unfailing sign of good morals and refined taste. *—C. W. Landon*

Music is God's gift to man, the only art of heaven given to earth, the only art of earth we take to heaven. *—Walter Savage Landor*

How many are there in these days to whom the finest preaching comes from the organ-loft!. . . there are those who declare that music is to be the Church of the future, wherein all creeds will unite like the tones in a chord. *—Sidney Lanier*

Music is love in search of a word.
—Sidney Lanier

It is incontestable that music induces in us a sense of the infinite and the contemplation of the invisible. *—Victor de LaPrade*

Music is never stationary; successive forms and styles are only like so many resting-places—like tents pitched and taken down again on the road to the Ideal.
—Franz Liszt

Music's the medicine of the mind.
—John A. Logan

And the night shall be filled with music,
And the cares that infest the day
Shall fold their tents like the Arabs
And as silently steal away.
—Longfellow

God sent His singers upon earth
With songs of sadness and of mirth,
That they might touch the hearts of men
And bring them back to heaven again.
—Longfellow

Show me the home wherein music dwells, and I shall show you a happy, peaceful, and contented home.
—Longfellow

Yea, music is the Prophet's art
Among the gifts that God hath sent,
One of the most magnificent!
—Longfellow

Then swelled the organ: up through choir and
nave
The music trembled with an inward thrill
Of bliss at its own grandeur.
—James Russell Lowell

Music, when it touches me, touches me too deeply for word, and has me utterly at its mercy. *—E. V. Lucas*

Music is a discipline, and a mistress of order and good manners.
—Martin Luther

Music is the art of the prophets, the only art that can calm the agitations of the soul; it is one of the most magnificent and delightful presents God has given us.
—Martin Luther

Those who are not touched by music, I hold to be like stocks and stones.
—Martin Luther

And when an audience disperses, can you guess what griefs the singer may have comforted, what hard hearts he may have softened, what high thoughts he may have awakened? *—Bulwer-Lytton*

Music, once admitted to the soul, becomes a sort of spirit, and never dies.
—Bulwer-Lytton

Music, the mosaic of the Air.
—Andrew Marvell

If it be true that music is, in sober fact, the only international language, the only emotional and spiritual coinage that is honored all over the world, then it must surely be an invaluable influence toward peace.
—Daniel Gregory Mason

Music is the harmonious voice of creation; an echo of the invisible world; one note of the divine concord which the entire universe is destined one day to sound. *—Mazzini*

What a divine calling is music! Though everything else may appear shallow and repulsive, even the smallest task in music is so absorbing, and carries us so far away from town, country, earth and all worldly things, that it is truly a blessed gift of God.
—Mendelssohn

There is nothing in the world so much like prayer as music is.
—William P. Merrill

The art is used too much as an amusement, as an exhibition of skill, as a means of attracting attention, and too little as a means of education. —*Karl Merz*

The power of music is so great, that in the legends of all nations, the invention of the art is ascribed to the gods. —*Karl Merz*

When Händel was told by his sovereign that the performance of the "Messiah" had afforded him pleasure, the composer replied: "Your majesty, I did not intend to amuse or to afford pleasure; I meant to make the world better." —*Karl Merz*

Sweet sounds, oh, beautiful music do not cease!
Reject me not into the world again!
With you alone is excellence and peace,
Mankind made plausible, his purpose plain.
—*Edna St. Vincent Millay*

But not in silence holy kept: the harp
Had work, and rested not; the solemn pipe
And dulcimer, all organs of sweet stop,
All sounds on fret by string or golden wire,
Temper'd soft tunings, intermix'd with voice
Choral and unison. . .
—*Milton*

Such sweet compulsion doth in music lie.
—*Milton*

There let the pealing organ blow
To the full-voiced choir below,
In service high and anthem clear,
As may, with sweetness through mine ear,
Dissolve me into ecstacies,
And bring all heaven before mine eyes.
—*Milton*

Music produces like effects on the mind as good medicine on the body. —*Mirandola*

Wherever there is good music there is harmony. Wherever there is harmony there are good citizens. —*J. Hampton Moore*

And music too—dear music! that can touch
Beyond all else the soul that loves it much.
—*Thomas Moore*

Music! Oh,how faint, how weak,
Language fades before thy spell,
Why should feeling ever speak,
Whence thou canst breathe her soul so well?
—*Thomas Moore*

'Twas not the air, 'twas not the words,
But that deep magic in the chords
And in the lips, that gave such power
As music knew not till that hour.
—*Thomas Moore*

Hark! the low music wakes, and soft and slow
Wanders at will through flowery fields of sound.
—*Lewis Morris*

Music—even in the most harrowing moment—ought never to offend the ear, but should always remain music, which desires to give pleasure. —*Mozart*

Of all the liberal arts music has the greatest influence over the passions, and is that which legislators ought to give the greatest encouragement. —*Napoleon I*

Without music life would be a mistake.
—*Friedrich Wilhelm Nietzsche*

Music's the cordial of a troubled breast,
The softest remedy that grief can find;
The gentle spell that charms our care to rest
And calms the ruffled passions of the mind.
—*John Oldham*

Music is a pleasing accomplishment; let the fair learn to sing. —*Ovid*

Music is to the mind as air to the body.
—*Plato*

In Heaven a spirit doth dwell
Whose heart-strings are a lute.
—*Edgar Allan Poe*

It is in music, perhaps, that the soul most nearly attains the great end for which, when inspired by the poetic sentiment, it struggles—the creation of supernal beauty.
—*Edgar Allan Poe*

He touched his harp, and nations heard, entranced,
As some vast river of unfailing source,
Rapid, exhaustless, deep, his numbers flowed,
And opened new fountains in the human heart.
—*Robert Pollok*

By music minds an equal temper know,
Nor swell too high nor sink too low;
If in the breast tumultous joys arise,
Music her soft assuasive voice applies,
Or when the soul is pressed with cares,
Exalts her in enlivening airs.
Warriors she fires with animated sounds,
Pours balm into the bleeding lovers' wounds,
Melancholy lifts her head,
Morpheus rouses from his bed,
Sloth unfolds her arms and wakes,
Listening envy drops her snakes.
Intestine war no more our passions wage,
And giddy factions bear away their rage.
—*Alexander Pope*

Music the fiercest grief can charm,
And fate's severest rage disarm.
Music can soften pain to ease,
And make despair and madness please;
Our joys below it can improve,
And antedate the bliss above.
—*Alexander Pope*

Light quirks of music, broken and uneven,
Make the soul dance upon a jig to Heav'n.
—*Alexander Pope*

Some to church repair,
Not for the doctrine, but the music there.
—*Alexander Pope*

Experience teaches that music does not remain where the devil rules, for the wicked are not worthy of the art.
—*Praetorius*

Musical compositions, it should be remembered, do not inhabit certain countries, certain museums, like paintings and statues. The Mozart Quintet is not shut up in Salzburg: I have it in my pocket.
—*Henri Rabaud*

Music is not a science any more than poetry is. It is a sublime instinct, like genius of all kinds. —*Louise De La Ramé*

The works of those who have stood the tests of ages have a claim to that respect and veneration which no modern can pretend. The duration and stability of their fame is sufficient to evince that it has not been suspended upon the slender thread of fashion and caprice, but bound to the heart by every tie of sympathetic approbation.
—*Sir Joshua Reynolds*

Art thou the evening breeze of this life, or the morning air of the future?
—*Jean Paul Richter*

Music is the poetry of the air.
—*Richter*

Forever old, forever young,
Immortal Music—Voice divine
Heard clearly, purely, here among
All tongues—thou Universal Tongue—
Since Morning Stars together sung,
Our souls are one with thee!
—*James Whitcomb Riley*

Music is for certain among us, more than a pleasure; it is a necessity.
—*Romain Rolland*

Let the love for literature, painting, sculpture, architecture and, above all, music, enter into your lives. —*Theodore Roosevelt*

All one's life is music, if one touches the notes rightly, and in time. —*Ruskin*

Music is the nearest at hand, the most orderly, the most delicate, and the most perfect, of all bodily pleasures. —*Ruskin*

And Saul's servants said unto him, Behold now, an evil spirit from God troubleth thee. Let our Lord now command thy servants, which are before thee, to seek out a man who is a cunning player upon the harp: and it shall come to pass, when the evil spirit from God is upon thee, that he shall play with his hand, and thou shalt be well.
I Samuel 16:15-16

Music is a shower-bath of the soul, washing away all that is impure.
—*Schopenhauer*

In music it is as with chess-playing—The Queen, melody, possesses supreme power; but it is the King, harmony, who ultimately decides. —*Schumann*

Major is the active and masculine; minor, the passive and feminine in music.
—*Schumann*

Play always as if a master were listening.
—*Schumann*

Ye pedlars in art, do ye not sink into the earth when ye are reminded of the words of Beethoven on his dying bed, "I believe I am yet but at the beginning"? —*Schumann*

There is a "reach" to music which the other arts have not; it seems to "get" you in an exhausted mood and quiets and refreshes where a book or a picture is not so sure.
—*Charles M. Schwab*

Ah Music, thou sweet sprite.
—*William Kean Seymour*

Give me some music. . . . . that piece of song,
That old and antique song we heard last
night;
Methought it did relieve my passion much,
More than light airs and recollected terms
Of these most brisk and giddy-paced times.
—*Shakespeare*

The man that hath no music in himself,
Nor is not moved with concord of sweet
sounds,
Is fit for treasons, stratagems, and spoils;
The motions of his spirit are dull as night,
And his affections dark as Erebus.
Let no such man be trusted.
—*Shakespeare*

When gripping grief the heart doth wound,
And doleful dumps the mind oppress,
Then music, with her silver sound,
With speedy help doth lend redress.
—*Shakespeare*

I pant for the music which is divine;
My heart in its thirst is a dying flower.
—Percy Bysshe Shelley

Music, when soft voices die,
Vibrates in the memory.
—Percy Bysshe Shelley

Every lovely fancy, every moment of delight, every thought and thrill of pleasure which music calls forth, or which already existing, is beautiful and hallowed by music, does not die. *—J. H. Shorthouse*

It will be in and through music that human thought will be carried beyond the point it has hitherto reached.
—J. H. Shorthouse

Musick! soft charm of heav'n and earth,
Whence didst thou borrow thy auspicious birth?
Or art thou of eternal date,
Sire to thyself, thyself as old as Fate?
—Edmund Smith

If I were to begin life again, I would devote it to music. It is the only cheap and unpunished rapture upon earth.
—Sydney Smith

Music: the paradise of the ears.
—Somaize

It is the funeral march. I did not think
That there had been such magic in sweet sounds!
—Robert Southey

The fine art which, more than any other, ministers to human welfare. Where there is beautiful music it is difficult for discontent to live. *—Herbert Spencer*

Just as my fingers on these keys
Make music, so the self-same sounds
On my spirit make a music, too.
—Wallace Stevens

Nature overflows with the raw material of music, but human art organizes this into musical strains. Here if ever man is face to face, ear to ear, heart to heart with God.
—J. W. Stimson

Lightlier move the minutes edged with music.
—Alfred Tennyson

There is sweet music here that softer falls
Than petals from blown roses on the grass,
Or night-dews on still waters between walls
Of shadowy granite, in a gleaming pass;
Music, that gentlier on the spirit lies
Than tired eyelids upon tired eyes;
Music that brings sweet sleep down from the blissful skies.
—Alfred Tennyson

Beethoven's music! From the mountain peaks
The strong, divine, compelling thunder rolls.
—Celia Thaxter

The God of Music dwelleth out of doors.
—Edith M. Thomas

Popular music, after all, is only familiar music. *—Theodore Thomas*

The human soul and music are alone eternal.
—George P. Upton

It is the universal language, which appeals to the universal heart of mankind.
—George P. Upton

Music is to the other arts, considered as a whole, what religion is to the church.
—Richard Wagner

Had I children, my utmost endeavors should be to make them musicians. Considering I have no ear, nor even thought of music, the preference seems odd, and yet it is embraced on frequent recollection. In short, as my aim would be to make them happy, I think it the most probable method. It is a resource which will last them their lives, unless they grow deaf; it depends upon themselves, not on others; always amuses and soothes, if not consoles; and of all fashionable pleasures, is the cheapest. *—Horace Walpole*

Lord, what music hast thou provided for thy saints in heaven, when thou affordest bad men such music on earth! *—Izaak Walton*

Nay, what is Nature's
Self, but an endless
Strife toward music,
Euphony, rhyme?
—William Watson

Since ever the world was fashioned,
Water, and air, and sod,
A music of divers meaning
Has flowed from the hand of God.
—F. E. Weatherly

What love is to man, music is to the arts and to mankind. Music is love itself,—it is the purest, most ethereal language of passion, showing in a thousand ways all possible changes of color and feeling.
K. M. von Weber

I see America go singing to her destiny.
—Walt Whitman

The man who disparages music as a luxury and non-essential is doing the nation an injury. Music now, more than ever before, is a national need. There is no better way to express patriotism than through music.
—Woodrow Wilson

The music in my heart I bore,
Long after it was heard no more.
—William Wordsworth

NEW YEAR'S DAY

Then welcome, welcome, glad New Year!
Dawn brightly on us all,
And bring us hope, our hearts to cheer,
Whatever may befall;
Bring patience, comfort, gladness, rest;
Bring blessings from above;
Bring happiness—the highest, best—
To us and those we love.

—Anon.

The tugging ship is unmoored; her sails are filling with the breeze; she sniffs the spray in her nostrils; her rigging grows taut like giant muscles; the course is set; the pilot is at the helm—the New Year is outward bound!

—W. W. W. Argow

It were good, therefore, that men, in their innovations, would follow the example of time itself, which indeed innovateth greatly, but quietly, and by degrees scarce to be perceived; for otherwise whatever is new is unlooked for; and ever it mends some and pains others; and he that is holpen takes it for a fortune, and thanks the time; and he that is hurt, for a wrong, and imputeth it to the author. *—Francis Bacon*

Now the New Year comes and the Old takes flight;
Dear God of our years, be close tonight!

—Mary Baldwin

Time flows from instants, and of these each one
Should be esteem'd as if it were alone;
The shortest space, which we so highly prize
When it is coming, and before our eyes,
Let it but slide into th' eternal main,
No realms, no worlds, can purchase it again.

—John Beaumont

Why slander we the times?
What crimes
Have days and years, that we
Thus charge them with iniquity?
. . . .
If thy desire it be
To see
The times prove good, be thou
But such thyself, and surely know
That all thy days to thee
Shall, spite of mischief, happy be.

—Joseph Beaumont

I see not a step before me as I tread on another year;
But I've left the Past in God's keeping—the Future His mercy shall clear;
And what looks dark in the distance, may brighten as I draw near.

—Mary Gardiner Brainard

Time! Time! in thy triumphal flight
How all life's phantoms fleet away!

—James Gordon Brooks

An' here's the Old Year goin' out before it's fair begun!
Heigh-ho!—Well, here's a Happy New Year to ye, all an' one!

—Alice Williams Brotherton

God's in His Heaven—
All's right with the world!

—Robert Browning

Even while we sing, he smiles his last,
And leaves our sphere behind.
The good Old Year is with the past,
O be the New as kind!

—William Cullen Bryant

Time! the corrector when our judgments err.

—Lord Byron

Out upon Time! It will leave no more
Of the things to come than the things before!
Out upon Time! who forever will leave
But enough of the past for the future to grieve.

—Lord Byron

Think'st thou existence doth depend on time?
It doth; but actions are our epochs.

—Lord Byron

On wide wing floats the angel Time,
That everlasting rover;
I listen for the midnight chime—
Twelve strokes—the year is over!
The stars shine clear above my roof,
The fire burns bright thereunder;
I think of the past year's mingled woof
Of sorrow, fear, and wonder.

—C.

That great mystery of TIME, were there no other; the illimitable, silent, never-resting thing called Time, rolling, rushing on, swift, silent, like an all-embracing ocean tide, on which we and all the Universe swim like exhalations, like apparitions which *are*, and then *are not*: this is forever very literally a miracle; a thing to strike us dumb,—for we have no word to speak about it. *—Carlyle*

I'll turn over a new leaf.

—Miguel de Cervantes

The value of moments, when cast up, is immense, if well employed; if thrown away, their loss is irrevocable.

—Lord Chesterfield

No! no arresting the vast wheel of time,
That round and round still turns with onward might.
—*Charles Cowden Clarke*

A happy new year! A happy new year to my dear country, the land of old integrity and truth! A happy new year to friends and enemies, Christians and Turks, Hottentots and Cannibals! To all on whom God permits his sun to rise and his rain to fall!
—*Matthias Claudius*

The merry year is born
Like the bright berry from the naked thorn.
—*Hartley Coleridge*

Time is the most undefinable yet paradoxical of things: the past is gone, the future is not come, and the present becomes the past even while we attempt to define it, and, like the flash of lightning, at once exists and expires. —*Charles Caleb Colton*

Time, the cradle of hope. . . Wisdom walks before it, opportunity with it, and repentance behind it: he that has made it his friend will have little to fear from his enemies, but he that has made it his enemy will have little to hope from his friends.
—*Charles Caleb Colton*

Then a welcome and cheer to the merry New Year!
While the holly gleams above us!
With a pardon for the foes who hate,
And a prayer for those who love us.
—*Eliza Cook*

A song for the Old, while its knell is tolled,
And its parting moments fly!
But a song and a cheer for the glad New Year,
While we watch the Old Year die!
—*George Cooper*

Let the ills we met,
And the sad regret,
With the Old be buried deep;
For what joy untold
Doth the New Year hold,
And what hopes within it sleep!
—*George Cooper*

Who comes dancing over the snow,
His soft little feet all bare and rosy?
Open the door, though the wild winds blow,
Take the child in and make him cozy.
Take him in and hold him dear,
He is the wonderful glad New Year.
—*Dinah Maria Mulock Craik*

I asked the New Year, "What am I to do
The whole year through?"
The answer came,
"Be true."
—*Grace Noll Crowell*

The new year begins in a snow-storm of white vows. —*George William Curtis*

"Happy New Year! happy New Year!" It is the day of hope and a fresh beginning. . . Ring out the old, ring in the new!
—*George William Curtis*

Old Time, that greatest and longest established spinner of all! . . . . his factory is a secret place, his work is noiseless, and his hands are mutes. —*Charles Dickens*

Time goes, you say? Ah no!
Alas, Time stays, *we* go.
—*Austin Dobson*

Let this auspicious morning be express'd
With a white stone distinguish'd from the rest,
White as thy fame, and as thy honour clear;
And let new joys attend on thy new-added date.
—*Dryden*

She shakes the rubbish from her mounting brow,
And seems to have renew'd her charter's date.
—*Dryden*

And now time's whiter series is begun,
Which in soft centuries shall smoothly run.
—*Dryden*

Time glides with undiscover'd haste;
The future but a length behind the past.
—*Dryden*

The specious panorama of a year
But multiplies the image of a day,—
A belt of mirrors round a taper's flame;
And universal Nature, through her vast
And crowded whole, an infinite paroquet,
Repeats one note.
—*Emerson*

As the bird trims her to the gale,
I trim myself to the storm of time,
I man the rudder, reef the sail,
Obey the voice at eve obeyed at prime:
"Lowly faithful, banish fear,
Right onward drive unharmed;
The port, well worth the cruise, is near,
And every wave is charmed."
—*Emerson*

And with the bells a New Year has begun;
Then beams the dawn of Hope, the night is done.
—*Thomas Hornsby Ferril*

Whether we wake or we sleep,
Whether we carol or weep,
The Sun with his Planets in chime,
Marketh the going of Time.
—*Edward Fitzgerald*

Dost thou love life? Then waste not time, for time is the stuff that life is made of.
—Benjamin Franklin

My inheritance how lordly wide and fair:
Time is my fair seed-field, to Time I'm heir.
—Goethe

Thus at Time's humming loom I ply.
—Goethe

The Old Year goes away; her eyes are sad—
The eyes of one who hopes or fears no more.
. . . .
The New Year enters in: a happy child,
Who looks for flowers to fill her outstretched hand,
And knows not fear although the winds be wild.
—Mary Gorges

Time! where didst thou those years inter
Which I have seene decease?
—William Habington

The present point of time is all thou hast:
The future doubtful, and the former past.
—Walter Harte

Ring, joyous chords! ring out again!
A swifter still, and a wilder strain!
And bring fresh wreaths! we will banish all
Save the free in heart from our festive hall.
—Felicia Hemans

Gather ye rose-buds while ye may;
Old Time is still a-flying;
And this same flower that smiles today,
Tomorrow will be dying.
—Robert Herrick

Old Time, in whose banks we deposit our notes
Is a miser who always wants guineas for groats;
He keeps all his customers still in arrears
By lending them minutes and charging them years.
—Oliver Wendell Holmes

For hark! the last chime of the dial has ceased,
And Old Time, who his leisure to cozen,
Has finish'd the Months, like the flasks at a feast,
Is preparing to tap a fresh dozen!
—Thomas Hood

And ye, who have met with Adversity's blast,
And been bow'd to the earth by its fury;
To whom the Twelve Months, that have recently pass'd
Were as harsh as a prejudiced jury—
Still, fill to the Future! and join in our chime,
The regrets of remembrance to cozen,
And having obtained a New Trial of Time,
Shout in hopes of a kindlier dozen.
—Thomas Hood

Wait thou for Time; it hath a sorcerer's power
To dim life's mockeries that gayly shine,
To lift the veil of seeming from the real,
Bring to thy soul a rich or fearful dower,
Write golden tracery on the sands of life,
And raise the drooping heart from scenes ideal
To a high purpose in the world of strife:
Wait thou for Time!
—Lucy Hooper

Years, following years, steal something every day;
At last thev steal us from ourselves away.
—Horace

Hark! bells of midnight are tolling the end!
Horns and loud whistles their choruses blend!
. . . .
Off with the old one, then, on with the new!
. . . .
Happy New Year—many, many!—to you!
—William Addison Houghton

What a mighty sum of events has been consummated; what a tide of passions and affections has flowed; what lives and deaths have alternately arrived; what destinies have been fixed forever! Once more our planet has completed one of those journeys in the heavens which perfect all the fruitful changes of its peopled surface, and mete out the few stages of our existence; and every day, every hour of that progress, has in all her wide lands, in all her million hearts, left traces that eternity shall behold. *—William Howitt*

The Old Year's heart its hopes laid down,
As in a grave; but, trusting, said:
"The flowers of the New Year's crown
Bloom from the ashes of the dead."
—Helen Hunt Jackson

The vicious count their years; virtuous, their acts. *—Samuel Johnson*

Sad, sad to think that the year is all but done.
—Charles Kingsley

Of all sounds, of all bells most solemn and touching, is the peal which rings out the Old Year. I never hear it without a gathering up of my mind to a concentration of all the images that have diffused over the past twelve-month. I begin to know the worth of that regretted time, as when a person dies.
—Charles Lamb

Beautiful is the year in its coming and in its going. *—Lucy Larcom*

"A New Year's gift to the world," said the Frost,
"Rich lace curtains which nothing cost."
—Charles Godfrey Leland

Then, too, the Old Year dieth,
And the forests utter a moan,
Like the voice of one who crieth
In the wilderness alone,
"Vex not his ghost!"

—*Longfellow*

Twelve throbs that tolled the zenith of the dark,
And mornward now the starry hands move on;
"Mornward!" the angelic watchers say,
"Passed is the sorest trial;
No plot of man can stay
The hand upon the dial;
Night is the dark stem of the lily Day."

—*James Russell Lowell*

New Year's eve is like every other night; there is no pause in the march of the universe, no breathless moment of silence among created things that the passage of another twelve months may be noted; and yet no man has quite the same thoughts this evening that come with the coming of darkness on other nights. —*Hamilton Wright Mabie*

With what a leaden and retarding weight
Does expectation load the wing of time!

—*William Mason*

A good New Year! Oh, let us all begin it
With cheerful faces turning to the light!

—*E. Matheson*

The old year is dead, and from its ashes blossoms bright
New Phoenix, spreading wings o'er the heavens far and near.

—*Adam Mickiewicz*

The old goes out, but the glad young year
Comes merrily in tomorrow.

—*Emily Huntington Miller*

Fly, envious time,
Call on the lazy leaden-stepping hours,
Whose speed is but the heavy plummet's pace.

—*Milton*

Swift years! but teach me how to bear,
To feel and act with strength and skill;
To reason wisely, nobly dare,
And speed your courses as you will.

—*A. Norton*

Old Time, who changes all below,
To wean men gently for the grave,
Hath brought us no increase of woe,
And leaves us all he ever gave.

—*Caroline Elizabeth Sarah Norton*

God bless our generation,
Who live both far and near,
And we wish them a happy, a happy New Year!

—*Old Carol*

God bless the Master of this house,
Likewise the Mistress too,
And all the little children
That round the table go.
Love and joy come to you,
And to you your wassail too,
And God bless you, and send you
A happy New Year.

—*Old English*

If New Year's Eve night-wind blow south,
It betokeneth warmth and growth;
If west, much milk, and fish in the sea:
If north, much cold and storms there will be;
If east, the trees will bear much fruit;
If north-east, flee it, man and brute.

—*Old English*

Now fare ye well for all this year,
Yet for my sake make ye good cheer!
Now have good day!

—*Old Manuscript*

Now the New Year reviving old Desires,
The thoughtful Soul to Solitude retires.

—*Omar Khayyam*

Let your past be not a ball and chain tied to your ankle to keep you back, but a journal to tell you what road you have traveled. Then, looking back only long enough to see where you are and what your course should be, forget the things that are behind and press forward.

—*Editorial. Outlook January 4, 1908*

You can make your New Year a happy New Year by forgetting the enmities and remembering the friendships, forgetting the failures and remembering the successes, forgetting the defeats and remembering the victories, forgetting the bitterness in sorrow and remembering its consolations.

—*Editorial. Outlook January 4, 1908*

E'en times are in perpetual flux, and run
Like rivers from their fountains, rolling on:
For time, no more than streams, is at a stay;
The flying hour is ever on her way;
And as the fountains still supply their store,
The wave behind impels the wave before;
Thus in successive course the minutes run,
And urge their predecessor minutes on,
Still moving ever new: for former things
Are laid aside, like abdicated kings;
And every moment alters what is done,
And innovates some act till then unknown.

—*Ovid*

It dies, the old year dies; and down the steep
Cold spaces of the sky there comes a word
That bids the new year rise.

—*Gilbert Parker*

O Time! whose verdicts mock our own,
The only righteous judge art thou.

—*Thomas William Parsons*

The present is our own; but while we speak,
We cease from its possession, and resign
The stage we tread on, to another race,
As vain, and gay, and mortal as ourselves.
—*Thomas Love Peacock*

"New leaves, to be sure! Let them turn them that are ashamed of their old ones."
—*Edward Payson Powell*

The Old Year has gone. Let the dead past bury its own dead. The New Year has taken possession of the clock of time. All hail the duties and possibilities of the coming twelve months!
—*Edward Payson Powell*

A casket with its gifts concealed—
This is the Year that for you waits
Beyond to-morrow's mystic gates.
—*Horatio Nelson Powers*

Gone! gone forever!—like a rushing wave
Another year has burst upon the shore
Of earthly being—and its last low tones,
Wandering in broken accents in the air,
Are dying to an echo.
—*George D. Prentice*

Do not crouch today, and worship
The old Past whose life is fled:
Hush your voice with tender reverence;
Crowned he lies, but cold and dead:
For the Present reigns our monarch,
With an added weight of hours:
Honor her, for she is mighty!
Honor her, for she is ours!
—*Adelaide A. Procter*

Let but the perfect Present, hour by hour,
Itself remember and itself repeat.
—*Adelaide A. Procter*

Shine, ye stars of heaven,
On the hours' slow flight!
See how Time, rewarding,
Gilds good deeds with light.
—*Adelaide A. Procter*

Noble things the great Past promised;
Holy dreams both strange and new;
But the Present shall fulfil them,
What he promised, she shall do.
—*Adelaide A. Procter*

Touch us gently, Time!
Let us glide adown thy stream
Gently,—as we sometimes glide
Through a quiet dream!
—*Bryan Waller Procter*

New Year, coming on apace,
What have you to give me?
Bring you scathe, or bring you grace,
Face me with an honest face;
You shall not deceive me.
—*Christina Rossetti*

"I bring you, friends, what the years have brought
Since ever men toiled, aspired, or thought—
Days for labor, and nights for rest;
And I bring you love, a heaven-born guest;
Space to work in, and work to do,
And faith in that which is pure and true.
Hold me in honor and greet me dear,
And sooth you'll find me a Happy Year."
—*Margaret E. Sangster*

O tell us, Year—we are fain to know—
What is thy charm that we hail thee so?
—*Margaret E. Sangster*

Time flies on restless pinions—constant never.
—*Schiller*

Threefold the stride of Time, from first to last:
Loitering slow, the Future creepeth—
Arrow-swift, the Present sweepeth—
And motionless forever stands the Past.
—*Schiller*

Speed the New Year, O ye attendant Hours!
Bring garlands, O ye fairy-footed Graces!
—*Clinton Scollard*

Time rolls his ceaseless course.
—*Sir Walter Scott*

See the minutes, how they run,
How many make the hour full complete;
How many hours bring about the day;
How many days will finish up the year;
How many years a mortal man may live.
—*Shakespeare*

Thy registers and thee I both defy,
Not wondering at the present nor the past;
For thy records and what we see doth lie.
Made more or less by thy continual haste;
This I do vow, and this shall ever be,
I will be true, despite thy scythe and thee.
—*Shakespeare*

Time is like a fashionable host,
That slightly shakes his parting guest by th' hand,
But with his arms outstretch'd, as he would fly,
Grasps in the comer: Welcome ever smiles,
And Farewell goes out sighing.
—*Shakespeare*

The swift years slip and slide adown the steep;
The slow years pass; neither will come again.
—*William Sharp*

The warm sun is failing, the bleak wind is wailing,
The bare boughs are sighing, the pale flowers are dying;
And the year
On the earth her deathbed, in a shroud of leaves dead,
Is lying.
Come, months, come away,
From November to May,
In your saddest array;
Follow the bier
Of the dead cold year,
And like dim shadows watch by her sepulchre.
—Shelley

As the wild air stirs and sways
The tree-swung cradle of a child,
So the breath of these rude days
Rocks the year:—be calm and mild,
Trembling hours; she will arise
With new love within her eyes.
—Shelley

The flood of time is rolling on;
We stand upon its brink, whilst *they* are gone
To glide in peace down death's mysterious stream.
Have ye done well?
—Shelley

"Orphan Hours, the Year is dead:
Come and sigh, come and weep."
"Merry Hours, smile instead,
For the Year is but asleep.
See, it smiles as it is sleeping,
Mocking your untimely weeping."
—Shelley

Time goes by turns, and chances change by course,
From foul to fair, from better hap to worse.
—Robert Southwell

Time wears all his locks before;
Take thy hold upon his forehead;
When he flies, he turns no more,
And behind his scalp is naked.
Works adjourn'd have many stays;
Long demurs breed new delays.
—Robert Southwell

"Just like the old page that God turned," I cried,
"This new one, too, is all alight with stars!"
—Violet Alleyn Storey

Time is painted with a lock before, and bald behind, signifying thereby that we must take time by the forelock; for, when it is once past, there is no recalling it.
—Swift

A wonderful stream is the River Time,
As it runs through the realms of Tears,
With a faultless rhythm, and a musical rhyme,
And a broader sweep, and a surge sublime
As it blends with the ocean of Years.
—Benjamin F. Taylor

I am the New Year, and I come to you pure and unstained,
Fresh from the hand of God.

....

All that I have I give with love unspoken.
All that I ask—*you keep the faith unbroken!*
—J. D. Templeton

Old year, you must not die;
You came to us so readily,
You lived with us so steadily,
Old year, you shall not die.
—Alfred Tennyson

The night is starry and cold, my friend,
And the New-year blithe and bold, my friend,
Comes up to take his own.
—Alfred Tennyson

Ring out the old, ring in the new,
Ring, happy bells, across the snow;
The year is going, let him go;
Ring out the false, ring in the true.
—Alfred Tennyson

Ring in the valiant man and free,
The larger heart, the kindlier hand;
Ring out the darkness of the land,
Ring in the Christ that is to be.
—Alfred Tennyson

I stood on a tower in the wet,
And New Year and Old Year met,
And winds were roaring and blowing:
And I said, "O years, that meet in tears,
Have ye aught that is worth the knowing?
Science enough and exploring,
Wanderers coming and going,
Matter enough for deploring,
But aught that is worth the knowing?"
—Alfred Tennyson

Time passes, Time the consoler, Time the anodyne.
—William Makepeace Thackeray

Behold, she stands and waits, the youthful Year!
A breeze of morning breathes about her brow;
She holds the storm and sunshine, bliss and fear,
Blossoms and fruit upon the ending boughs,
She brings these gifts. What blessing wilt thou choose?
—Celia Thaxter

I went to the throne, with trembling heart.
The year was done.
"Have you a New Year for me, dear Master?
I have spoiled this one!"
He took my year, all soiled and blotted
And gave me a new one, all unspotted,
Then, into my tired heart he smiled:
"Do better now, my child!"
—Unknown

Over the threshold a gallant new-comer
  Steppeth with tread that is loyal to see;
White as the winter-time, rosy as summer,
  Hope in his eyes, and with laugh ringing free.
Lo! in his hands there are gifts overflowing,
  Promises, prophecies, come in his train;
O'er him the dawn in its beauty is glowing,
  Banishing shadows of sorrow and pain.

—Unknown

Good-bye, Old Year! Tried, trusty friend, thy tale at last is told;
O New Year! write thou thine for us in lines of brightest gold.

—Unknown

Our time consumes like smoke, and posts away;
Nor can we treasure up a month or day:
The sand within the transitory glass
Doth haste, and so our silent minutes pass.

—Rowland Watkyns

Onward the chariot of the Untarrying moves;
  Nor day divulges him nor night conceals;
Thou hearest the echo of unreturning hooves
  And thunder of irrevocable wheels.

—William Watson

The great eventful Present hides the Past; but through the din
Of its loud life hints and echoes from the life behind steal in.

—Whittier

We meet today
To thank Thee for the era done,
And trust Thee for the opening one.

—Whittier

This is the New Year, entering
Our house. Who knows what it may bring?
The times are strange; all this tonight
Of bells and horns and whirling light
May be the drums and flags unfurled
Of an unknown, new-builded world.

—Margaret Widdemer

For look! how the light of the New Year is gilding
  The worn, wan face of the bruised old world!

—Ella Wheeler Wilcox

Fleetly hath passed the year; the seasons came
Duly as they were wont,—the gentle Spring,
And the delicious Summer, and the cool
Rich Autumn, with the nodding of the grain,
And Winter, like an old and hoary man,
Frosty and stiff,—and so are chronicled.

—Nathaniel Parker Willis

God stands winding his lonely horn,
And time and the world are ever in flight.

—W. B. Yeats

Each moment has its sickle, emulous
Of Time's enormous scythe, whose ample sweep
Strikes empires from the root.

—Edward Young

Time, in advance, behind him hides his wings,
And seems to creep decrepit with his age;
Behold him when past by: what then is seen,
But his broad pinions swifter than the winds?

—Edward Young

PATRIOTISM

He who looks with pride upon this history which his fathers have written by their heroic deeds, who accepts with gratitude the inheritance which they have bequeathed to him, and who highly resolves to preserve this inheritance unimpaired and to pass it on to his descendants enlarged and enriched, is a true American, be his birthplace or his parentage what it may. —*Lyman Abbott*

A nation is made great, not by its fruitful acres, but by the men who cultivate them; not by its great forests, but by the men who use them; not by its mines, but by the men who build and run them. America was a great land when Columbus discovered it; Americans have made of it a great nation.
—*Lyman Abbott*

O liberty! thou goddess heavenly bright,
Profuse of bliss, and pregnant with delight!
—*Addison*

Let freedom never perish in your hands,
But piously transmit it to your children.
—*Addison*

But what avail her unexhausted stores,
Her blooming mountains, and her sunny shores,
With all the gifts that heaven and earth impart,
The smiles of nature and the charms of art,
While proud oppression in her valleys reigns,
And tyranny usurps her happy plains?
—*Addison*

O Liberty, white Goddess! is it well
To leave the gates unguarded? On thy breast
Fold Sorrow's children, soothe the hurts of fate,
Lift the down-trodden, but with hand of steel
Stay those who to thy sacred portals come
To waste the gifts of freedom.
—*Thomas Bailey Aldrich*

America is rising with a giant's strength. Its bones are yet but cartilages.
—*Fisher Ames*

Laws, freedom, truth, and faith in God
Came with those exiles o'er the waves;
And, where their pilgrim feet have trod,
The God they trusted guards their graves.
—*Leonard Bacon*

America! half-brother of the world!
With something good and bad of every land.
—*Philip James Bailey*

For, O America, our country! —land
Hid in the west through centuries, till men
Through countless tyrannies could understand
The priceless worth of freedom,—once again
The world was new-created when thy shore
First knew the Pilgrim keels.
—*Arlo Bates*

America! America!
God mend thine every flaw,
Confirm thy soul in self-control,
Thy liberty in law!
—*Katharine Lee Bates*

Let power and justice side by side
Bring civil peace and civic pride;
Still may the ancient order bide
Of law and liberty.
—*Louis F. Benson*

"Freedom!" their battle-cry,—
"Freedom! or leave to die!"
Ah! and they meant the word,
Not as with us 'tis heard,
Not a mere party shout:
They gave their spirits out;
Trusted the end to God.
—*George Henry Boker*

Our country, made under Washington, saved under Lincoln, it is ours to keep it.
—*Edwin C. Bolles*

Give us, again, leaders of courage, men of vision, men who believe that right makes might, men with faith in the efficiency, the strength, the permanency and the ultimate triumph of this blessed old Republic.
—*William E. Borah*

This is the Land we love, our heritage,
Strange mixture of the gross and fine, yet sage
And full of promise,—destined to be great.
—*Robert Bridges ("Droch")*

In a nation like ours, where the government is founded upon the principle of equality and derives its just powers from the consent of the governed; in a land like ours, where every citizen is a sovereign and where no one cares to wear a crown—every year presents a battlefield, and every day brings forth occasion for the display of a patriotism whose essence is service.
—*William Jennings Bryan*

What heroes from the woodland sprung,
When, through the fresh-awakened land,
The thrilling cry of freedom rung.
—*William Cullen Bryant*

Great were the hearts, and strong the minds,
Of those who framed, in high debate,
The immortal league of love that binds
Our fair broad empire, state with state.
—*William Cullen Bryant*

Our country is not the only thing to which we owe our allegiance. It is also owed to justice and to humanity. Patriotism consists not in waving the flag, but in striving that our country shall be righteous as well as strong. —*James Bryce*

Liberty, such as deserves the name, is an honest, equitable, diffusive, and impartial principle. It is a great and enlarged virtue, and not a sordid, selfish, and illiberal vice. It is the portion of the mass of the citizens, and not the haughty license of some potent individual or some predominant faction.
—*Edmund Burke*

In a free country, every man thinks he has a concern in all public matters; that he has a right to form and a right to deliver an opinion upon them. They sift, examine, and discuss them. They are curious, eager, attentive, and jealous; and by making such matters the daily subjects of their thoughts and discoveries, vast numbers contract a very tolerable knowledge of them, and some a very considerable one. And this it is that fills free countries with men of ability in all stations. Whereas in other countries, none but men whose office calls them to it having not much care or thought about public affairs, and not daring to try the force of their opinions with one another, ability of this sort is extremely rare in any station in life.
—*Edmund Burke*

For Freedom outlives the old crowns of the earth,
And Freedom shall triumph forever.
—*Hezekiah Butterworth*

For Freedom's battle, once begun,
Bequeathed from bleeding sire to son,
Though baffled yet, is ever won.
—*Lord Byron*

The very essence of a free government consists in considering offices as public trusts, bestowed for the good of the country, and not for the benefit of an individual or party.
—*John C. Calhoun*

Is American Independence over when the last Fourth of July rocket dies in the darkness? Independence ascends stage by stage, from its infancy in political freedom, on toward a vigorous youth of material and economic emancipation, while the Delectable Mountains of the future beckon us to a national maturity of moral liberty and social redemption. —*W. J. Cameron*

Peace! Independence! Truth! go forth
Earth's compass round;
And your high priesthood shall make earth
All hallowed ground.
—*Thomas Campbell*

Nothing so sweete as is our countrie's earth,
And joy of those from whom we claime our birth.
George Chapman

Freedom has a thousand charms to show,
That slaves, howe'er contented, never know.
—*Cowper*

He is the freeman whom the truth makes free,
And all are slaves beside.
—*Cowper*

They held—to be free is the birthright of man. —*Arthur Cleveland Coxe*

To Thee we pray: Bless us and keep us free;
All that is past forgive;
Teach us henceforth to live
That, through our country we may honor Thee.
—*Francis Marion Crawford*

It is the common fate of the indolent to see their rights become a prey to the active. The condition upon which God hath given liberty to man is eternal vigilance; which condition if he break, servitude is at once the consequence of his crime and the punishment of his guilt. —*John Philpot Curran*

A man's country is not a certain area of land, but it is a principle; and patriotism is loyalty to that principle.
—*George William Curtis*

We of America, with our soil sanctified and our symbol glorified by the great ideas of liberty and religion,—love of freedom and love of God,—are in the foremost vanguard of this great caravan of humanity. . . Our heritage is all the love and heroism of liberty in the past; and all the great of the Old World are our teachers.
—*George William Curtis*

Much is being said and written about saving the democracies. The best and wisest way to save our democracy is to use it. You are the sovereign people. The gentlemen in the government and in Congress are the servants of the people. Do not forget this important fact. And do not let them forget it.
—*Dorothy Detzer*

Some laws there are too sacred for the hand
Of man to approach: recorded in the blood
Of patriots, before which, as the Rood
Of faith, devotional we take our stand;
Time-hallowed laws! Magnificently planned
When Freedom was the nurse of public good,
And Power paternal: laws that have withstood
All storms, unshaken bulwarks of the land!
Free will, frank speech, an undissembling mind,
Without which Freedom dies and laws are vain,
On such we found our rights, to such we cling;
In them shall power his surest safeguard find.
Tread them not down in passion or disdain;
Make man a reptile, he will turn and sting.

—Aubrey de Vere

I repeat . . . that all power is a trust; that we are accountable for its exercise; that from the people and for the people all springs, and all must exist. *—Benjamin Disraeli*

O freedom! first delight of human kind!

—Dryden

Patriots, in peace, assert the people's right,
With noble stubbornness resisting might.

—Dryden

Americans believe. . . In the dignity and strength of common human nature and therefore in democracy and its ultimate triumph.

—Charles W. Eliot

Those persons who are burning to display heroism may rest assured that the course of social evolution will offer them every opportunity. *—Havelock Ellis*

By the rude bridge that arched the flood,
Their flag to April's breeze unfurled,
Here once the embattled farmers stood,
And fired the shot heard round the world.

—Emerson

For what avail the plough or sail,
Or land or life, if freedom fail?

—Emerson

United States! the ages plead—
Present and Past in under-song,—
Go put your creed into your deed,
Nor speak with double tongue.

—Emerson

Ye sons of Columbia, unite in the cause
Of liberty, justice, religion, and laws.

—Thomas Green Fessenden

My country! if a wretch shall e'er arise
Out of thy countless sons, who would curtail
Thy freedom, dim thy glory,—while he lives
May all earth's peoples curse him.

—Festus

If our country is worth dying for in time of war let us resolve that it is truly worth living for in time of peace.

—Hamilton Fish

He is a poor patriot whose patriotism does not enable him to understand how all men everywhere feel about their altars and their hearthstones, their flags and their fatherland.

—Harry Emerson Fosdick

They that can give up essential liberty to obtain a little temporary safety deserve neither liberty nor safety. *—Benjamin Franklin*

For to all He gave
Eternal rights, which none may violate;
And, by a mighty hand, the oppressed He yet shall save!

—William Lloyd Garrison

Liberty is worth whatever the best civilization is worth. *—Henry Giles*

National injustice is the surest road to national downfall.

—William Ewart Gladstone

I have always regarded that Constitution as the most remarkable work known to me in modern times to have been produced by the human intellect, at a single stroke (so to speak), in its application to political affairs.

—William Ewart Gladstone

Patriotism belongs to the men and women who are the conscience of a nation.

—Guy D. Goff

Ill fares the land, to hastening ills a prey,
Where wealth accumulates, and men decay.

—Oliver Goldsmith

Such is the patriot's boast where'er we roam:
His first, best country ever is his own.

—Oliver Goldsmith

If liberty, after being extinguished on the Continent, is suffered to expire here, whence is it ever to emerge in the midst of that thick night that will invest it?

—Robert Hall

The greatest glory of a free-born people
Is to transmit that freedom to their children.

—William Harvard

For Freedom is its own eternal law:
It makes its own conditions, and in storm
Or calm alike fulfils the unerring Will.
Let us not then despise it when it lies
Still as a sleeping lion, while a swarm
Of gnat-like evils hover round its head.

—John Hay

Please God we use, and not abuse
The land so hardly won!

—Caroline Hazard

The history of the world is none other than the progress of the consciousness of Freedom.
—*Georg Wilhelm Friedrich Hegel*

I know not what course others may take, but as for me, give me liberty, or give me death! —*Patrick Henry*

Citizen I—by birth or grant of court.
Yet am I citizen? What this estate
Which gives me right to share in my own rule,
And all my country's progress help dictate?
—*Leigh Mitchell Hodges*

Wake in our breasts the living fires,
The holy faith that warmed our sires.
—*Oliver Wendell Holmes*

Heaven keep her ever free,
Wide as o'er land and sea
Floats the fair emblem her heroes have won!
—*Oliver Wendell Holmes*

A nation is great not through dams in its rivers or its ships on the sea or the deposits in its banks. It is great by the moral fiber and character of its citizens. Nations die when these weaken. —*Herbert Hoover*

In the weaving of our destiny, the pattern may change, yet the woof and warp of our weaving must be those inspired ideals of unity, of ordered liberty, of equality of opportunity, of popular government, and of peace to which this Nation was dedicated.
—*Herbert Hoover*

The cause we supported was just, and was glorious;
When men fight for freedom, they must be victorious.
—*Joseph Hopkinson*

O Lord, stretch forth Thy mighty hand,
And guard and bless our fatherland.
—*W. Walsham How*

The American people will advance step by step, surely and inevitably, to a realization of their ideals, and nothing whatever will stand in the way in the course of time of that equality of opportunity and of equal rights before the law which the Declaration of Independence announced, and which the Constitution was intended to conserve.
—*Charles Evans Hughes*

A community is like a ship; every one ought to be prepared to take the helm.
—*Henrik Ibsen*

The patriot nearly always believes, or thinks he believes, that he desires the greatness of his country because his country stands for something intrinsically great and valuable. Where this conviction is absent we cannot speak of patriotism, but only of the cohesion of a wolf-pack. —*W. R. Inge*

When a man assumes a public trust, he should consider himself as public property.
—*Thomas Jefferson*

All private virtue is the public fund:
As that abounds, the state decays or thrives:
Each should contribute to the general stock,
And who lends most is most his country's friend.
—*Robert Jephson*

What constitutes a State?
Not high-raised battlement or laboured mound,
Thick wall or moated gate;
Not cities proud with spires and turrets crowned;
Not bays and broad-armed ports,
Where, laughing at the storm, rich navies ride;
Not starred and spangled courts,
Where low-browed baseness wafts perfume to pride.
No:—men, high-minded men,
With powers as far above dull brutes endued
In forest, brake, or den,
As beasts excel cold rocks and brambles rude,—
Men who their duties know,
But know their rights, and, knowing, dare maintain.
Prevent the long-aimed blow,
And crush the tyrant while they rend the chain;
These constitute a State.
—*Sir William Jones*

Those that by their deeds will make it known
Whose dignity they do sustain;
And life, state, glory, all they gain,
Count the republic's, not their own.
—*Ben Jonson*

Your world, by factions rent,
Shall watch this new world grow
. . . .
From east to western sea,
One nation—mine for me!
—*Arthur W. Jose*

In the long vista of the years to roll,
Let me not see my country's honour fade;
Oh! let me see our land retain its soul!
Her pride in Freedom, and not Freedom's shade.
—*John Keats*

O! thus be it ever, when freemen shall stand
Between their loved homes and the war's desolation!
Blest with victory and peace, may the heav'n rescued land
Praise the power that hath made and preserved us a nation.
—*Francis Scott Key*

All we have of freedom, all we use or know—
This our fathers bought for us long and long ago.

—Rudyard Kipling

Judge of the Nations, spare us yet,
Lest we forget—lest we forget!

—Rudyard Kipling

The world has never had a good definition of the word liberty, and the American people, just now, are much in want of one.

—Abraham Lincoln

I have never had a feeling politically that did not spring from the sentiments embodied in the Declaration of Independence.

—Abraham Lincoln

O Liberty! can man resign thee,
Once having felt thy generous flame?
Can dungeons, bolts, or bars confine thee,
Or whips thy noble spirit tame?

—Rouget de L'Isle

Mere vaporizing and boasting become a nation as little as a man. But honest, outspoken pride and faith in our country are infinitely better and more to be respected than the cultivated reserve which sets it down as ill-bred and in bad taste ever to refer to our country except by way of depreciation, criticism or general negation.

—Henry Cabot Lodge

Borne on the night-wind of the Past,
Through all our history, to the last,
In the hour of darkness and peril and need,
The people will waken and listen to hear
The hurrying hoof-beats of that steed,
And the midnight message of Paul Revere.

—Longfellow

Thou, too, sail on, O Ship of State!
Sail on, O Union, strong and great!
Humanity, with all its fears,
With all the hopes of future years,
Is hanging breathless on thy fate!

—Longfellow

It has been said so often and it is everlastingly true, that America is the best and last hope of mankind; and if we should fail—which God forbid; where in all the world may the broken spirit find refuge? Where beneath the shining heavens will there be found a haven for those who seek a land of Liberty?

—Frank O. Lowden

When a deed is done for Freedom, through the broad earth's aching breast,
Runs a thrill of joy prophetic, trembling on from east to west.

—James Russell Lowell

We need a type of patriotism that recognizes the virtues of those who are opposed to us. We must get away from the idea that America is to be the leader of the world in everything. She can lead in some things. The old "manifest destiny" idea ought to be modified so that each nation has the manifest destiny to do the best it can—and that without cant, without the assumption of self-righteousness and with a desire to learn to the uttermost from other nations.

—Francis John McConnell

What do we need to keep the nation whole,
To guard the pillars of the State? We need
The fine audacities of honest deed;
The homely old integrities of soul;
The swift temerities that take the part
Of outcast right—the wisdom of the heart.

—Edwin Markham

I touch my country's mind.

—John Masefield

The wretched have no country; that dear name
Comprises home, kind kindred, fostering friends,
Protecting laws, all that binds man to man.

—Charles Maturin

Nations grown corrupt
Love bondage more than liberty;
Bondage with ease than strenuous liberty.

—Milton

I would remember now
My country's goodliness, make sweet her name.

—William Vaughn Moody

Take, Freedom, take thy radiant round;
When dimmed, revive: when lost, return;
Till not a shrine through earth be found
On which thy glories shall not burn!

—Thomas Moore

When will the world shake off such yokes? oh, when
Will that redeeming day shine out on men
That shall behold them rise, erect and free,
As heav'n and nature meant mankind should be?

—Thomas Moore

Unite for the public safety, if you would remain an independent nation. *—Napoleon I*

Unite for the public safety, if you would remain an independent nation.

—Napoleon I

And we who have toiled for freedom's law, have we sought for freedom's soul?
Have we learned at last that human right is not a part but the whole?

—John Boyle O'Reilly

In a chariot of light from the regions of day,
The Goddess of Liberty came:
Ten thousand celestials directed the way
And hither conducted the dame.
—Thomas Paine

Those who expect to reap the blessings of freedom, must, like men, undergo the fatigue of supporting it. *—Thomas Paine*

A democracy,—that is a government of all the people, by all the people, for all the people; of course a government of the principles of eternal justice, the unchanging law of God; for shortness' sake I will call it the idea of Freedom.
—Theodore Parker

Pity the land whose law destroys
The reach of Thought, the quest of Truth,
In the heart of its radiant youth.
—Kathryn Peck

There is no other land like thee,
No dearer shore;
Thou art the shelter of the free;
The home, the port of liberty
Thou hast been, and shalt ever be,
Till time is o'er.
—James Gates Percival

Oh, let freemen be our sons!
—John Pierpont

He serves me most who serves his country best. *—Pope*

A country fit for liberty—
For men who love their fellow men.
—Woodbury Pulsifer

My Countrymen, hats off! with heart and will
Thank God that you are free, and then
Arise and don your nationhood like men.
—Roderic Quinn

A Nation born in fearlessness stands forth before the world
With God her shield, the Right her sword, and Freedom in her eyes.
—Wallace Rice

Our country cannot well subsist without liberty, nor liberty without virtue.
—Jean Jacques Rousseau

Help us to father a nation, strong
In the comradeship of an equal birth,
In the wealth of the richest bloods of earth.
—Robert Haven Schauffler

Breathes there a man with soul so dead
Who never to himself hath said,
This is my own, my native land!
Whose heart hath ne'er within him burn'd,
As home his footsteps he hath turn'd
From wandering on a foreign strand?
—Sir Walter Scott

To the love and favour of my country
Commit myself, my person and the cause.
—Shakespeare

I do love
My country's good with a respect more tender
More holy and profound than mine own life.
—Shakespeare

Not active trade and victorious armies, but religion and morality are the safeguards of freedom. *—Robert Payne Smith*

Long may our land be bright
With freedom's holy light;
Protect us by thy might,
Great God our King.
—Samuel Francis Smith

Thy spirit, Independence, let me share.
—Tobias Smollett

After all,
'Tis Freedom wears the loveliest coronal.
—Frank L. Stanton

And statesmen at her council met
Who knew the seasons when to take
Occasion by the hand, and make
The bounds of freedom wider yet.
—Alfred Tennyson

Hail! Independence, hail! Heaven's next best gift
To that of life and an immortal soul!
—James Thomson

O thou! by whose almighty nod the scale
Of empire rises, or alternate fails,
Send forth the saving virtues round the land
In bright patrol.
—James Thomson

A private man, however successful in his own dealing, if his country perish is involved in her destruction; but if he be an unprosperous citizen of a prosperous city, he is much more likely to recover. Seeing, then, that States can bear the misfortunes of individuals, but individuals cannot bear the misfortunes of States, let us all stand by our country. *—Thucydides*

Let me not faction's partial hate
Pursue to *this land's woe.*
—Unknown

So its home again, and home again, America for me!
My heart is turning home again, and there I long to be,
In the land of youth and freedom beyond the ocean bars,
Where the air is full of sunlight and the flag is full of stars.
—Henry van Dyke

O dearest country, is it well with thee
Indeed, and is thy soul in health?
—Henry van Dyke

My ardent desire is, and my aim has been, (as far as depended upon the executive department,) to comply strictly with *all* our engagements, foreign and domestic, but to keep the United States free from political connexions with *every* other country, to see them independent of *all* and under the influence of *none*. In a word, I want an *American* character, that the powers of Europe may be convinced we act for *ourselves,* and not for *others*. This, in my judgment, is the only way to be respected abroad and happy at home. —*George Washington*

The people's government, made for the people, made by the people, and answerable to the people. —*Daniel Webster*

May the sun in his course visit no land more free, more happy, more lovely, than this our own country! —*Daniel Webster*

Democracy is an experiment, and the right of the majority to rule is no more inherent than the right of the minority to rule; and unless the majority represents sane, righteous, unselfish public sentiment, it has no inherent right. —*William Allen White*

Around our gift of freedom draw
The safeguards of Thy righteous law.
—*John Greenleaf Whittier*

The Declaration of Independence . . . was a vital piece of practical business, not a piece of rhetoric. —*Woodrow Wilson*

Freedom exists only where the people take care of the government.
—*Woodrow Wilson*

America started right with a Declaration addressed to "a decent respect to the opinions of mankind." It is necessary that we get back to that fundamental belief.
—*Woodrow Wilson*

The commands of democracy are as imperative as its privileges and opportunities are wide and generous. Its compulsion is upon us. —*Woodrow Wilson*

For thou art founded in the eternal fact
That every man doth greaten with the act
Of freedom.
—*George Edward Woodberry*

Slaves who once conceive the glowing thought
Of freedom, in that hope itself possess
All that the contest calls for;—spirit, strength,
The scorn of danger, and united hearts,
The surest presage of the good they seek.
—*William Wordsworth*

PEACE DAY

Then sheathes in calm repose the vengeful blade,
For gentle peace in Freedom's hallowed shade.
—*John Quincy Adams*

A great Kingdom of Peace lies close at hand, ready to come into being if we would but turn toward it. To make it real is the task of the men and women who live upon the earth at this moment. —*Jane Addams*

From hence, let fierce contending nations know
What dire effects from civil discord flow.
—*Joseph Addison*

Although two thousand years have passed away,
We, in our vaunted peaceful Christian age,
See death, rapine and robbery hold sway,
And war's wild revelry of bloodshed rage,
At empire's call see life and freedom cease:
They make a solitude and call it peace.
—*James Allman*

War is honorable
In those who do their native rights maintain;
In those whose swords an iron barrier are
Between the lawless spoiler and the weak;
But is, in those who draw th' offensive blade
For added power or gain, sordid and despicable
As meanest office of the worldly churl.
—*Joanna Baillie*

If there is anything in which earth, more than any other, resembles hell, it is its wars.
—*Albert Barnes*

If we accept the philosophy that man has not the moral force and power to rise above his present obvious destiny, then by one more act of final universal folly he will have reached his goal of self-annihilation.
—*Richard B. Bennett*

War is not all war, and there lies the heart of the monster. —*Edmund Blunden*

War has been "found out," overwhelmingly found out. War is an ancient impostor, but none of his masks and smiles and gallant trumpets can any longer delude us; he leads the way through the cornfields to the cemetery of all that is best. The best is, indeed, his special prey. What men did in the battle of the Somme, day after day, and month after month, will never be excelled in honour, unselfishness, and love; except by those who come after and resolve that their experience shall never again fall to the lot of human beings. —*Edmund Blunden*

I should say that he who desires peace should speak of peace more often than of war. —*Aristide Briand*

Nothing has been done by war for the good of mankind that could not have been better accomplished by Peace.
—*Phillips Brooks*

I abominate war as unchristian. I hold it to be the greatest of human crimes, and to involve all others—violence, blood, rapine, fraud—everything that can deform the character, alter the nature, and debase the name of man. —*Lord Brougham*

The world is coming to understand that armies and navies, however numerous and strong, are impotent to stop thought.
—*William Jennings Bryan*

A warless world will come as men develop warless hearts. —*Charles Wesley Burns*

Let those who love turmoil arm for turmoil: their very arming will bring it; and let those who love peace disarm for peace: the disarming will hasten it.
—*John Burroughs*

It is not each nation's desire for national expression which makes peace impossible; it is the fact that thus far in the world's history such desire has been bound up with militarism. The nation whose frontier bristles with bayonets and with forts is like the individual with a magazine pistol in his pocket. Both make for murder. Both in their hearts really mean murder.
—*Nicholas Murray Butler*

There are enough young men and young women enrolled in the American colleges and universities today to require our Government quickly to take its proper place in rebuilding this broken world and in leading the way, as our instructed public opinion would so gladly have us do, in the restoration of prosperity at home and in the reestablishment of public confidence and peace throughout the world.
—*Nicholas Murray Butler*

And the sight
Of blood, which spouts through hoary scalps, is not,
To me, a thing of triumph, nor the death
Of men surprised, a glory.
—*Lord Byron*

All that the mind would shrink from, of excesses;
All that the body perpetrates, of bad;
All that we read, hear, dream, of man's distresses;
All that the devil would do, if run stark mad;

All that defies the worst which pen expresses;
All by which hell is peopled, or is sad
As hell—mere mortals who their power abuse—
Was here (as heretofore and since) let loose.
—*Lord Byron*

The possession of peace like ours is not a thing to be hugged in selfish enjoyment, it is endangered unless it can be shared.
—*W. J. Cameron*

There is one thing no people have ever done; that is, to oppose a threatening war with intelligent and vigorous purpose some years before it was due to arrive.
—*Carrie Chapman Catt*

War is nothing more than a reflection or image of the soul. It is the fiend within coming out.
—*William Ellery Channing*

Peace is the fairest form of happiness.
—*William Ellery Channing*

There are two ways of ending a dispute—discussion and force; the latter manner is simply that of the rude beasts; the former is proper to beings gifted with reason.
—*Cicero*

Oh for a lodge in some vast wilderness,
Some boundless contiguity of shade,
Where rumour of oppression and deceit,
Of unsuccessful or successful war,
Might never reach me more.
—*Cowper*

War is a game which were their subjects wise, kings would not play at.
—*Cowper*

Peace, daughter of a strife sublime,
Abide with us till strife be lost in endless time.
—*Francis Marion Crawford*

There may have been excuse for men of the stone age to use physical force for the preservation of their species, but none can defend such practices in the light of twentieth century civilization. . . . Man has eliminated many things that have stood in the path of the march of progress, but has continued to allow the most serious menace of all to loom large, as a hideous monster ready to strike at a moment's notice.
—*A. C. Davis*

Give me full charge of the education of the youth of this nation for the next twenty-five years and I will rear a race of men who would no more fight on the field of battle than they would offer human sacrifices on the altars of the gods.
—*John H. Dietrich*

Once we can transform moral sentiment to the point of stamping men who advocate violence in international affairs as criminals and outcasts, just as we stamp the men today who advocate violence within the nation, wars will be few and far between.
—*John H. Dietrich*

War is never a solution; it is an aggravation.
—*Benjamin Disraeli*

If there be greater calamity to human nature than famine, it is that of an exterminat-
—*Benjamin Disraeli*

And raw in fields the rude militia swarms,
Mouths without hands; maintain'd at vast expense,
In peace a charge, in war a weak defence.
—*Dryden*

War, he sung, is toil and trouble;
Honour but an empty bubble;
Never ending, still beginning,
Fighting still, and still destroying.
—*Dryden*

The patriot should never speak of war, but as the ruin of nations; the philanthropist, but as the ruin of men; the Christian, but as in utter and irreconcilable conflict with the principles and teachings of the Prince of Peace; and all, with honor and loathing, as the very spirit of a darker world, seeking to anticipate perdition in this.
—*Tryon Edwards*

The development of military technique is on such a scale that the life of human beings will prove unbearable, unless they soon find a way of averting war. —*Albert Einstein*

He who loves the bristle of bayonets only sees in the glitter what beforehand he feels in his heart. It is avarice and hatred; it is that quivering lip, that cold, hating eye, which built magazines and powder-houses.
—*Ralph Waldo Emerson*

Nothing can bring you peace but the triumph of principles.
—*Ralph Waldo Emerson*

If there is in the affairs of mortal men any one thing which it is proper to explode, and incumbent upon every man by every lawful means to avoid, to deprecate, to oppose, that one thing is, doubtless, war. —*Erasmus*

Peace—we shall have it soon on the same condition that we got war. We must fight for it in the moral sphere as we did in the physical sphere. Peace has been promised since the first night of Christianity only to men of good will.
Good will must be in the bottom of the heart; without it, it is only a sham peace.
—*Ferdinand Foch*

Organizations will stampede us into war again if we allow them to keep on.
—Henry Ford

I hate war for its consequences, for the lies it lives on and propagates, for the undying hatreds it arouses, for the dictatorships it puts in the place of democracies, and for the starvation that stalks after it. I hate war, and never again will I sanction or support another. *—Harry Emerson Fosdick*

Eternal God, Father of all Souls;
Grant unto us such clear vision of the sin of War,
That we may earnestly seek that
Co-operation between nations
Which alone can make War impossible.
—Harry Emerson Fosdick

Mad wars destroy in one year the works of many years of peace. *—Benjamin Franklin*

All wars are follies, very expensive and very mischievous ones. In my opinion, there never was a good war or a bad peace. When will mankind be convinced and agree to settle their difficulties by arbitration?
—Benjamin Franklin

You are not going to get peace with millions of armed men. The chariot of peace cannot advance over a road littered with cannon.
—David Lloyd George

A great war leaves the country with three armies—an army of cripples, an army of mourners, and an army of thieves.
—German Proverb

As long as mankind shall continue to bestow more liberal applause on their destroyers than on their benefactors, the thirst of military glory will ever be the vice of exalted characters. *—Gibbon*

After contemplating the events preceding the catastrophe of 1914, we remain unconvinced as to the wisdom of our predecessors. . . . We respect the noble war dead, but we question the judgment of those responsible for their death. . . . Organized slaughter, we realize, does not settle a dispute; it merely silences an argument. *—James Frederick Green*

Millions of citizens, in many lands are beginning to believe that mankind is entering a new era, when war may and should cease; that while every nation, race and people has rights to be maintained, yet there are better ways than war of achieving security, of maintaining rights and honor and of solving controversies. *—Sidney L. Gulick*

War is nothing less than a temporary repeal of the principles of virtue. It is a system out of which almost all the virtues are excluded, and in which nearly all the vices are included. *—Robert Hall*

If the press of the world would adopt and persist in the high resolve that war should be no more, the clangor of arms would cease.
—John Hay

Lord, bid war's trumpet cease;
Fold the whole earth in peace.
—Oliver Wendell Holmes

A day of battle is a day of harvest for the devil. *—William Hooke*

Peace is not made in documents, but in the hearts of men. *—Herbert Hoover*

Bid the din of battle cease!
Folded be the wings of fire!
—Julia Ward Howe

There is one armor that the world of men and women, as a world, has never yet put on. The churches have long bungled with its fastenings, but the world has gone unfended, and few have been those in whose hands the mystical sword of the spirit has shone with daily use.

This armor, waiting to be worn, is the armor of brotherhood and sacrifice, the sword of unselfishness, a conquering sword, with the power, where used, to unite the world in love. And there are none who may not put it on.
—M. A. DeWolfe Howe

We are a peaceful people, and it is well for us to remember that we rely on friendship and good will, not on force and threats of force, to extend our influence and win adherence to our international proposals.
—Charles Evans Hughes

The pathway of peace is the longest and most beset with obstacles the human race has to tread; the goal may be distant, but we must press on.
—Charles Evans Hughes

War should be made a crime, and those who instigate it should be punished as criminals. *—Charles Evans Hughes*

A day will come when a cannon will be exhibited in museums, just as instruments of torture are now, and the people will be astonished that such a thing could have been.
—Victor Hugo

National and international patience and self-restraint; avoidance of force in the pursuit of policy; non-interference in the internal affairs of other nations; the use of peaceful means to adjust differences; the faithful observance of agreements; the modification of such agreements, when essential, by mutual understanding and orderly process; the reduction and limitation of overburdening military armaments, and cooperation and interchange in the economic field. *—Cordell Hull*

They shall beat their swords into ploughshares, and their spears into pruning-hooks; nation shall not lift up sword against nation, neither shall they learn war any more.
Isaiah 2:4

Pacts count for nothing when nations are armed to the teeth.
—Charles E. Jefferson

I recoil with horror at the ferociousness of man. Will nations never devise a more rational umpire of differences than force? Are there no means of coercing injustice more gratifying to our nature than a waste of the blood of thousands and of the labor of millions of our fellow creatures?
—Thomas Jefferson

War is an instrument entirely inefficient toward redressing wrong; and multiplies, instead of indemnifying losses.
—Thomas Jefferson

Dress it as we may, feather it, daub it with gold, huzza it, and sing swaggering songs about it, what is war, nine times out of ten, but murder in uniform?
—Douglas Jerrold

In times of peace there is no slaughter of the strong, no sacrifice of the courageous.
—David Starr Jordan

Other things being equal, the nation which has known least of war is the one most likely to develop the "strong battalions" with whom victory must rest. *—David Starr Jordan*

The era of true peace on earth will not come as long as a tremendous percentage of your taxes goes to educate men in the trades of slaughter. *—Reginald Wright Kauffman*

When the strength of man is shattered,
And the powers of earth are scattered,
From beneath the ghastly ruin
Peace shall rise!
—Archibald Lampman

Lord, let war's tempests cease,
Fold the whole world in peace
Under Thy wings.
Make all the nations one,
All hearts beneath the sun,
Till Thou shalt reign alone,
Great King of Kings.
—Longfellow

Down the dark future, through long generations,
The echoing sounds grow fainter, and then cease;
And like a bell, with solemn, sweet vibrations,
I hear once more the voice of Christ say, "Peace!"
—Longfellow

Were half the power that fills the world with terror,
Were half the wealth bestowed on camps and courts,
Given to redeem the human mind from error,
There were no need of arsenal or forts.
The warrior's name would be a name abhorred;
And every nation that should lift again
Its hand against a brother, on its forehead
Would wear forever more the curse of Cain!
—Longfellow

Ef you take a sword an' dror it,
An' go stick a feller thru,
Guv'ment ain't to answer for it,
God'll send the bill to you.
—James Russell Lowell

Ez fer war, I call it murder,—
There you hev it plain an' flat.
—James Russell Lowell

We kind o' thought Christ went agin war an' pillage. *—James Russell Lowell*

It is easy for clever governments to induce men to surrender their lives. *—Emil Ludwig*

War is one of the greatest plagues that can afflict humanity; it destroys religion, it destroys states, it destroys families. Any scourge, in fact, is preferable to it. Famine and pestilence become as nothing in comparison with it. *—Martin Luther*

Take away the sword;
States can be saved without it.
—Bulwer-Lytton

We shall never be able to effect physical disarmament until we have succeeded in effecting moral disarmament.
—J. Ramsay MacDonald

We have all taken risks in the making of war. Isn't it time that we should take risks to secure peace? *—J. Ramsay MacDonald*

He who makes war his profession, cannot be otherwise than vicious. *—Machiavelli*

Then through the clamor of arms was heard
A whisper of the Master's word.
"Fling down your swords; be friends again:
Ye are not wolf-packs: ye are men.
Let brother-counsel be the law:
Not serpent fang, not tiger claw."
—Edwin Markham

O Christ of Olivet, you husht the wars
Under the far Andean stars:
Light now your strong, nail-wounded hands
Over all peoples, over all lands—
Stretch out those comrade hands to be
A shelter over land and sea!
—Edwin Markham

We are the Dead.
Give ear O Peace!
A thousand thousand empty hearths
And wives un-husbanded
And children fatherless, cry out to thee:
Be it not said
Thou hast forgotten why these tears are shed.
—W. W. Marsh

Peace hath her victories
No less renown'd than war.
—John Milton

It is historically true, and will remain so, that the nation which faces starvation will go out and fight for something to eat.
—John S. Moore

Surely we have received proof as never before that war serves no good ends, even for the side that wins. *—Fridtjof Nansen*

War is the business of barbarians.
—Napoleon I

The more I study the world, the more I am convinced of the inability of brute force to create anything durable. *—Napoleon I*

Set the struggling peoples free!
Crown with Law their Liberty!
—Alfred Noyes

When the world—all of it—consents to organize for peace then we shall have peace.
—John F. O'Ryan

Five great enemies to peace inhabit with us: avarice, ambition, envy, anger, and pride. If those enemies were to be banished, we should infallibly enjoy perpetual peace.
—Petrarch

I hate war—but I believe; believe that the song of the angels above Bethlehem is a prophecy; believe that right is ultimate might; believe in the fatherhood of God; in the brotherhood of man, and have cast the anchor of my faith behind the Prince of Peace.
—Daniel A. Poling

As men of reason we scoff at war; as men of business we fear it; as men of religion and good-will we loathe it; and as artists we love it. *—Ernest Raymond*

It is imbecile to prate about the glamour of war and the infection of the military spirit. There is no glamour left in war. We know the truth about it.
—Agnes Repplier

The greatest hope of peace lies neither in legal enactment, nor in the individual's announcement that he personally will have nothing to do with any future war. Behind both is the problem of the world's learning to live on a human basis. The real advance in peace up to this moment rests more than anything upon advances in the human art of living together. *—Sidney S. Robins*

The noblest monument to peace and to neighborly economic and social friendship in all the world is not a monument in bronze or stone, but the boundary which unites the United States and Canada—3,000 miles of friendship with no barbed wire, no gun or soldier and no passport on the whole frontier.
—Franklin D. Roosevelt

Permanent friendships between nations, as between men, can be sustained only by scrupulous respect for the pledged word.
—Franklin D. Roosevelt

Among the grassy mountain paths the glittering troops increase—
They come! They come!—how fair their feet!—they come that publish peace!
—John Ruskin

Oh, rare, divinest life
Of Peace, compared with Strife!
Yours is the truest splendor, and the most enduring fame. *—Charles Sangster*

Peace is rarely denied to the peaceful.
—Schiller

Farewell the neighing steed and the shrill trump,
The spirit-stirring drum, the ear-piercing fife,
The royal banner, and all quality,
Pride, pomp, and circumstance of glorious war!
And, O you mortal engines, whose rude throats
The immortal Jove's dread clamours counterfeit,
Farewell! *—Shakespeare*

Peace is of the nature of a conquest;
For then both parties nobly are subdued,
And neither party loser.
—Shakespeare

O war! thou son of hell. *—Shakespeare*

'Tis death to me to be at enmity; I hate it, and desire all good men's love.
—Shakespeare

Still in thy right hand carry gentle peace,
To silence envious tongues.
—Shakespeare

I confess without shame that I am tired and sick of the war. Its glory is all moonshine. Even success the most brilliant is over dead and mangled bodies, the anguish and lamentation of distant families appealing to me for missing sons, husbands, and fathers. It is only those who have not heard a shot nor heard the shrieks and groans of the wounded and lacerated, that cry aloud for more blood, more vengeance, more desolation.
—General Sherman

Avoid shame, but do not seek glory,—nothing so expensive as glory.
—Sydney Smith

God is forgotten in war; every principle of Christianity is trampled upon.
—Sydney Smith

War loves to seek its victims in the young.
—Sophocles

War! that mad game the world so loves to play. *—Swift*

Nation with nation, land with land,
Unarmed shall live as comrades free;
In every heart and brain shall throb
The pulse of one fraternity.
—John Addington Symonds

I would that wars should cease,
I would the globe from end to end
Might sow and reap in peace.
—Alfred Tennyson

Ah, when shall all men's good
Be each man's rule, and universal peace
Lie like a shaft of light across the land,
And like a lane of beams athwart the sea,
Thro' all the circle of the golden year?
—Alfred Tennyson

Ring out the thousand wars of old,
Ring in the thousand years of peace!
—Alfred Tennyson

For I digged into the Future, far as human eye could see,
Saw the Vision of the world, and all the wonder that would be. . . . .
Till the war-drum throbbed no longer, and the battle-flags were furled,
In the Parliament of man, the Federation of the world.
—Alfred Tennyson

War on the one hand is such a terrible, such an atrocious thing, that no man, especially no Christian man, has the right to assume the responsibility of beginning it.
—Count Lyof Tolstoi

Our Country! Save us, Lord,
From wielding vengeful sword
At Right's expense.
—Robert Woods Van Kirk

My first wish is to see this plague to mankind (war) banished from the earth and the sons and daughters of this world employed in more pleasing and innocent amusements than in preparing implements and exercising them for the destruction of mankind.
—George Washington

Let us thank God that we live in an age when something has influence besides the bayonet. *—Daniel Webster*

Nothing except a battle lost can be half so melancholy as a battle won.
—Duke of Wellington

Take my word for it, if you had seen but one day of war, you would pray to Almighty God, that you might never see such a thing again. *—Duke of Wellington*

"Hate hath no harm for love," so ran the song;
"And peace unweaponed conquers every wrong."
—John Greenleaf Whittier

"Put up the sword!" The voice of Christ once more
Speaks, in the pauses of the cannon's roar, . . .
O men and brothers! let that voice be heard.
War fails, try peace; put up the useless sword!
—John Greenleaf Whittier

We cannot fight forever; when the domes
Of Truth's avoided temple surely gleam
Above wrecked cities and forsaken homes,
Men will desert the battle for the dream—
For dreams are stronger than armies in the end.
—Frank Wilmot

The only basis of peace is justice. I do not object to war because it is cruel and unjust, but because it is a clumsy and brutal instrument to get at justice.
—Woodrow Wilson

"Peace is not bought with dead men slain."
—Barbara Young

How much longer, O Lord, shall we bear it all?
How many more red years?
—Ruth Comfort Mitchell Young

SAFETY WEEK

The secret of accident-free motoring is to anticipate situations before they develop. . . After an emergency has developed, it is often too late to avoid a collision. So take it easy—think—live and let live!

—Aetna Casualty and Surety Company

Safety features must be an intrinsic part of the design of the machine, and of the physical layout and operation of the plant.

—P. G. Agnew

It is an indefensible system that trains thousands of men to chase and fight fires, but virtually no men to chase and fight those who build the fires. How long would our cities stand unburned if on' their firemen rested also all responsibility for the observance of laws governing fire hazard and arson, for detecting violations, and for bringing all evidence before the courts?

—E. T. Allen

Not fire, but the owner of the hand that lights it is the public's enemy.

—E. T. Allen

THE FOUR HORSEMEN—death, permanent disability, injuries and economic loss—ride rough-shod into many homes over the nation every day in the year, extracting their toll as the result of accidents that occur due to unsafe habits or unsafe conditions. Deaths resulting from these accidents are not counted in hundreds but ten of thousands; permanent disabilities in hundreds of thousands; injuries in millions. The tragic part of it all is that these home accidents could, in most instances, be prevented by the use of corrective measures at little cost or effort.

—American National Red Cross

To arouse interest in safety is one thing, to sustain it another.

—Editorial. Annals of the American Academy of Political and Social Science January '26

I submit that training in safety is exactly the same sort of training, as an educative process, as training in the English language, or training in politeness, or training in any other thing which one wishes a child to know.

—Ada Hart Arlitt

Road sense is the offspring of courtesy and the parent of safety.

—Australian traffic rules

One very practical way of reducing the cost of living would be by eliminating needless accidents. Production today is seriously handicapped by thousands of workmen who are either permanently or temporarily thrown out of employment through accidents which could be avoided.

—Roger Babson

He that cannot see well, let him go softly.

—Francis Bacon

Human life is no less precious and costly now than it was during the war. Homes and streets and factories must be made at least as safe as the trenches were!

—Harriet E. Beard

Good order is one of the first requisites for safety anywhere.

—Harriet E. Beard

Since all of the safety devices that it is possible to invent for the safeguarding of human life are of less value than individuals who are trained in self-control, the importance of self-control in connection with any phase of accident prevention cannot be given too much emphasis.

—Harriet E. Beard

A statistician made a few calculations and discovered that since the birth of our nation more lives had been lost in celebrating independence than in winning it.

—Curtis Billings

Safety teaches us to stop and weigh the value of our acts to see whether the chance taken is really worth while—to distinguish between what is good sport and what is poor sport.

—Boy Scouts of America

It is not possible to make the world "fool-proof," but it *is* possible, though not easy, for people to train themselves to such habits of alertness, self-control, common-sense and skill that they are safe almost anywhere.

—Boy Scouts of America

Safety is not a matter of "Every man for himself"—it means looking out for the other person as well, and doing everything in one's power to prevent accidents to others, from whatever cause.

—Boy Scouts of America

When we come to know the true meaning of safety we realize that far from taking the adventure *out* of life, it is the very thing that is going to help us put adventure *into* life.

—Boy Scouts of America

For the most part we are contributing most effectively to universal safety through simple acts of consideration for others, and by looking after ourselves. . . By a simple observance of the rules of safety, we have the opportunity to be heroes, though unrecognized ones, a dozen times a day.

—Boy Scouts of America

Danger which can not be removed must be avoided, except for some good reason. We cannot change the swift current of a river nor slacken the drag of the under-tow at the seashore, but we do not have to risk drowning by bathing in an obviously dangerous place. We can choose a safe place in which to swim. We can not remove a railroad trestle, but we do not have to run the risk of falling off or of being caught by an unexpected train by using it as a pathway. We can not make the lake freeze faster than the weather permits, but we do not have to go skating until the ice will bear us.

—Boy Scouts of America

Where the road bends abruptly take short steps. *—Ernest Bramah*

Children should be seen and not hurt.

—David Broderick

Look twice before you leap.

Charlotte Brontë

Early and provident fear is the mother of safety. *—Edmund Burke*

The basic "Three E's" of traffic safety—education, engineering and enforcement.

—C. F. Butcher

Oh! are they safe? we ask not of success.

—Lord Byron

Make haste slowly. *—Caesar Augustus*

Public safety is the first responsibility of a municipal government. *—F. C. Cain*

Safety is sane and practicable, . . .it is a national asset of inestimable value.

—W. H. Cameron

Earnest effort in reducing the casualties of peace is an expression of the highest type of patriotism to one's country and of service to humanity as a whole. *—W. H. Cameron*

An earthquake, a famine, a pestilence compel universal attention and the most generous financial response; the dropping of a worker here and there, day by day and in remote places, is taken little heed of—there is a moment's grief in the neighborhood—and the rush of life goes on. Similarly, each worker thinks of an accident as something that is likely to happen to the other fellow, but not to himself. These instinctive barriers the safety worker must overcome.

—W. H. Cameron

We now have unshakable conviction that accident causes are man-made and that a man-made problem can be solved by men and women. *—W. H. Cameron*

If life is worth while, if it is worth continuing, then the safe piloting of life's adventure must depend upon facing the risks of life fearlessly, but with a knowledge of their inherent qualities. Some of the thrill of life is in meeting its dangers. Our workers, our citizens, must first understand what safety is; it must become a desirable and sought-for attribute of living. It must be worked into the habits of consciousness of children as they are taught to talk and live.

—W. H. Cameron

It is the part of a wise man to keep himself today for tomorrow.

—Miguel de Cervantes

Precaution is better than cure.

—Sir Edward Coke

The cautious seldom err. *—Confucius*

There is no right to strike against the public safety by anybody, anywhere, any time.

—Calvin Coolidge

If the death and disaster that now fall upon innocent people, through the year and over our country as a whole, were concentrated into one calamity we would shudder at the tremendous catastrophe. The loss is no less disastrous because diffused in time and space.

—Calvin Coolidge

I will train myself to recognize all hazards of accidents before I get to them.

—Paul de Kruif

When thou buildest a new house, then thou shalt make a battlement for thy roof, that thou bring not blood upon thine house, if any man fall from thence.

—Deuteronomy 22:8

The sense of security more frequently springs from habit than from conviction. The lapse of time during which a given event has not happened is, in this logic of habit, constantly alleged as a reason why the event should never happen, even when lapse of time is precisely the added condition which makes the event imminent. A man will tell you that he has worked in a mine for forty years unhurt by an accident, and offer this as a reason why he should apprehend no danger, though the roof is beginning to sink. The older a man gets, the more difficult it is to him to retain a believing conception of his own death. *—George Eliot*

Safe ways of thinking and acting acquired in youth, before carelessness becomes a habit, will be instinctive in adult years and will make for better and safer conditions in our homes, our industries and our public places.

—M. B. Elson

Accident prevention is a world problem, and public safety is an attainable ideal. It is certainly not a far-off millenium or a faint gleam through the mist. Each year gives evidence that within the heart of man is heard and understood a universal command, "Thou shalt not kill." *—Eleanor Everet*

For safety is not a gadget but a state of mind. —*Eleanor Everet*

If we owe it to our men to care for them when they are hurt, we certainly owe it to them to do everything in our power to keep them from getting hurt; and if it would be a good investment for us to build a larger industrial hospital, it certainly will be a better investment for us to get rid of accidents. . . *Prevent accidents,* even if you have to redesign our machines or methods to do so.
—*Henry Ford*

Production without safety is inefficient. Accident prevention is absolutely an essential part of the industrial program. While we take great pleasure in giving employment to maimed men, we believe that we are doing a far greater work in preventing this maiming of men. We feel that accidents are absolutely unnecessary. —*Henry Ford*

A stitch in time save nine.
—*Thomas Fuller*

Accident prevention is not only good morals and good ethics but also good business.
—*Elbert H. Gary*

No greater service to humanity can be given than that which seeks to prevent accidents and occupational diseases. It is an amazing price we pay for the terrible slaughter in the industrial life of our country.
—*Samuel Gompers*

It would be a contravention of good educational principles if we were to use a sense of fear as the prime agency in safety instruction. —*Thomas Gosling*

Know, one false step is ne'er retriev'd,
And be with caution bold.
—*Thomas Gray*

We are not proving ourselves spiritually worthy of our material progress. We have not been neighborly, courteous, and kind upon the highway. Our lack of decency toward our fellow men is a definite black mark against us. —*Cary T. Grayson*

The grim reaper smiles in his sleeve as he takes his daily toll from humanity's stupidity and carelessness. —*Ernest Greenwood*

Just as accidents in the factory are stupid and a reflection of inefficiency somewhere in the management, so are accidents in the home a reflection of inefficiency on the part of the home manager—the mother, or the father, or both. —*Ernest Greenwood*

Accidents, and particularly street and highway accidents, do not happen—they are caused.
—*Ernest Greenwood*

The Boldest Farmer heeds the Cautious Rule
To stand Behind the Bull, Before the Mule.
—*Arthur Guiterman*

Rome was not built in a day and a problem as old as safety cannot be controlled overnight. It is all a matter of keeping everlastingly at it. —*Julien H. Harvey*

It is better to obey laws than to appeal for mercy in the courts. —*Charles M. Hayes*

Remember the street car cannot turn out.
—*Charles M. Hayes*

"Safety First" is "Safety Always."
—*Charles M. Hayes*

Who can hope to be safe? who sufficiently cautious?
Guard himself as he may, every moment's an ambush.
—*Horace*

Man never heeds enough from hour to hour what he should shun. —*Horace*

Caution is the oldest child of wisdom.
—*Victor Hugo*

A lot of people. . .confuse *prudence* and *timidity.* They forget about the fundamental doctrine of *safety through skill*: a much more wholesome attitude than that of *safety through fear.*
Paul W. Kearney

Our wanton accidents take root, and grow
To vaunt themselves God's laws.
—*Charles Kingsley*

Nothing under the sun is accidental.
Gotthold Ephraim Lessing

It is the duty of every man to protect himself and those associated with him from accident which may result in injury and death.
—*Abraham Lincoln*

Horrors happen on the straightaways because an open stretch invites fool minds.
—*Los Angeles Times*

The purpose to save life is the noblest of all purposes;
It embodies the highest ideal of humanity;
Conserves the best asset of the nation;
Provides the best protection for the nation;
Creates the real glory of the nation;
It incarnates the only spirit which offers a solution for all our modern problems, namely, the spirit of democracy and brotherhood;
It answers in the affirmative—we *are* our brother's keeper, and, more than that, we are our brother's brother.
—*John McDowell*

"Safe at home" is an expression frequently heard. However, when we consider the fact that home accident fatalities are exceeded only by accidental deaths from motor vehicle operation, and that nearly one-

third of all accidental deaths occur at home, the hazards confronting us in our daily home life are more serious than supposed.

—*Metropolitan Life Insurance Company*

It should be noted that the teaching of safety is far more than the mere inculcation of specific habits and techniques. The problem of safety is one of the fundamental problems of the human race and has its root deep in the psychological and philosophical bases for right living, so that a course in safety if rightly conducted is of far-reaching significance from a cultural and character-forming point of view.

—*National Conference on Street and Highway Safety*

Except in rare instances, traffic accidents are not acts of God. They are acts of men. They can be prevented.

—*National Conference on Street and Highway Safety*

Safety means something more than accident prevention—it means also conservation of all that goes to make life worth while—health, opportunity, and the material resources upon which life itself depends.

—*National Safety Council*

Safety is the opposite of waste.

—*National Safety Council*

Unavoidable accidents are so rare that we can almost say there are none.

—*National Safety Council*

We must become prevention-minded rather than punishment-minded, because prevention removes the need of punishment—both man's punishment and nature's punishment, which is death or injury.

—*National Safety Council*

These fatal accidents are a challenge to the decency and sanity of the United States.

—*Editorial. New York Globe*

A monetary payment for an accident or a life lost in the service of an industrial plant is no true offset to the injury suffered or the misery entailed. No money can compensate for these sufferings. —*G. A. Orth*

He that looketh not before he leapeth
May chance to stumble before he sleepeth.

—*William Painter*

Recklessness is a species of crime and should be so regarded on our streets and highways. —*Marlen E. Pew*

As a national humanitarian movement it is one in which all interests should harmoniously pull together in the common aim of lessening one of the heaviest burdens imposed upon civilization. —*J. A. A. Pickard*

Were human nature perfect, the one cardinal "Safety First" rule would be "Thou shalt use thy common sense."

—*J. A. A. Pickard*

The prudent man looketh well to his going.

—*Proverbs 14:15*

He is free from danger who, even when he is safe, is on his guard.

—*Publilius Syrus*

Prevention is the daughter of intelligence.

—*Sir Walter Raleigh*

Safety is an unselfish service rendered to humanity. —*J. Harry Reid*

If people could be made to understand that only the *undertaker*, the *doctor* and the *ambulance chaser* win when they take chances, perhaps an improvement could be brought about. —*Ralph C. Richards*

We are a nation of chance takers.

—*Ralph C. Richards*

Modern thought is recognizing that the basis of national progress, whether industrial or social, is the health, efficiency and spiritual development of the people.

—*John D. Rockefeller, Jr.*

This country will not be a good place for any of us to live in unless we make it a good place for all of us to live in.

—*Theodore Roosevelt*

Safety education is a conception of life, a state of mind, a point of view. But it is more than that. It clothes itself in clearly stated ideals, sets up a constructive philosophy of living together in a well-ordered world.

—*Harold Rugg*

All adventures involve uncertainty and danger. A danger courageously met and intelligently controlled is part of the substance of a normal life. A danger carelessly met and ineffectively controlled results in defeat of purpose and even in tragedy.

—*Editorial. Safety Education Magazine*

The first law of nature is self-preservation; but, like all of the wonderful advances in human endeavor, it required the vision and faith of far-seeing men to make safety of the workers an essential feature of good management in the industries of our country. It is my sincere wish and hope that the day will come when the protecting arms of Universal Safety will spread out over all industry and reach all the millions of workers who make industry possible.

—*Charles M. Schwab*

We may outrun
By violent swiftness
And lose by over-running.

—*Shakespeare*

They stumble that run fast.
—*Shakespeare*

Out of this nettle, danger, we pluck this flower, safety. —*Shakespeare*

Be wary, then; best safety lies in fear.
—*Shakespeare*

Physical education and safety go hand in hand—the one stimulating adventure and experience, the other trying to do away with the unfortunate accidents of life that frustrate adventure and bring so much pain and unhappiness. —*Herbert J. Stack*

May our consideration of the safety of labor and the toiler be rewarded by a higher respect for humanity as a whole, a greater regard for law, a purer and deeper and higher patriotism; and may this great country continue to be the beacon to the world, lighting toward liberty and toward progress.
—*Edwin A. Steiner*

We are not a cruel people, neither are we indifferent to human life and suffering. Let a city be burned or a district be flooded, and we pour out our money to the distressed as no other people in the world. It seems necessary that the situation be spectacular, however, before we become aroused. —*Ethelbert Stewart*

Automobiles are not ferocious. . . .it is man who is to be feared.
—*Robbins B. Stoeckel*

To be a good driver in the terms of applied ethics is to be a person of good manners, ready to see and appreciate the problems of others, to make proper allowances for them and to exercise even a little more patience, care and consideration than is actually called for by the letter of the law.
—*Robbins B. Stoeckel*

Greed wrecks many men and nations; so do temper and hate. But all Man's destroyers can take lessons from the demon of CARELESSNESS. —*Editorial. Sunday Mirror*

There is a new industrial philosophy abroad. . . Nothing is so valuable economically as the man. To injure or to kill him is to destroy the one essential element in the scheme of world-wide civilization and prosperity. . . The stronger, the longer lived, the happier, the more ambitious he is, the better for mankind. —*Ida M. Tarbell*

Look ere you leap, see ere you go,
It may be for thy profit so.
—*Thomas Tusser*

Look ere thou leap, whose literal sense is, Do nothing suddenly or without advisement.
—*William Tyndale*

"A chain is no stronger than its weakest link." Likewise, a shop is no safer than its least safe worker.
—*United States Compensation Commission*

Effective work in the field of accident prevention consists of something far more than tom-tom beating. To get good results we must focus our safety selling campaign on the individual worker.
—*United States Compensation Commission*

The problem of safety is closely linked with health, thrift, and many other elements which taken together make up the great problem of developing a finer citizenship.
—*United States Department of Commerce*

Remember that the best safety device known is a careful man.
—*United States Navy Department*

You're enjoying good health.
That's fine.
You want to remain well.
That's natural.
You may be careless.
That's possible.
You may have an accident.
That's probable.
You sincerely hope not.
That's obvious.
Then practice safety first.
That's wisdom.
—*United States Navy Department*

An electric iron is a great improvement over the old-fashioned "sad iron," but nothing could be sadder than an electric iron left attached. —*M. T. W.*

Few people have risen in life by means of a shaky stepladder. —*M. T. W.*

We'd say that a lad who always obeys the traffic signals is a signally reliable person.
—*M. T. W.*

An accident is therefore something that balks the order or purpose of the world and safety is something that lets it have its way. Safety is then a part as it were of the great order itself. —*Albert W. Whitney*

A better slogan than "Safety First" for school use would be "Safety for More and Better Adventures."
Albert W. Whitney

Safety is primarily a matter of the head rather than the hand and hence pre-eminently educational. —*Albert W. Whitney*

Safety then, guardian of the unfolding world-purpose, instead of diminishng the adventure of life is precisely that which makes it possible. Instead of making the world safe *from* danger we are in a far deeper sense making the world safe *for* adventure or in a still fuller sense we are saving the world from the bad adventure which mere chance has waiting for it and for the good adventure which it is within the purpose of the world that we should have.

—Albert W. Whitney

Survival of the fittest is the survival of the safe, if the word is used in its broadest sense.

—Albert W. Whitney

The essence of safety is cooperation. . .no man can be sure of his own safety or that of his family, without the cooperation of his fellows. *—Sidney J. Williams*

SLOGANS:

Better too much vigilance than a lifetime of regret.

If you drink, don't drive! If you drive, don't drink!

Carelessness is our hungriest killer.

One Man at Work is Worth Two in the Hospital.

He who stops to look each way
May live to look another day.

Death is your playmate when you play in the street.

Fire, a good friend, a bad fóe. Watch it when it works, fight it when it runs away.

When Mr. Careful comes to stay, Mr. Danger runs away.

Knowledge plus Caution equals Safety.

Long Life, Not Lost Life.

Better a thousand times careful than once dead.

Preach safety first, and practice what you preach.

Safety saves sickness, suffering, sorrow.

Safety means first aid to the uninjured.

Safety is the cornerstone of efficiency.

Be safe or you'll be sorry.

The chance-taker is the accident-maker.

The path of the careless is beset with dangers.

Behold how great a matter a little fire kindleth.

The only safe match is a burned match.

Fire is a good servant but a poor master.

Touch not, taste not.

If it's trouble you want to hatch
Look for gas with a lighted match.

A live boy should let a live wire alone.

Crossed wires cause fires.

Cross Crossings Cautiously.

Two good legs are worth a thousand crutches.

Better lose the ball than your life.

If you dive like a feather and swim like a stone
Stay out of deep water, let swimming alone.

Stop! Look! Listen!

Care, not Dare.

All accidents have causes.

Chance travels on crutches.

Make safety a habit, not a happening.

Better be careful than crippled.

Better cause a delay than an accident.

If hurry interferes with safety, cut out the hurry.

The speedway ends at the cemetery.

Don't monkey with the buzz saw.

Forethought is better than afterthought.

Goosey, goosey gander, why do you wander
Off the curb, off the curb, always into danger?

Little Miss Muffet
Instead of a tuffet
Sat on the curb one day.
Along came an auto
And soon she was caught, Oh!
Her feet having got in the way.

The First Rule of the Road is Courtesy

Be a Safe Driver and a Careful Pedestrian

Govern Your Driving by the Conditions Ahead

An ounce of caution is better than a pound of charity.

Don't gamble with your life; it is the biggest stake you possess.

Don't take a long chance; it often spells the last.

Invest a few moments in thinking. It will pay good interest.

It is better to be careful a thousand times than injured once.

The cost of Safety is only a thought.

"Didn't think" kills thousands annually.

The living may learn a lesson from the dead.

ST. PATRICK'S DAY

We're one at heart, if you be Ireland's friend,
Though leagues asunder our opinions tend:
There are but two great parties in the end.
—*William Allingham*

With due condescension, I'd call your attention
To what I shall mention of Erin so green,
And without hestitation, I will show how that nation
Became of creation the gem and the queen.
—*Anon.*

What color should be seen
Where our fathers' homes have been
But their own immortal Green?
—*Anon.*

The Harp melodiously shall sound,
When Erin's sons shall be unbound,
St. Patrick's Day they'll dance around
The blooming laurel tree.
—*Anon.*

Oh, Paddy dear, an' did ye hear the news that's goin' round?
The shamrock is forbid by law to grow on Irish ground!
No more St. Patrick's Day we'll keep, his colour can't be seen,
For there's a cruel law agin' the Wearin' o' the green!
—*Anon.*

When law can stop the blades of grass from growin' as they grow,
An' when the leaves in summer time their color dare not show,
Then I will change the color, too, I wear in my caubeen;
But till that day, plaise God, I'll stick to the Wearin' o' the Green.
—*Anon.*

There in groups were hundreds kneeling
Keen remorse and anguish feeling,
Brooding o'er the awful story
Of St. Patrick's Purgatory.
—*Anon.*

Oh! St. Patrick was a gentleman
Who came of decent people;
He built a church in Dublin town,
And on it put a steeple.
—*Henry Bennett*

So, success attend St. Patrick's fist,
For he's a saint so clever;
Oh! he gave the snakes and toads a twist,
And bothered them forever!
—*Henry Bennett*

For 'tis green, green, green, where the ruined towers are gray,
And it's green, green, green, all the happy night and day;
Green of leaf and green of sod, green of ivy on the wall,
And the blessed Irish shamrock with the fairest green of all.
—*Mary Elizabeth Blake*

Since the rule
Of Heremon, the noble man of grace,
There was worshipping of stones
Until the coming of good Patrick of Macha.
—*Book of Leinster*

A man full of the grace and favors of the Holy Spirit, like John. A fair garden with plants of virtues. A vine-branch with fruitfulness. A flashing fire for kindling charity. A lion for great strength and might. A dove for gentleness and simplicity. A serpent for cunning and prudence. A man gentle and humble, tender to the sons of Life, but rough and ungentle to the sons of Death. A slave in labour and service to Christ. A king in rank and might for binding and loosing, for freeing and ensnaring, for quickening and killing. —*Book of Lismore*
(*Praise of Patrick*)

He was a terror to any snake that came in his path, whether it was the cold, slimy reptile sliding along the ground or the more dangerous snake that oppresses men through false teachings. And he drove the snakes out of the minds of men, snakes of superstition and brutality and cruelty.
—*Arthur Brisbane*

Erin, an exile bequeaths thee his blessing!
Land of my forefathers, Erin go bragh!
—*Thomas Campbell*

The greatest of St. Patrick's miracles was that of driving the venomous reptiles out of Ireland, and rendering the Irish soil, for ever after, so obnoxious to the serpent race, that they instantaneously die on touching it. Colgan seriously relates that St. Patrick accomplished this feat by beating a drum, which he struck with such fervor that he knocked a hole in it, thereby endangering the success of the miracle. But an angel appearing mended the drum; and the patched instrument was long exhibited as a holy relic.
—*Chambers Book of Days*

The shamrock, or small white clover (*trifolium repens* of botanists), is almost universally worn in the hat over all Ireland, on St. Patrick's day. The popular notion is, that when St. Patrick was teaching the doctrine

of the Trinity to the pagan Irish, he used this plant, bearing three leaves upon one stem, as a symbol or illustration of the great mys'ery.
—*Chambers Books of Days*

There's a dear little plant that grows in our isle,
'Twas St. Patrick himself, sure, that set it;
And the sun on his labor with pleasure did smile,
And with dew from his eye often wet it.
It thrives through the bog, through the brake, and the mireland;
And he called it the dear little shamrock of Ireland—
The sweet little shamrock, the dear little shamrock,
The sweet little, green little, shamrock of Ireland!
—*Andrew Cherry*

"Well, here's thank God for the race and the sod!"
Said Kelly and Burke and Shea.
—*J. I. C. Clarke*

Before I came across the sea
To this delightful place,
I thought the native Irish were
A funny sort of race;
I thought they bore shillelagh-sprigs,
And that they always said:
'Och hone, acushla, tare-an-ouns,"
"Begorra," and "bedad!"
—*Converted Saxon*

Oh, thou tormenting Irish lay!
I've got thee buzzing in by brain,
And cannot turn thee out again.
—*Eliza Cook*

Dear Erin, how sweetly thy green bosom rises!
An emerald set in the ring of the sea.
Each blade of thy meadows my faithful heart prizes,
Thou queen of the west, the world's cushla-ma-chree.
—*John Philpot Curran*

"Who says that the Irish are fighters be birth?"
Says little Dan Crone.
"Faix, there's not a more peaceable race on th' earth,
If ye lave 'em alone."
—*Thomas Augustin Daly*

Oh, the music in the air!
An' the joy that's ivrywhere—
Shure, the whole blue vault of heaven is wan grand triumphal arch,
An' the earth below is gay
Wid its tender green th'-day,
Fur the whole world is Irish on the Seventeenth o' March!
—*Thomas Augustin Daly*

When Erin first rose from the dark-swelling flood
God blessed the green Island, he saw it was good.
The Emerald of Europe, it sparkled, it shone
In the ring of this world, the most precious stone.
—*William Drennen*

Oh, never fear for Ireland, for she has so'gers still,
For Remy's boys are in the wood, and Rory's on the hill;
And never had poor Ireland more loyal hearts than these—
May God be kind and good to them, the faithful Rapparees!
The fearless Rapparees!
The jewel waar ye, Rory, with your Irish Rapparees!
—*Sir Charles Gavan Duffy*

The shamrock on an older shore
Sprang from a rich and sacred soil
Where saint and hero lived of yore,
And where their sons in sorrow toil.
—*Maurice Francis Egen*

If you would like to see the height of hospitality,
The cream of kindly welcome, and the core of cordiality:
Joys of all the olden time—you're wishing to recall again?
Come down to Donovans, and there you'll meet them all again.
—*Francis A. Fahy*

A plenteous place is Ireland for hospitable cheer,
Uileacan dubh O!
—*Sir Samuel Ferguson*

And let the Orange lily be
Thy badge, my patriot-brother—
The everlasting Green for *me*;
And we for one another.
—*John de Jean Frazer*

When after the Winter alarmin',
The Spring steps in so charmin',
So fresh and arch
In the middle of March,
Wid her hand St. Patrick's arm on,
Let us all, let us all be goin',
Agra, to assist at your sowin',
The girls to spread
Your iligant bed,
And the boys to set the hoe in.
—*Alfred Percival Graves*

The list of Irish saints is past counting; but in it all no other figure is so human, friendly, and lovable as St. Patrick—who was an Irishman only by adoption.
—*Stephen Gwynn*

Every Irishman has a potato in his head.
—*J. C. and A. W. Hare*

Help me, St. Patrick,
Or else I swear I'll serve thee a trick,
For if I wear thy Cross and Shamrogue
Next seventeenth of March, I am a rogue
Nor will I more believe the Story
Of thy famed Northern Purgatory.
—*Irish Rendezvous*

Nine hundred thousand vipers blue he charmed with sweet discourses,
And dined on them at Killaloo in soups and second courses.
—*Irish song*

The shamrock I'm pressin'
An' while I'm confessin'
I'm praisin' St. Patrick an' "wearin' the green."
—*Ben King*

Oh, while a man may dream awake,
On gentle Irish ground,
'Tis Paradise without the snake—
That's easy to be found.
—*Frederick Langbridge*

O kindly, generous, Irish land
So leal and fair and loving!
No wonder the wandering Celt should think
And dream of you in his roving.
—*John Locke*

O Ireland isn't it grand you look—
Like a bride in her rich adornin'?
And with all the pent-up love of my heart
I bid you the top o' the mornin'!
—*John Locke*

On the eighth day of March it was, some people say,
That St. Patrick at midnight he first saw the day,
While others declare 'twas the ninth he was born. . . . .
Till Father Mulcahy, who showed them their sins,
Said, "No one could have two birthdays, but a twins."

Says he, "Boys, don't be fightin' for eight or for nine,
Don't be always dividin', but sometimes combine;
Combine eight and nine, and seventeen is the mark,
So let that be his birthday." "Amen!" says the clerk.
—*Samuel Lover*

"If you hold a four-leaf shamrock in your left hand at dawn on St. Patrick's Day you get what you want very much but haven't wished for." —*Patricia Lynch*

Bless the dear old verdant land!
Brother, wert thou born of it?
As thy shadow life doth stand
Twining round its rosy band,
Did an Irish Mother's hand
Guide thee in the morn of it?
Did a father's first command
Teach thee love or scorn of it?
—*Denis Florence MacCarthy*

"God be with you, dear Ireland," he gasped with a sigh,
"I have lived to behold you—I'm ready to die."
—*Thomas D'Arcy McGee*

But if an emblem o'er my dust should rise,
Let it be this: Our Harp within a wreath
Of Shamrocks twining round it lovingly.
—*Thomas D'Arcy McGee*

Far are the Gaelic tribes and wide
Scattered round earth on every side,
For good or ill;
They aim at all things, rise or fall,
Succeed or perish—but, through all,
Love Erin still.
—*Thomas D'Arcy McGee*

It is somewhat suggestive that the apostle of Ireland was himself a foreign-born citizen. He acquired a better right to speak for Ireland than any man that was ever born in it, before or since. And that should be a lesson to moderate certain Irish patriots who would have it that there is nothing good that does not come from Ireland. . . .and while it is permissible for us on this one day of the year to blow our own horn a little, it is well for us to be modest enough to acknowledge and to be thankful for the apostle who was not an Irishman and yet was the best Irishman that ever lived.
—*Edward McGlynn*

It would be hard, indeed, to find a patron saint in any land better beloved than St. Patrick. The Irish are devoted to his memory, and countless thousands of their little lads are christened Patrick, which speedily becomes shortened to Pat. Even the girls do not escape, as the many Patricias can testify.
—*J. Walker McSpadden*

The Irish believe that the celebration of this day aids to promote good-fellowship and to keep up old acquaintance, besides helping forward the cause of charity, which in this case means the caring for the orphans and the comforting of the aged.
—*J. Walker McSpadden*

You've heard, I suppose, long ago,
How the snakes, in a manner most antic,
He marched to the county Mayo,
And trundled them into th' Atlantic.
—*William Maginn*

With deep affection and recollection
I often think of the Shandon bells,
Whose sound so wild would, in days of childhood,
Fling round my cradle their magic spells.
Or this I ponder, where'er I wander,
And thus grow fonder, sweet Cork, of thee;
With thy bells of Shandon,
That sound so grand on
The pleasant waters of the river Lee.
—Francis Sylvester Mahony

O'Ruark, Maguire, those souls of fire, whose names are shrined in story:
Think how their high achievements once made Erin's greatest glory.
—James Clarence Mangan

Take a blessing from my heart to the land of my birth,
And the fair Hills of Eiré, O!
—James Clarence Mangan

Over the Isle his spirit went
Like fire across the firmament.
Kings at Tara caught the word,
Churl and kern and chieftain heard.
Lo, the Druid's mystic rod
Fell down withered before God!
—Edwin Markham

With the frost he kindled fire;
Drove the snakes from brake and brier,
Hurling out the writhing brood
With the lightning of his rood.
—Edwin Markham

O, the Shamrock, the green, immortal Shamrock!
Chosen leaf of Bard and Chief,
Old Erin's native Shamrock.
—Thomas Moore

St. Patrick set up the Church in Ireland; he fills up its first age; sixty years of the fifth century, the whole period of the conversion of the country, belong to him.
—William Bullen Morris

My love is pledged to Ireland's fight;
My love would die for Ireland's weal.
—John Francis O'Donnell

In Connaught is St. Patrick's Reek,
His Purgatory in Ulster seek.
William O'Kelly

Seit Patryk come thorou goddes grace
To preche in Irlande
To teche men the right beileve
Of jhu crist to understande
So ful of wormes that londe he fonde
That no man might gone
In som stede for wormes
But that he was hurt on one.
—Old English Manuscript

There's ne'er a mile in Ireland's Isle where the dirty vermin musters;
Where'er he put his dear forefoot he murdered them in clusters.
The toads went hop, the frogs went flop, slap-dash into the water,
And the beasts committed suicide to save themselves from slaughter.
—Old Irish Song

And if the field of fame be lost,
It won't be by an Irishman.
—James Orr

The savage loves his native shore,
Though rude the soil and chill the air;
Then well may Erin's sons adore
Their isle, which nature formed so fair.
What flood reflects a shore so sweet
As Shannon great, or pastoral Bann?
Or who a friend or foe can meet
So generous as an Irishman?
—James Orr

As the rapture of martyrs all agony endeth,
As the rivers of Aidenn 'mid earth's turbid waters,
As Una the Pure One 'mid Eve's fallen daughters,
So is Erin, my shining one,
So is Erin, my peerless one!
—Fanny Parnell

At Tara today in this fateful hour
I place all Heaven with its power,
And the sun with its brightness,
And the snow with its whiteness,
And fire with all the strength it hath,
And lightning with its rapid wrath,
And the winds with their swiftness along their path,
And the sea with its deepness,
And the rocks with their steepness,
And the earth with its starkness:
All these I place,
By God's almighty help and grace,
Between myself and the powers of darkness.
—Rune of St. Patrick

I am born of a father who was a decurion but I sold my noble rank, I blush not to state it nor am I sorry, for the profit of others. *—St. Patrick's Confession*

God inspired me beyond others that I should faithfully serve the nation to whom the love of Christ conveyed me.
—St. Patrick's Confession

I bind myself today to a strong virtue, an invocation of the Trinity.
I believe in a Threeness with confession of a Oneness in the Creator of the Universe!
—Patrick's Hymn

To the Emerald Isle, where our kindred are dwelling,
And where the remains of our forefathers sleep,
Our eyes turn today. . .
—John Pierpont

In a quiet watered land, a land of roses,
Stands St. Kiernan's city fair;
And the warriors of Erin in their famous generations
Slumber there.

—Thomas W. Hagen Rolleston

The Abraham and Moses of the Irish.

—Thomas Joseph Shahan

We'll toast Old Ireland!
Dear Old Ireland!
Ireland, boys, hurrah!

—Timothy Daniel Sullivan

The land of faith, the land of grace,
The land of Erin's ancient race!

—Michael Tormey

O, the red rose may be fair,
And the lily statelier;
But my shamrock, one in three
Takes the very heart of me!

—Katherine Tynan

Wandered from the Antrim hills,
Wandered from Killalas rills,
Patrick heard upon the breeze
Voices from the Irish seas.

—Unknown

O, love is the soul of a true Irishman;
He loves all that's lovely, loves all that he can,
With his sprig of shillelagh and shamrock so green.

—Unknown

Och, Dublin City, there is no doubtin',
Bates every city upon the say.

—Unknown

Long may the shamrock,
The plant that blooms forever,
With the rose combined,
And the thistle twined,
Defy the strength of foes to sever.

—Unknown

The white and the orange, the blue and the green, boys,
We'll blend them together in concord to-night;
. . . .
For union is beauty, and strength is victorious,
In hues, tones, or hearts, on St. Patrick's Day.

—John Francis Waller

Then, "Fusion of hearts, and confusion of colors!"
Be the Irishman's toast on St. Patrick's Day.

—John Francis Waller

Saint Patrick, slave to Milcho of the herds
Of Ballymena, sleeping, heard these words:
"Arise and flee
Out from the land of bondage, and be free!"
. . . .
So went he forth: but in God's time he came
To light on Uilline's hills a holy flame;
And, dying, gave
The land a Saint that lost him as a Slave.

—John Greenleaf Whittier

Then away to the Moyne, o'er the moors of Mayo,
Still onward, still welcomed by high and by low—
Blake, Burke, and O'Malley, Lynch, Kirwan and Browne;
By forest, lake, mountain, through village and town.

—James Wills

O Erin! O my mother! I will love thee!
Whether upon thy green Atlantic throne
Thou sitt'st august, majestic and sublime;
Or on thy empire's last remaining fragment
Bendest forlorn, dejected and forsaken,—
Thy smiles, thy tears, thy blessings and thy woes,
Thy glory and thy infamy, be mine!

—Charles Wolfe

ST. VALENTINE'S DAY

Endless torments dwell about thee:
Yet who would live, and live without thee!
—Joseph Addison

Who is Lydia, pray, and who
Is Hypatia? Softly, dear,
Let me breathe it in your ear—
They are you, and only you.
—Thomas Bailey Aldrich

Life is so short, so fast the lone hours fly,
We ought to be together, you and I.
—Henry Alford

One sweet, sad secret holds my heart in thrall;
A mighty love within my breast has grown,
Unseen, unspoken, and of no one known;
And of my sweet, who gave it, least of all.
—Felix Arvers

I loved thee once, I'll love no more:
Thine be the grief as is the blame:
Thou are not what thou wast before—
What reason I should be the same?
—Robert Ayton

I cannot love as I have loved,
And yet I know not why:
It is the one great woe of life
To feel all feeling die.
—P. J. Bailey

For you are to me what the bowstring is to the shaft,
Speeding my purpose aloft and aflame and afar.
William Rose Benét

So as you come, and as you do depart,
Joys ebb and flow within my tender heart.
—Charles Best

On paper curiously shaped
Scribblers today of every sort,
In verses Valentines yclep'd,
To Venus chime their annual court.
—Henry G. Bohn

I thought when love for you died, I should die.
It's dead. Alone, most strangely, I live on.
—Rupert Brooke

There is musick, even in the beauty and the silent note which Cupid strikes, far sweeter than the sound of an instrument.
—Sir Thomas Browne

Beloved, let us love so well,
Our work shall still be better for our love,
And still our love be sweeter for our work,
And both commended, for the sake of each,
By all true workers and true lovers born.
—Elizabeth Barrett Browning

How do I love thee? Let me count the ways.
I love thee to the depth and breadth and height
My soul can reach, when feeling out of sight
For the ends of Being and ideal Grace.
I love thee to the level of everyday's
Most quiet need, by sun and candle-light.
I love thee freely, as men strive for Right;
I love thee purely, as they turn from Praise.
—Elizabeth Barrett Browning

Say thou dost love me, love me, love me—toll
The silver iterance!—only minding, Dear,
To love me also in silence, with thy soul.
—Elizabeth Barrett Browning

Tho' father an' mither an' a' should gae mad,
O whistle, an' I'll come to ye, my lad.
—Robert Burns

Or were I in the wildest waste,
Sae black and bare, sae black and bare,
The desert were a Paradise,
If thou wert there, if thou wert there.
—Robert Burns

Oh, my luve's like a red, red rose,
That's newly sprung in June;
Oh, my luve's like a melodie
That's sweetly played in tune.
—Robert Burns

When things were as fine as could possibly be
I thought 'twas the spring; but alas it was she.
—John Byrom

Give, oh give me back my heart!
—Lord Byron

Be thou the rainbow to the storms of life,
The evening beam that smiles the clouds away.
—Lord Byron

Oh, come with me and be my love!
—Calder Campbell

My love-lies-bleeding.
—Thomas Campbell

Cold in the dust this perished heart may lie,
But that which warmed it once shall never die!
—Thomas Campbell

Then come, you fairies, dance with me a round,
Dance in this circle, let my Love be center,
Melodiously breathe out a charming sound,
Melt her hard heart, that some remorse may enter.
—Thomas Campion

Let Time and Chance combine, combine!
Let Time and Chance combine!
The fairest love from heaven above,
That love of yours was mine,
My Dear!
That love of yours was mine.
—*Thomas Carlyle*

Long have I waited for this day of days
When some small sign from you should loose my tongue. . .
—*Guy Wetmore Carryl*

For this was on St. Valentine's day,
When every fowl cometh there to choose his mate.
—*Chaucer*

Throned in my heart I see thee still.
—*Willis Gaylord Clarke*

Her very frowns are fairer far
Than smiles of other maidens are.
—*Hartley Coleridge*

I have heard of reasons manifold
Why Love must needs be blind,
But this the best of all, I hold,—
His eyes are in his mind.
—*Samuel Taylor Coleridge*

If there's delight in love, 'tis when I see
That heart which others bleed for, bleed for me.
—*William Congreve*

I know not when the day shall be,
I know not when our eyes shall meet;
What welcome you may give to me,
Or will your words be sad or sweet,
It may not be 'till years have passed,
'Till eyes are dim and tresses gray;
The world is wide, but, love, at last,
Our hands, our hearts, must meet some day.
—*Hugh Conway*

If I were a star of even,
I'd rise and set for thee.
—*Rose Terry Cooke*

A mighty pain to love it is
And 'tis a pain that pain to miss;
But of all pains, the greatest pain
It is to love, but love in vain.
—*Abraham Cowley*

I love you,
Not only for what you are,
But for what I am
When I am with you.
—*Roy Croft*

All my life's sweet consists in her alone;
So much I love the most Unloving one.
—*Samuel Daniel*

I love thee for a heart that's kind—
Not for the knowledge in thy mind.
—*William H. Davies*

How long I've loved thee, and how well—
I dare not tell! —*Margaret Deland*

Muse, bid the Morn awake!
Sad Winter now declines,
Each bird doth choose a mate;
This day's Saint Valentine's.
For that good bishop's sake
Get up and let us see
What beauty it shall be
That Fortune us assigns.
—*Michael Drayton*

How happy the lover,
How easy his chain,
How pleasing his pain,
How sweet to discover
He sighs not in vain.
—*John Dryden*

Thou art to me a delicious torment.
—*Ralph Waldo Emerson*

In Beauty's name, I love you.
—*Arthur Davison Ficke*

Lo! you, enshrined.
—*Ford Madox Ford*

I count my time by times that I meet thee;
These are my yesterdays, my morrows, noons,
And nights; these my old moons and my new moons.
—*Richard Watson Gilder*

Not from the whole wide world I chose thee,
Sweetheart, light of the land and the sea!
The wide, wide world could not inclose thee,
For thou art the whole wide world to me.
—*Richard Watson Gilder*

Or love me less, or love me more;
And play not with my liberty:
Either take all, or all restore;
Bind me at least, or set me free!
—*Sidney Godolphin*

I'll be this abject thing no more
Love, give me back my heart again.
—*George Granville*

Dear as the light that visits these sad eyes,
Dear as the ruddy drops that warm my heart.
—*Thomas Gray*

Ah, what is love? It is a pretty thing,
As sweet unto a shepherd as a king.
—*Robert Greene*

Cupid, thou naughty boy, when thou wert loathèd,
Naked and blind, for vagabonding noted,
Thy nakedness I with my reason clothèd,
Mine eyes I gave thee—so was I devoted.
Fie, wanton, fie! Who would show children kindness?
No sooner he into mine eyes was gotten
But straight he clouds them with a seeming blindness,
Makes Reason wish that Reason were forgotten.
—*Sir Fulke Greville (Lord Brooke)*

Though I am dead my soul shall love thee still. —*James Hammond*

Woman much missed, how you call to me, call to me. —*Thomas Hardy*

When every lip invokes young loveliness,
Whom, whom but you should I commemorate?
—*Lucy Hawkins*

Open your heart and take us in,
Love—love and me.
—*W. E. Henley*

Thou art my love, my life, my heart,
The very eyes of me.
—*Robert Herrick*

Bid me to live, and I will live
Thy Protestant to be:
Or bid me love, and I will give
A loving heart to thee,
A heart as soft, a heart as kind,
A heart as sound and free
As in the whole world thou canst find,
That heart I'll give to thee.
—*Robert Herrick*

Oft I have heard both youths and virgins say,
Birds choose their mates, and couple too, this day:
But by their flight I never can divine
When I shall couple with my Valentine.
—*Robert Herrick*

Heart of my heart, O come with me
To walk the ways of Arcadie.
—*Norah M. Holland*

Too young for love?
Ah, say not so!
Too young? Too young?
Ah, no! no! no!
—*Oliver Wendell Holmes*

I love thee—I love thee!
'Tis all that I can say;
It is my vision in the night,
My dreaming in the day.
—*Thomas Hood*

Oh, if it be to choose and call thee mine,
Love, thou art every day my Valentine!
—*Thomas Hood*

With thee I fain would live, with thee I'd gladly die! —*Horace*

If you lak-a me lak I lak-a you.
—*Rosamond Johnson*

Drink to me only with thine eyes,
And I will pledge with mine;
Or leave a kiss but in the cup,
And I'll not look for wine.
—*Ben Jonson*

No lady is so fair as mine.
Joyce Kilmer

The heart of a man to the heart of a maid—
Light of my tents, be fleet—
Morning awaits at the end of the world,
And the world is all at our feet.
—*Rudyard Kipling*

Sing, for faith and hope are high—
None so true as you and I—
Sing the Lovers' Litany:
"Love like ours can never die!"
—*Rudyard Kipling*

Hail to thy returning festival, old Bishop Valentine! Great is thy name in the rubric, thou venerable Archflamen of Hymen! Immortal Go-between; who and what manner of person art thou? Art thou but a *name*, typifying the restless principle which impels poor humans to seek perfection in union? or wert thou indeed a mortal prelate, with thy tippet and thy rochet, thy apron on, and decent lawn sleeves? Mysterious personage! like unto thee, assuredly, there is no other mitred father in the calendar.
—*Charles Lamb*

Thou comest attended with thousands and ten thousands of little Loves. . . Singing Cupids are thy choristers and thy precentors; and instead of the crosier, the mystical arrow is borne before thee.
—*Charles Lamb*

This is the day on which those charming little missives, ycleped Valentines, cross and inter-cross each other at every street and turning. The weary and all forespent two-penny postman sinks beneath a load of delicate embarrassments, not his own. . . In these little visual interpretations, no emblem is so common as the *heart*—that little three-cornered exponent of all our hopes and fears,—the bestuck and bleeding heart.
—*Charles Lamb*

The sunshine of thine eyes,
Oh, let it fall on me!
—*George Parsons Lathrop*

I love a lassie, a bonnie, bonnie lassie;
She's as pure as the lily in the dell.
She's as sweet as the heather,
The bonnie, bloomin' heather,
Mary, ma Scotch Blue-bell.
—*Harry Lauder and Gerald Grafton*

Your name is in the whisper of the woods.
—*Francis Ledwidge*

The charms, alas! that won me,
I never can forget:
Although thou hast undone me,
I own I love thee yet.
—*William Leggett*

You were a Mending Flower to me
To cure my heart and mind.
—*Vachel Lindsay*

I love thee, as the good love heaven.
—*Longfellow*

Does not all the blood within me
Leap to meet thee, leap to meet thee,
As the springs to meet the sunshine?
—*Longfellow*

I could not love thee, dear, so much,
Lov'd I not honour more.
—*Richard Lovelace*

Not as all other women are
Is she that to my soul is dear;
Her glorious fancies come from far,
Beneath the silver evening-star,
And yet her heart is ever near.
—*James Russell Lowell*

Come live with me, and be my love;
And we will all the pleasures prove
That hills and valleys, dales and fields,
Woods or steepy mountain yields.
—*Christopher Marlowe*

O, thou art fairer than the evening air
Clad in the beauty of a thousand stars.
—*Christopher Marlowe*

Love! thy love pours down on mine
As the sunlight on the vine,
As the snow-rill on the vale,
As the salt breeze in the sail;
As the song unto the bird,
On my lips thy name is heard.
—*George Meredith*

I loved you ere I knew you; know you now,
And having known you, love you better still.
—*Owen Meredith*

Thou art the shape of melodies,
And thou the ecstasy of prayers!
—*Alice Meynell*

"There are many To-morrows, my Love, my Love,—
"There is only one To-day."
—*Joaquin Miller*

So dear I love him, that with him all deaths
I could endure, without him live no life.
—*John Milton*

With thee conversing. I forget all time,
All seasons, and their change.
—*John Milton*

I but know that I love thee, whatever thou art.
—*Thomas Moore*

A boat at midnight sent alone
To drift upon the moonless sea,
A lute, whose lending chord is gone,
A wounded bird, that hath but one
Imperfect wing to soar upon,
Are like what I am, without thee.
—*Thomas Moore*

Wert thou more fickle than the restless sea,
Still should I love thee, knowing thee for such.
—*William Morris*

I've wandered east, I've wandered west,
I've bourne a weary lot;
But in my wanderings far or near
Ye never were forgot.
The fount that first burst frae this heart
Still travels on its way
And channels deeper as it rins
The luve o' life's young day.
—*William Motherwell*

Two souls with but a single thought,
Two hearts that beat as one.
—*Münch-Bellinghausen*

Think of my loyal love, my last adieu;
Absence and love are naught if we are true.
—*Alfred de Musset*

O Love! I know not why, when you are glad,
Gaily my glad heart leaps.
O Love, I know not why, when you are sad,
Wildly my sad heart weeps.
—*Sarojini Naidu*

How shall I woo thee, O Dearest?
With the delicate silence of love.
—*Sarojini Naidu*

I do not love thee!—no! I do not love thee!
And yet when thou art absent I am sad.
—*Caroline Elizabeth Sarah Norton*

Heart of my heart, the world is young;
Love lies hidden in every rose.
—*Alfred Noyes*

One, we are one, O heart of my heart,
One, still one, while the world grows old.
—*Alfred Noyes*

In dream let me my true love see.
In dream let me my lover see.
—*Old Rhyme*

Ah, dearer than my soul. . . .
Dearer than light, or life, or fame.
—*John Oldham*

A Book of Verses underneath the Bough,
A Jug of Wine, a Loaf of Bread—and Thou
Beside me singing in the Wilderness—
Oh, Wilderness were Paradise enow!
—*Omar Khayyám*

Your heart is a music-box, dearest!
With exquisite tunes at command,
. . . .
It begins with and ends with "I love!"
"I love!"
My heart echoes to it "I love!"
—*Frances S. Osgood*

Angels are painted fair, to look like you.
—Thomas Otway

Ah me! love can not be cured by herbs.
—Ovid

But bid her eyes to me incline—
I'll ask no other sun to shine.
—Thomas Nelson Page

Take all the pearls are in the brine,
Sift heaven for stars; earth's flowers entwine—
But be her heart my Valentine.
—Thomas Nelson Page

O dear my love, I unto thee have given
Pledge that I am thy vassal evermore.
—Gilbert Parker

Ah, lady, when I gave my heart to thee,
It passed into thy lifelong regency.
—Gilbert Parker

"O Love, O Life, O more than life to me,
How can I live without the surety
Of thy sweet presence till we meet again!"
—Gilbert Parker

Let those love now who never loved before;
Let those who always loved, now love the more.
—Thomas Parnell

Ah. . .I would break the bars of years asunder
To bring you back to me.
—Theodocia Pearce

My merry, merry, merry roundelay
Concludes with Cupid's curse:
They that do change old love for new,
Pray gods, they change for worse!
—George Peele

What thing is love?—for (well I wot) love is a thing.
It is a prick, it is a sting.
It is a pretty, pretty thing;
It is a fire, it is a coal,
Whose flame creeps in at every hole!
—George Peele

And how should I know your true love
From many another one?
—Thomas Percy

Sweeter far and of fairer hue
Is a flower that never in garden grew—
I cannot name it, but dear—'tis you!
—Sarah Metcalf Phipps

I fill this cup to one made up
Of loveliness alone,
A woman, of her gentle sex
The seeming paragon.
—Edward Coate Pinkney

On the stars thou gazest, my star; would I were heaven, that I might look on thee with many eyes. *—Plato*

Thou wast all that to me, love,
For which my soul did pine:
A green isle in the sea, love,
A fountain and a shrine.
—Edgar Allan Poe

Ye gods, annihilate but space and time,
And make two lovers happy.
—Alexander Pope

Apollo has peeped through the shutter,
And awaken'd the witty and fair;
The boarding-school belle's in a flutter,
The twopenny post's in despair;
The breath of the morning is flinging
A magic on blossom and spray,
And cocknevs and sparrows are singing
In chorus on Valentine's day.
—Winthrop Mackworth Praed

Love me if I live!
Love me if I die!
What to me is life or death,
So that thou be nigh?
—Bryan Waller Procter

If she undervalue me,
What care I how fair she be?
—Sir Walter Raleigh

Love me and the world is mine.
—David Reed

So, little loveliest lady mine,
Here's my heart for your valentine!
—Laura E. Richards

My debt to you, Belovèd,
Is one I cannot pay
In any coin of any realm
On any reckoning day.
—Jessie B. Rittenhouse

Still so gently o'er me stealing,
Mem'ry will bring back the feeling,
Spite of all my grief revealing
That I love thee, love thee still.
—Felice Romani

For one man is my world of all the men
This wide world holds; O love, my world is you.
—Christina Georgina Rossetti

More shower than shine
Brings sweet St. Valentine.
—Christina Georgina Rossetti

And still you reign my Queen of Hearts
And I'm your Valentine.
—Christina Georgina Rossetti

O love, my love! if I no more should see
Thyself, nor on the earth the shadow of thee,
Nor image of thine eyes in any spring,—
How then should sound upon Life's darkening slope
The ground-whirl of the perish'd leaves of Hope,
The wind of Death's imperishable wing?
—Dante Gabriel Rossetti

You and I have found the secret way,
None can bar our love or say us nay.
—George William Russell

You brought and gave the infinite
To me who had despaired of it.
—Robert Haven Schauffler

My heart shall o'ertake you
Wherever you are.
—Clinton Scollard

Love rules the court, the camp, the grove,
And men below and saints above,
For love is heaven, and heaven is love.
—Sir Walter Scott

As I am true to thee and thine,
Do thou be true to me and mine!
—Sir Walter Scott

Shall I compare thee to a summer's day?
Thou art more lovely and more temperate.
—Shakespeare

Doubt thou the stars are fire;
Doubt that the sun doth move;
Doubt truth to be a liar;
But never doubt I love.
—Shakespeare

Forty thousand brothers
Could not, with all their quantity of love,
Make up my sum.
—Shakespeare

Perdition catch my soul,
But I do love thee! and when I love thee not,
Chaos is come again.
—Shakespeare

My bounty is as boundless as the sea,
My love as deep; the more I give to thee
The more I have, for both are infinite.
—Shakespeare

But if the while I think on thee, dear friend,
All losses are restored and sorrows end.
—Shakespeare

She is mine own,
And I as rich in having such a jewel
As twenty seas, if all their sands were pearls,
The water nectar, and the rocks pure gold.
—Shakespeare

O mistress mine, where are you roaming?
O, stay and hear! your true-love's coming.
—Shakespeare

"Good morrow, 'tis St. Valentine's day,
All in the morning betime,
And I a maid at your window,
To be your Valentine."
—Shakespeare

O fair! O sweet! when I do look on thee,
In whom all joys so well agree,
Heart and soul do sing in me.
—Sir Philip Sidney

Thy fatal shafts unerring move;
I bow before thine altar, Love.
—Tobias Smollett

Where, whenas Death shall all the world subdue,
Our love shall live, and later life renew.
—Edmund Spenser

I hate the day, because it lendeth light
To see all things, but not my love to see.
—Edmund Spenser

Sweetheart, when you walk my way,
Be it dark or be it day;
Dreary winter, fairy May,
I shall know and greet you.
—Frank L. Stanton

You are so beautiful that time and space
Have held none other like you, nor shall hold.
—George Sterling

Take thou my life, ah, take it,
But spare me thy disdain!
—Richard Henry Stoddard

When, dearest, I but think of thee,
Methinks all things that lovely be
Are present, and my soul delighted.
—Sir John Suckling

I prithee send me back my heart,
Since I cannot have thine;
For if from yours you will not part,
Why, then, shouldst thou have mine?
—Sir John Suckling

In all I wish, how happy should I be,
Thou grand Deluder, were it not for thee!
—Jonathan Swift

Yet leave me not; yet, if thou wilt, be free;
Love me no more, but love my love of thee.
—Algernon Charles Swinburne

Were you the earth, dear Love, and I the skies,
My love should shine on you like to the sun
And look upon you with ten thousand eyes
Till heaven wax'd blind and till the world were done.
—Joshua Sylvester

Were I as high as heaven above the plain,
And you, my Love, as humble and as low
As are the deepest bottoms of the main,
Wheresoe'er you were, with you my love should go.
—Joshua Sylvester

Open the door of thy heart,
And open thy chamber door,
And my kisses shall teach thy lips
The love that shall fade no more
Till the sun grows cold,
And the stars are old,
And the leaves of the Judgment
Book unfold!
—Bayard Taylor

The red rose cries, "She is near, she is near";
And the white rose weeps, "She is late";
The larkspur listens, "I hear; I hear";
And the lily whispers, "I wait."
—Alfred Tennyson

O love! O fire! once he drew
With one long kiss my whole soul through
My lips, as sunlight drinketh dew.
—Alfred Tennyson

Thou idol of my constant heart.
—Celia Thaxter

'Tis said that absence conquers love;
But oh believe it not!
I've tried, alas! its power to prove,
But thou art not forgot.
—Frederick W. Thomas

O be true
To your soul, dearest, as my life to you!
—Francis Thompson

I fear to love thee, Sweet, because
Love's the ambassador of loss.
—Francis Thompson

O love, my love, I love but thee!
Come back to me! Come back to me!
—Theodore Tilton

I'd leave my happy home for you.
—Harry von Tilzer

Ah me! why may not love and life be one?
—Henry Timrod

I need the starshine of your heavenly eyes,
After the day's great sun.
—Charles Hanson Towne

I believe if I should die
And you should kiss my eyelids where I lie
Cold, dead, and dumb to all the world contains,
The folded orbs would open at thy breath,
And from its exile in the Isles of Death
Life would come gladly back along my veins.
—Mary Ashley Townsend

Come, let us make love deathless, thou and I.
—Herbert Trench

The seamen on the wave, love,
When storm and tempest rave, love,
Look to one star to save, love,
Thou art that star to me!
—John Tyler

O, I do adore her,
My own heart's dear.
—Pierson Underwood

Whoe'er thou art, thy master see;
He was—or is—or is to be.
—Voltaire

Will you love me in December as you do in May,
Will you love me in the good old fashioned way?
When my hair has all turned gray,
Will you kiss me then and say,
That you love me in December as you do in May?
—James J. Walker

Go, lovely rose!
Tell her that wastes her time and me
That now she knows,
When I resemble her to thee,
How sweet and fair she seems to be.
—Edmund Waller

Trooly it is with us as it was with Mr. and Mrs. Ingomer in the Play, to whit—
2 soles with but a single thawt
2 harts which beet as 1.
—Artemus Ward

World-wide apart, and yet so near,
I breathe her charmèd atmosphere.
—John Greenleaf Whittier

No lance have I, in joust or fight,
To splinter in my lady's sight;
But, at her feet, how blest were I
For any need of hers to die!
—John Greenleaf Whittier

But there is no fear, and hell has no terror,
To change or alter a love like mine.
—Ella Wheeler Wilcox

O dearer far than light and life are dear.
—William Wordsworth

She gave me eyes, she gave me ears. . .
And love and thought and joy.
—William Wordsworth

Hearts were made to give away
On Valentine's dear day.
—Annette Wynne

Art thou not dearer to mine eyes than light?
Dost thou not circulate through all my veins?
Mingle with life, and form my very soul?
—Edward Young

THANKSGIVING DAY

If gratitude is due from man to man, how much more from man to his Maker! The Supreme Being does not only confer upon us those bounties which proceed more immediately from His hand, but even those benefits which are conveyed to us by others.
—Joseph Addison

There is not a more pleasing exercise of the mind than gratitude. It is accompanied with such an inward satisfaction that the duty is sufficiently rewarded by the performance.
—Joseph Addison

Come, ye thankful people, come,
Raise the song of Harvest-home!
All is safely gathered in,
Ere the winter storms begin;
God, our Maker, doth provide
For our wants to be supplied.
—Henry Alford

For our country extending from sea unto sea,
The land that is known as the "Land of the Free"—
Thanksgiving! Thanksgiving!
—Anon.

Singing the reapers homeward come, Io! Io!
Merrily singing the harvest home, Io! Io!
—Anon.

This is the feast-time of the year,
When plenty pours her wine of cheer,
And even humble boards may spare
To poorer poor a kindly share.
—Anon.

Praise Him that He gave the rain
To mature the swelling grain;
And hath bid the fruitful field
Crops of precious increase yield.
Praise Him for our harvest-store,
He hath filled the garner-floor.
—H. W. Baker

Thanksgiving is the holiday of peace, the celebration of work and the simple life . . . a true folk-festival that speaks the poetry of the turn of the seasons, the beauty of seed-time and harvest, the ripe product of the year—and the deep, deep connection of all these things with God.
—Ray Stannard Baker (David Grayson)

Flocks that whiten all the plain,
Yellow sheaves of ripened grain,
Clouds that drop their fattening dews,
Suns that temperate warmth diffuse;
. . . .
These to Thee, my God, we owe,
Source whence all our blessings flow.
—Anna L. Barbauld

Then lift up the head with a song!
And lift up the hand with a gift!
To the ancient Giver of all
The spirit in gratitude lift!
—Amelia E. Barr

Remember God's bounty in the year. String the pearls of His favor. Hide the dark parts, except so far as they are breaking out in light! Give this one day to thanks, to joy, to gratitude! *—Henry Ward Beecher*

Because for all of us there is the sunshine of human betterment which we may reach if we seek it with every fiber of our being,
Because those of us who live today are preparing a great harvest, altruistic and assured for tomorrow,
Let us give thanks.
—Marguerite Ogden Bigelow

Famine once we had,
But other things God gave us in full store,
As fish and ground-nuts to supply our strait,
That we might learn on Providence to wait;
And know, by bread man lives not in his need,
But by each word that doth from God proceed.
But a while after plenty did come in,
From His hand only who doth pardon sin,
And all did flourish like the pleasant green,
Which in the joyful spring is to be seen.
—William Bradford

But for the quiet homes where love is queen
And life is more than baubles, touched and seen,
And old folks bless us, and dear children play:
For these, O Lord, our thanks!
—Robert Bridges ("Droch")

Stand up, on this Thanksgiving Day, stand upon your feet. Believe in man. Soberly and with clear eyes, believe in your own time and place. There is not, and there never has been a better time, or a better place to live in. *—Phillips Brooks*

Heap high the board with plenteous cheer, and gather to the feast,
And toast the sturdy Pilgrim band whose courage never ceased.
Give praise to that All-Gracious One by whom their steps were led,
And thanks unto the harvest's Lord who sends our "daily bread."
—Allice Williams Brotherton

Some people always sigh in thanking God.
—Elizabeth Barrett Browning

On Thanksgiving Day we acknowledge our dependence.

—*William Jennings Bryan*

Some hae meat and canna eat,—
And some wad eat that want it;
But we hae meat, and we can eat,
Sae let the Lord be thankit.

—*Robert Burns*

"Praise ye the Lord!" the leader called:
"Praise ye the Lord!" spake he.
"Give thanks to God with fervent lips,
Give thanks to God to-day,"
The anthem rose from all the ships,
Safe moored in Boston Bay.

—*Hezekiah Butterworth*

"Praise ye the Lord!" The psalm to-day
Still rises on our ears,
Borne from the hills of Boston Bay
Through five times fifty years.

—*Hezekiah Butterworth*

It is literally true, as the thankless say, that they have nothing to be thankful for. He who sits by the fire, thankless for the fire, is just as if he had no fire. Nothing is possessed save in appreciation, of which thankfulness is the indispensable ingredient. But a thankful heart hath a continual feast.

—*W. J. Cameron*

When a wise man of old declared, "It is a *good* thing to give thanks," he meant it is a saving thing, a restorative thing, an invigorating and fortifying and nourishing thing—the sense of thankfulness.

—*W. J. Cameron*

. . . for the ability to be of service to a fellow-creature, we ought to *give* thanks, not demand it, since in any true act of helpfulness it is the helper who is most helped. Thanksgiving, after all, is a word of action: it imports something done. —*W. J. Cameron*

When our perils are past, shall our gratitude sleep?
No,—here's to the pilot that weathered the storm!

—*George Canning*

Thanksgiving-day, I fear,
If one the solemn truth must touch,
Is celebrated, not so much
To thank the Lord for blessings o'er,
As for the sake of getting more!

—*Will Carleton*

We thank Thee, O Father of all, for the power
Of aiding each other in life's darkest hour;
The generous heart and the bountiful hand
And all the soul-help that sad souls understand.

—*Will Carleton*

O men, grown sick with toil and care,
Leave for awhile the crowded mart;
O women, sinking with despair,
Weary of limb and faint of heart,
Forget your years to-day and come
As children back to childhood's home.

—*Phoebe Cary*

Over the river and through the wood—
Now grandmother's cap I spy!
Hurrah for the fun!
Is the pudding done?
Hurrah for the pumpkin-pie!

—*Lydia Maria Child*

O give thanks unto the Lord; for he is good: for his mercy endureth forever.

—*I Chronicles 16:34*

A thankful heart is not only the greatest virtue, but the parent of all the other virtues.

—*Cicero*

O God, while here for present good I bring
Thee grateful praise,
I thank Thee too for all the joy of old
Thanksgiving Days.

—*Martha Haskell Clark*

We thank Thee, then, O Father,
For all things bright and good,
The seed-time and the harvest,
Our life, our health, our food.

—*Matthias Claudias*

Praise the bridge that carried you over.

—*George Colman the Younger*

Pumpkin pies as yellow as gold—
Melting lusciousness untold!
Puddings, pickles, sauces various.
These to tender lads precarious!
Last of all—by no means least—
Crowning all the jolly feast,
Making all the air quite murky,
Smoked the plump and light brown turkey.

—*George Cooper*

But O! Thou bounteous Giver of all good,
Thou art, of all Thy gifts, Thyself the crown!
Give what Thou cans't, without Thee we are poor,
And with Thee rich, take what Thou wilt away.

—*Cowper*

Gratitude for benefits is eternal.

—*Quintus Rufus Curtius*

For, after all, put it as we may to ourselves, we are all of us from birth to death guests at a table which we did not spread. The sun, the earth, love, friends, our very breath are parts of the banquet. . . Shall we think of the day as a chance to come nearer to our Host, and to find out something of Him who has fed us so long?

—*Rebecca Harding Davis*

The harvest swaths are gathered in the garth,
The aftermath is floating in the fields,
The house-carl bides beside the roaring hearth,
And clustered cattle batten in the shields.
Thank ye the gods, O dwellers in the land,
For home and hearth and ever-giving hand.
—Daniel Lewis Dawson

Thou shalt observe the feast of tabernacles seven days, after that thou hast gathered in thy corn and thy wine: And thou shalt rejoice in thy feast, thou, and thy son, and thy daughter, and thy manservant and thy maidservant, and the Levite, the stranger, and the fatherless, and the widow, that are within thy gates. Seven days shalt thou keep a solemn feast unto the Lord thy God . . . because the Lord thy God shall bless thee in all thine increase, and in all the work of thine hands, and thou shalt surely rejoice.
—Deuteronomy 16:13-15

If you have lived, take thankfully the past.
—Dryden

You seem not high enough your joys to rate;
You stand indebted a vast sum to fate,
And should large thanks for the great blessing pay. *—Dryden*

Choppin' suet in de kitchin,
Stonin' raisins in de hall,
Beef a-cookin' fo' de mince-meat,
Spices groun'—I smell 'em all.
—Paul Laurence Dunbar

Why, it's the climax of the year—
The highest time of living—
Till naturally its bursting cheer
Just melts into Thanksgiving!
—Paul Laurence Dunbar

Be thankful f'r what ye have not, Hinnissy—'tis the only safe rule.
—Finley Peter Dunne

Amongst the many acts of gratitude we owe to God, it may be accounted one, to study and contemplate the perfections and beauties of his works of creation. Every new discovery must necessarily raise in us a fresh sense of the greatness, wisdom, and power of God. He hath so ordered things that almost every part of the creation is for our benefit, either to the support of our being, the delight of our senses, or the agreeable exercise of the rational faculty. *—Jonathan Edwards*

On Thanksgiving Day no servile labor may be performed, and thanks should be offered for the increase and abundance of His fruits upon the face of the earth.
—Elizabeth, Queen of England

For flowers that bloom about our feet;
For tender grass, so fresh, so sweet;
For song of bird, and hum of bee;
For all things fair we hear or see,
Father in heaven, we thank Thee!
—Ralph Waldo Emerson

Consider the bodily gifts which God has given you. . .
Consider your gifts of mind. . .
Consider your spiritual graces. . .
Consider in detail how good and gracious God has been to you.
—Francis de Sales, Saint

For the beautiful face of the year; for the glory of the seasons and the sure and bountiful harvests,
We thank Thee, our Father.
For our homes and our friends, for the humble, the faithful and the loving people of the world,
We thank Thee, Our Father.
—William C. Gannett

Come forth, come forth, to the festal board,
As our sires were won't in the days of old;
. . . .
Come forth, come forth, with your heart-felt praise,
To swell the songs at the altar's side.
—Hannah E. Garey

Thy bountiful care what tongue can recite?
It breathes in the air; it shines in the light;
It streams from the hills; it descends to the plain;
And sweetly distils in the dew and the rain.
—Sir Robert Grant

Let us praise God
For the Day, for the glory and warmth of the sun, for the stir of life, and for honest toil that wins food and rest.
God be praised for the Day.
For the gift of Children; may He help us to train them to be reverent and truthful, that they may gladden our hearts and bring joy to the world.
God be praised for Children.
For good Friends to rejoice with us in our joys, to cheer us in trouble and to lighten our tasks; may He help us to repay them in fellowship and service.
God be praised for our Friends.
—Gray Book

Ay, call it holy ground,—
The soil where first they trod!
They have left unstained what there they found—
Freedom to worship God!
—Felicia Hemans

Lord, 'tis Thy plenty-dropping hand
That soils my land,
And giv'st me for my bushel sowne
Twice ten for one.
All this, and better, Thou dost send
Me, to this end,
That I should render, for my part,
A thankful heart. *—Robert Herrick*

Lord, I confess too, when I dine,
The pulse is thine,
And all those other bits that be
There placed by thee.
—Robert Herrick

Thanksgiving for a former doth invite
God to bestow a second benefit.
—*Robert Herrick*

It is the Puritan's Thanksgiving Eve;
And gathered home from fresher homes around,
The old man's children keep the holiday—
In dear New England, since the fathers slept—
The sweetest holiday of all the year.
—*J. G. Holland*

For summer's bloom and autumn's blight,
For bending wheat and blasted maize,
For health and sickness, Lord of light,
And Lord of darkness, hear our praise.
—*J. G. Holland*

Concerning the blessings of God, whether they tend unto this life or the life to come, there is great cause why we should delight more in giving thanks than in making requests for them, inasmuch as the one hath pensiveness and fear, the other always joy annexed. —*Richard Hooker*

Lord, for the erring thought
Not into evil wrought:
Lord, for the wicked will
Betrayed and baffled still:
For the heart from itself kept,
Our thanksgiving accept.
—*William Dean Howells*

"What's the cause of your day of Thanksgiving?
Tell me, pray," cried the King in his ire.
Said the minister, "This is the reason—
That things are no worse, O my sire!"
—*Helen Hunt Jackson*

And they went out into the fields, and gathered their vineyards, and trode the grapes, and made merry, and went into the house of their God, and did eat and drink.
—*Judges 9:27*

Season of mists and mellow fruitfulness!
Close bosom-friend of the maturing sun;
Conspiring with him how to load and bless
With fruit the vines that round the thatch-eaves run;
To bend with apples the moss'd cottage trees,
And fill all fruit with ripeness to the core;
To swell the gourd, and plump the hazel shells
With a sweet kernel.
—*John Keats*

And taught by thee the Church prolongs
Her hymn of high thanksgiving still.
—*John Keble*

Thanksgiving stirs her ruddy fire;
The glow illuminates November:
She sees new glimmerings of desire
Flash up from every fading ember.
—*Lucy Larcom*

When gratitude o'erflows the swelling heart,
And breathes in free and uncorrupted praise
For benefits received: propitious heaven
Takes such acknowledgment as fragrant incense,
And doubles all its blessings.
—*George Lillo*

With the sacrifice of thanks, as with the sacrifice of alms, "if there be first a willing mind, it is accepted according to that a man hath, and not according to that he hath not."
—*Editorial. Living Age Nov. 28, 1908*

For the gladness life has brought,
For the beauties passing thought,
For the song, the dream, the quest,
. . . .
Lord of gladness, hope and dream,
. . . .
Thee we praise!
—*Elizabeth Roberts Macdonald*

Give thanks, O heart, for the high souls
That point us to the deathless goals—
. . . .
Souls that have built our faith in man,
And lit the ages as they ran.
—*Edwin Markham*

Thanksgiving Day comes, by statute, once a year; to the honest man it comes as frequently as the heart of gratitude will allow, which may mean every day, or once in seven days, at least.
—*Edward Sandford Martin*

Let us be thankful, then, for all the right choices we make when we have to choose; for all the unseen influences that help us to choose right; for whatever withholds us, or diverts from a course that is not our true course; for any denial of apparent advantage or present ease which constrains us toward the fulfilment of a nobler destiny.
—*Edward Sandford Martin*

For hearts that are kindly, with virtue and peace, and not seeking blindly a hoard to increase; for those who are grieving o'er life's sordid plan; for souls still believing in heaven and man; for homes that are lowly with love at the board; for things that are holy, I thank thee, O Lord! —*Walt Mason*

Join voices, all ye living souls, ye birds,
That singing up to heaven's gate ascend,
Bear on your wings and in your notes
His praise.
—*John Milton*

All things living He doth feed;
His full hand supplies their need.
—*John Milton*

Sing to the Lord of harvest,
Sing songs of love and praise;
With joyful hearts and voices
Your Alleluias raise.
—*John S. B. Monsell*

And be the future bright or dark, God grant we never may
Forget the reverent spirit of that first Thanksgiving Day!

—*J. J. Montague*

Fountain of mercy! whose pervading eye
Can look within and read what passes there,
Accept my thoughts for thanks; I have no words:
My soul, o'erfraught with gratitude, rejects
The aid of language: Lord,—behold my heart!

—*Hannah More*

Then he said unto them: Go your way, eat the fat, and drink the sweet, and send persons unto them for whom nothing is prepared: for this day is holy unto our Lord: neither be ye sorry; for the joy of the Lord is your strength. —*Nehemiah 8:10*

Forever on Thanksgiving Day
The heart will find the pathway home.

—*Wilbur D. Nesbit*

It is strange men cannot praise the bridge they go over, or be thankful for favours they have had. —*Roger North*

Harvest home! harvest home!
We've ploughed, we've sowed,
We've reaped, we've mowed,
We've brought home every load.
Hip, hip, hip, harvest home!

—*Old Song*

All deep and genuine gratitude is touched with humility. . . Self-satisfaction, content with what one is or has done, are alien to the spirit of Thanksgiving.

—*Editorial. Outlook Dec. 1, 1906*

Thanks are justly due for boons unbought.

—*Ovid*

Our rural ancestors, with little blest,
Patient of labour when the end was rest,
Indulged the day that housed their annual grain,
With feasts, and off'rings, and a thankful strain.

—*Alexander Pope*

O God of Years, the Earth is full of Thy Plenitude,
And we, Thy humble and contrite servants,
Bow before Thee, with hearts of Thanksgiving.

—*Emery Pottle*

"I feel it in my bones," said the little mother. . . "Yes; Thanksgiving is in the air!" "To be sure," said the father, "it is a law of nature. What could one do if he could not give thanks?" —*E. P. Powell*

"Thanksgiving Day is a jewel, to set in the hearts of honest men; but be careful that you do not take the day, and leave out the gratitude." —*E. P. Powell*

"But see, in our open clearings, how golden the melons lie;
Enrich them with sweets and spices, and give us the pumpkin-pie!"

—*Margaret Junkin Preston*

And therefore, I, William Bradford (by the grace of God to-day,
And the franchise of this good people), governor of Plymouth, say—
Through virtue of vested power—ye shall gather with one accord
And hold in the month of November, thanksgiving unto the Lord.

—*Margaret Junkin Preston*

My God, I thank Thee who hast made
The Earth so bright;
So full of splendor and of joy,
Beauty and light;
So many glorious things are here,
Noble and right!

—*Adelaide A. Procter*

Thou crownest the year with thy goodness; and thy paths drop fatness.
They drop upon the pastures of the wilderness; and the little hills rejoice on every side.
The pastures are clothed with flocks; the valleys also are covered over with corn:
They shout for joy, they also sing.

—*Psalms 65:11-13*

Sing unto the Lord with thanksgiving; sing praise upon the harp unto our God:
Who covereth the heaven with clouds,
Who prepareth rain for the earth,
Who maketh grass to grow upon the mountains.

—*Psalms 147:7,8*

The Pilgrims rose, at this, God's word,
And sailed the wintry seas:
With their own flesh nor blood conferred,
Nor thought of wealth nor ease.

—*Jeremiah Eames Rankin*

The gratitude of most men is but a secret desire of receiving greater benefits.

—*François Duc de la Rochefoucauld*

If I have enjoyed the hospitality of the Host of this universe, Who daily spreads a table in my sight, surely I cannot do less than acknowledge my dependence.

—*G. A. Johnston Ross*

Oh, the rapture of that release! Feasting instead of fasting!
Happiness in the heart of the home, and hope with its silver ray!
Oh, the songs of prayer and praise to the Lord God everlasting
That mounted morn and noon and eve on that first Thanksgiving Day!

—*Clinton Scollard*

Nothing is more honorable than a grateful heart. —*Seneca*

Let never day nor night unhallow'd pass,
But still remember what the Lord hath done.
—*Shakespeare*

Such thanks as fits a king's remembrance.
—*Shakespeare*

He who thanks but with the lips
Thanks but in part;
The full, the true Thanksgiving
Comes from the heart.
—*J. A. Shedd*

For what I give, not what I take,
For battle, not for victory,
My prayer of thanks I make.
—*Odell Shepard*

The grateful person, being still the most severe exacter of himself, not only confesses, but proclaims, his debts. —*Robert South*

Dear the people coming home,
Dear glad faces long away,
Dear the merry cries, and dear
All the glad and happy play.
Dear the thanks, too, that we give
For all of this, Thanksgiving Day.
—*Harriet Prescott Spofford*

Gather the gifts of earth with equal hand;
Henceforth ye too may share the birthright soil,
The corn, the wine, and all the harvest-home. —*E. C. Stedman*

Lord, behold our family here assembled. We thank Thee for this place in which we dwell; for the love that unites us; for the peace accorded us this day; for the hope with which we expect the morrow; for the health, the work, the food, and the bright skies, that make our lives delightful; for our friends in all parts of the earth, and our friendly helpers. . . Let peace abound in our small company. —*Robert Louis Stevenson*

Great as the preparations were for the dinner, everything was so contrived that not a soul in the house should be kept from the morning service of Thanksgiving in the church. —*Harriet Beecher Stowe*

And who gives thanks? He who with helping touch
Revives the thirsty plant; who pities much
The tired beast; to poor gives alms of love,
Has writ his thanks, in words of fire, above.
—*Edith A. Talbot*

The privative blessings—the blessings of immunity, safeguard, liberty, and integrity—which we enjoy deserve the thanksgiving of a whole life. —*Jeremy Taylor*

At opening your eyes, enter upon the day with thanksgiving for the preservation of you the last night. —*Jeremy Taylor*

And though I ebb in worth, I'll flow in thanks.
—*John Taylor*

In everything give thanks.
I Thessalonians 5:18

Give thanks, O heart, O soul,
As the bright year doth roll
To a perfect end, like a perfect scroll.
—*Charles Hanson Towne*

But whether we have less or more,
Always thank we God therefor.
—*Unknown*

For the freedom of our land, and the challenge which that freedom brings,
We thank Thee, our Heavenly Father.
—*Unknown*

Whereas it is the duty of all nations to acknowledge the providence of Almighty God, to obey his will, to be grateful for his benefits, and humbly to implore his protection and favor. . . Now therefore, I do recommend and assign Thursday, the twenty-sixth day of November next, to be devoted by the people of these States to the service of that great and glorious Being, who is the Beneficent Author of all the good that was, that is, or that will be; that we may then all unite in rendering unto him our sincere and humble thanks for his kind care and protection of the people of this country.
—*George Washington*

With songs and honors sounding loud,
Address the Lord on high;
Over the heav'ns He spreads His cloud,
And waters veil the sky.
He sends His showers of blessing down,
To cheer the plains below;
He makes the grass the mountains crown,
And corn in valleys grow.
—*Isaac Watts*

Thanksgiving Day does not mark merely a specific festival. It marks a continuity of life and all that is in or of it.
—*Edward Elwell Whiting*

Ah! on Thanksgiving Day, when from East and from West,
From North and from South come the pilgrim and guest;
When the gray-haired New Englander sees round his board
The old broken links of affection restored;
When the care-wearied man seeks his mother once more,
And the worn matron smiles where the girl smiled before;
What moistens the lip and what brightens the eye,
What calls back the past, like the rich Pumpkin pie?
—*Whittier*

And let these altars, wreathed with flowers
And piled with fruits, awake again
Thanksgivings for the golden hours,
The early and the latter rain!
—*Whittier*

For the land that gave me birth;
For my native home and hearth;
For the change and overturning
Of the times of my sojourning;
For the world's step forward taken;
For an evil way forsaken;
For cruel law abolished;
For all that man upraises
I sing the song of praises.

—Whittier

Heap high the farmer's wintry hoard!
Heap high the golden corn!
No richer gift has Autumn poured
From out her lavish horn!

—Whittier

Sing,. O my soul, rejoicingly, on evening's twilight calm
Uplift the loud thanksgiving, pour forth the grateful psalm.

—Whittier

Our harvests being gathered in, our governor sent four men on a fowling, so that we might after a special manner rejoice together after we had gathered the fruit of our labors. *—Edward Winslow*

For peaceful homes, and healthful days,
For all the blessings earth displays,
We owe thee thankfulness and praise,
Who givest all.

—Christopher Wordsworth

THRIFT WEEK

By sowing frugality we reap liberty, a golden harvest.

—*Agesilaus*

Thrift in the use of things precludes personal waste in consumption.

—*Benjamin Richard Andrews*

Thrift substitutes a plan based on foresight and a candid examination of needs for an impulsive ill-considered spending.

—*Benjamin Richard Andrews*

He that despiseth small things
Shall fall by little and little.

—*Apocrypha: Ecclesiasticus 1:58*

The beginning of a savings-bank account is often a crisis in a man's moral destiny, a revolution destined to make over his whole life.

—*Albert W. Atwood*

There is only one object in economy for any decent person, and that of course is to have the money to spend when you really need it or want it for a useful object.

—*Albert W. Atwood*

Thrift before marriage makes for happiness after the ceremony.

—*Albert W. Atwood*

Thrift is paramount but habits of thrift cannot be inculcated by precept.

—*H. L. Baldensperger*

Economy is not meanness. True economy consists in always making the income exceed the outgo. —*P. T. Barnum*

Successful savers are straight thinking spenders. —*Harvey A. Blodgett*

Saving is a means to ten thousand ends. The realization of almost every personal ambition, the possession of things greatly longed for, depend on money one has saved, and upon habits which control his use of money. —*Harvey A. Blodgett*

Ability to save is first *wanting* to—deciding to—and then saving consistently until the habit is formed. After the habit is formed it is second nature to save.

—*Harvey A. Blodgett*

The person who saves money and puts it out at interest not only helps himself but is a public benefactor. He helps make the wheels of industry go round, for all great enterprises are made possible through savings. —*Harvey A. Blodgett*

The practising of thrift in one direction will be found to encourage the practising of it in others, and saving will be realized to be no hardship when it is learned that present denial is going to make possible some future gratification. —*Mary Willcox Brown*

To hide money away, and keep it out of use, is a very thriftless thing to do. The thrifty person is not a miser. —*T. N. Carver*

A little in one's own pocket is better than much in another man's purse. 'Tis good to keep a nest-egg. Every little makes a mickle.

—*Cervantes*

Keep thy shop, and thy shop will keep thee.

—*George Chapman*

Make ducks and drakes with shillings.

—*George Chapman*

For of fortune's sharpe adversite,
The worst kind of infortune is this,—
A man that has been in prosperite,
And it remember whan it passed is.

—*Chaucer*

The world is fast becoming aroused to the fact, that saving is one of the chief, vital principles of existence; that the extravagant, wasteful practices of the past mean ruin to the nation continuing them.

—*W. Rockwood Conover*

Our wasted oil unprofitably burns,
Like hidden lamps in old sepulchral urns.

—*Cowper*

Every family should work for an emergency fund equal to six months' living expenses, and this should be held on deposit in a sound bank and in Government bonds and regarded as a protection and not as a means to make money. —*Samuel Crowther*

The soundest investment is a home free from mortgage. That has now been proved.

—*Samuel Crowther*

"Annual income, twenty pounds; annual expenditure, nineteen six; result—happiness. Annual income, twenty pounds; annual expenditure, twenty pounds ought and six; result—misery." —*Charles Dickens*

They poor, I rich; they beg, I give;
They lack, I have; they pine, I live.

—*Edward Dyer*

Wouldst thou shut up the avenues of ill,
Pay every debt as if God wrote the bill.

—*Ralph Waldo Emerson*

If a man could keep on working and having enough for his needs, that man would have a fortune stored up within himself. But some die in harness and others must rest, so it is necessary to save.

—*William Felsinger*

But dost thou love life? Then do not squander time, for that is the stuff life is made of. —*Benjamin Franklin*

Buy what thou hast no Need of and ere long thou shalt sell thy Necessaries.

—*Benjamin Franklin*

A penny saved is twopence clear:
A pin a day's a groat a year.

—*Benjamin Franklin*

A shilling spent idly by a fool may be picked up by a wiser person, who knows better what to do with it; it is, therefore, not lost. —*Benjamin Franklin*

The way to wealth is as plain as the way to market. It depends chiefly on two words, industry and frugality; that is, waste neither time nor money, but make the best use of both. Without industry and frugality nothing will do; with them, everything.

—*Benjamin Franklin*

A thrifty person sets traps to catch the waste, and changes it into things worth having. —*Jane Eayre Fryer*

Wilful waste brings woeful want.

—*Thomas Fuller*

The social revolution will be accomplished not through violence and class struggle but through the homely virtue of persistent and constant saving. —*Alvin H. Hansen*

The principal theme of thrift is independence.

—*M. W. Harrison*

The thrift that does not make a man charitable sours into avarice.

—*M. W. Harrison*

The waste of money cures itself, for soon there is no more to waste.

—*M. W. Harrison*

Wouldst thou both eat thy cake and have it?

—*George Herbert*

The wise man sayeth, store is no sore.

—*John Heywood*

When the sun shineth, make hay.

—*John Heywood*

He that will not when he may,
When he would he shall have nay.

—*John Heywood*

If you want to know whether you are going to be a success or a failure in life, you can easily find out. The test is simple and infallible. Are you able to save money? If not, drop out. You will lose. You may not think it, but you will lose as sure as you live. The seed of success is not in you.

—*James J. Hill*

There can be no freedom or beauty about a home life that depends on borrowing and debt.

—*Henrik Ibsen*

Have you ever considered that if you are spending all of your money as it comes to you, week by week or month by month, you are working in a tread mill? At the end of the month you are no nearer the end of your ambitions than you were at the beginning.

—*J. A. Jayne*

One thing all lives have in common: uncertainty; one maxim all men may take to heart: be prepared; and for the vast majority of us, thrift is essential to being prepared.

—*Alvin Johnson*

He that is extravagant will quickly become poor, and poverty will enforce dependence and invite corruption. —*Samuel Johnson*

Without frugality few can become rich, and with it few would become poor.

—*Samuel Johnson*

As he brews, so shall he drink.

—*Ben Jonson*

Though we may be forced to admit that personal thrift alone is not in all cases enough to give economic security, none of the remedies likely to be adopted now will make it any less desirable. . . . For practically all of us the skillful use of our resources will continue to be an important factor in the quality of our living.

—*Editorial. Journal of Home Economics*

The thrift habit teaches a man to earn largely, that he may save wisely, so as to be able to spend advantageously in the time of need or opportunity, when the need will be greater or the opportunity better than that of the present. —*W. H. Kniffen*

Waste not the smallest thing created, for grains of sand make mountains, and atomies infinity. Waste not the smallest time in imbecile infirmity, for well thou knowest that seconds form eternity. —*E. Knight*

With every dollar that the depositor saves he strengthens the barrier between himself and possible want in times when work is not to be found. —*William E. Knox*

A lack of knowledge of the value of money on the part of women is the most powerful enemy to domestic happiness that exists.

—*Judge Arthur Lacy*

Thrift is broader than mere saving. It is to the individual what conservation is to the nation. —*John A. Lapp*

Mither wadna waste, and I wad be disgracing her memory if I wasted.
—*Harry Lauder*

Behave to your purse as you would to your best friend. —*Harry Lauder*

A bank book makes good reading—better than some novels. —*Harry Lauder*

Don't throw away the crusts—eat them. They are as nourishing as beef.
—*Harry Lauder*

Thrift is care and prudence in the management of one's affairs, the foundation upon which every successful and enduring business enterprise is based.
—*William Mather Lewis*

Teach economy; that is one of the first virtues. —*Abraham Lincoln*

If it were possible to inject the quality of saving into every boy, we would have a great many more real men.
—*Sir Thomas Lipton*

He looks the whole world in the face for he owes not any man.
—*Longfellow*

How much you should save, or how little, is not nearly so important as saving something —anything—regularly. —*J. P. McEvoy*

You should save because it is good discipline.
—*J. P. McEvoy*

Thrift is more than prudence, which is merely good judgment and foresight in the practical affairs of life. It is more than economy, which is a disposition to save. It is more than frugality, which is prudent economy in the care of money or goods.
—*T. D. MacGregor*

Extravagance causes financial ills in the nation, but its effects on individual citizens is of primary importance, because no nation can be more prosperous than its people.
—*T. D. MacGregor*

The habit of thrift proves your power to rule your own self. You are captain of your soul. You are able to take care of yourself, and then out of the excess of your strength you produce a surplus.
—*William A. McKeever*

The little savings bank in the home means more for the future of the children of a family almost than all the advice in the world. It gives them the right start.
—*William McKinley*

The times call for all of us to "Stop, Look, Listen", and having done that, to work and save. —*Frank L. McVey*

A great many temptations come to the spendthrift which pass by one who has learned to save. —*Orison Swett Marden*

Thrift means that you should always have the best you can possibly afford, when the thing has any reference to your physical and mental health, to your growth in efficiency and power. —*Orison Swett Marden*

Thrift, or saving, is at the foundation of civilization. —*James B. Morman*

The waste of plenty is the resource of scarcity. —*T. L. Peacock*

But first of all, and all the time, it is a prerequisite to the practice of thrift, that the people be thriftily minded.
—*Raymond Pearl*

Go to the ant, thou sluggard; consider her ways, and be wise: Which having no guide, overseer, or ruler, Provideth her meat in the summer, and gathereth her food in the harvest. *Proverbs 6:6-8*

A rolling stone gathers no moss.
—*Publilius Syrus*

I had my sleeping car in mind for many years. I wanted to build the car and made up my mind that to succeed in my life's dream, it was necessary to have some money and a good deal of it. I began by eliminating a number of things to which I had grown accustomed. Cigars were among them. I had been in the habit of paying five cents apiece for my cigars. I gave them up and many other things too. The total did not amount to much, but the habit was valuable, for I learned I could do without many other things that before that time I thought were absolutely essential to my well-being. —*George M. Pullman*

Extravagance is our national curse.
—*John D. Rockefeller*

Extravagance rots character; train your youth away from it. On the other hand, the habit of saving money, while it stiffens the will, also brightens the energies.
—*Theodore Roosevelt*

Whatever thrift is, it is not avarice. Avarice is not generous; and, after all, it is the thrifty people who are generous.
—*Lord Rosebery*

Thrift comes too late when you find it at the bottom of your purse. —*Seneca*

He that wants money, means, and content is without three good friends.
—*Shakespeare*

He that keeps nor crust nor crumb,
Weary of all, shall want some.
—*Shakespeare*

Neither a borrower nor a lender be;
For loan oft loses both itself and friend;
And borrowing dulls the edge of husbandry.
—*Shakespeare*

Here's to the flaunting, extravagant quean,
And here's to the housewife that's thrifty!
—*Richard Brinsley Sheridan*

In saving waste, we have inspired the workers of hand and head. EVERYTHING HAS A VALUE. —*George W. Sherman*

Make no mistake. The habit of thrift robs one of no proper pleasure, clouds no worthy outlook, narrows no life, hampers no laudable ambition. On the contrary, it adds immensely to the joys of human existence, widens every prospect for usefulness and honor, broadens the horizon of opportunity enormously, and makes possible the realization of lofty aspirations. —*W. G. Sibley*

Those families who get on in the world invariably practice economies, accumulate property, establish incomes, and finally become more valuable to the business interests of their communities than those who spend for gratifications all they earn. —*W. G. Sibley*

Thrift was never more necessary in the world's history than it is today.
—*Francis H. Sisson*

He has spent all his life in letting down empty buckets into empty wells; and he is frittering away his age in trying to draw them up again. —*Sydney Smith*

He that won't look ahead looks behind with a tear in his eye. —*Spanish Proverb*

We must understand that the pennies are to be saved as well as the dollars, that the little scraps of food, little bits of land and the smallest amounts of our various resources and commodities must be guarded just as assiduously as our mightiest storehouse of wealth. —*S. W. Straus*

In addition to the money we save, we should be thrifty of our time, our health, our strength and our talents. —*S. W. Straus*

Thrift is not a mere forced rule: it is a virtue; it is a principle. Thrift is not an affair of the pocket, but an affair of character. Thrift is not niggardliness, but wisdom.
—*S. W. Straus*

Beware of all enterprises that require new clothes. —*Henry D. Thoreau*

Thrift should then be begun with the rich, important, able, and popular. So long as it is advocated as the virtue of the poor and lowly, the young and struggling, the propaganda will be largely self destructive.
—*Edward L. Thorndike*

The worst form of thriftlessness is expenditure for objects or conditions which give no essential satisfaction to the buyer or anybody else. —*Edward L. Thorndike*

I may be a pessimist, but the philosophy of anti-thrift just now coming into being seems to me the greatest danger to the peace of the world. —*Adriano Tilgher*

Forethought and temperance are the virtues which produced thrift, and with thrift the economic progress of society. And those are the virtues which today are gravely compromised. —*Adriano Tilgher*

Who goeth a borrowing
Goeth a sorrowing.
—*Thomas Tusser*

Keep adding little to little, and soon there will be a great heap. —*Virgil*

One must be economical in order to be liberal.
—*Voltaire*

The difference between the clerk who spends all of his salary and the clerk who spends part of it is the difference—in ten years—between the owner of a business and the man out of a job. —*John Wanamaker*

Economy makes happy homes and sound nations; instill it deep.
—*George Washington*

Make all you can, save all you can, give all you can. —*John Wesley*

If a man does not provide for all who are dependent upon him, and if he has not that vision of conditions to come and that care for the days that have not yet dawned which we sum up in the whole idea of thrift and saving, then he has not opened his eyes to any adequate conception of human life.
—*Woodrow Wilson*

Bad spending makes the poor poorer.
—*Hartley Withers*

The task of making out of the American people a nation of thrifty men and women is a work of years, but the enormous national and individual benefits accruing therefrom will justify whatever time and effort is expended on it. —*George F. Zook*

WASHINGTON'S BIRTHDAY

More than all, and above all, Washington was master of himself.
—Charles Francis Adams

His example is complete, and it will teach wisdom and virtue to magistrates, citizens, and men, not only in the present age, but in future generations, as long as our history shall be read. *—John Adams*

If I were to characterize George Washington's feelings toward his country, I should be less inclined than most people to stress what is called Washington's *love* of his country. What impresses me as far more important is what I should call Washington's *respect* for his country. *—Randolph G. Adams*

How cheapened of distinction and impoverished of dignity would be our national life if it were bereft of the glorified common sense of George Washington!
—Edwin Anderson Alderman

Washington stands high, clean, spotless, like the shaft that commemorates his fame.
—Edwin Anderson Alderman

The historical figure of George Washington is characterized by a moral balance and by a serenity of mind which constitute the greatest gifts of a truly republican ruler.
—Ricardo J. Alfaro

I venture to say, that, from the Latin American point of view, the greatest glory of George Washington consists in having governed with success the first republican nation established in modern times and in having set examples and standards that will last as long as justice and righteousness, honesty and wisdom, unselfishness and patriotism preside over the destinies of free and civilized nations.
—Ricardo J. Alfaro

Exalted chief, in thy superior mind
What vast resource, what various talents joined!
—Richard Alsop

He changed mankind's ideas of political greatness. *—Fisher Ames*

Contact with his sound thinking, his firm unemotional acting and his benign masterful leadership cannot fail to steady us and to help direct us in our choice of statesmen to lead us out of present national troubles.

Supreme in war, in council, and in peace.
—Anon.

But why for him vain marbles raise?
Can the cold sculpture speak his praise?
Illustrious shade! we can proclaim
Our gratitude, but not thy fame.
Long as Columbia shall be free,
She lives a monument of thee.
—Anon.

That name in the days of peace was a loadstone, attracting to itself a whole people's confidence, a whole people's love, and the whole world's respect. *—Anon.*

Let us today reverently thank the God of our fathers that Washington's influence is still a shining light. It illuminates as none other the soul of America. It is today, as it has ever been, a vital force. From his grave in Mount Vernon he still guides the destinies of the American people. When the seas are smooth we little feel his presence, but when the ship of state plunges into a storm and is threatened by angry seas his mighty shade is again our helmsman.
—James M. Beck

He was the noble promoter of social reform.
—Simón Bolívar

The great citizen, the first-born son of the New World. *—Simón Bolívar*

The work of Washington is still the most potent influence for the advancement of civilization and the freedom of the race.
—William Edgar Borah

Simple and brave, his faith awoke
Ploughmen to struggle with their fate;
Armies won battles when he spoke,
And out of Chaos sprang the state.
—Robert Bridges ("Droch")

It will be the duty of the historian and the sage, in all ages, to let no occasion pass of commemorating this illustrious man; and until time shall be no more, will a test of the progress which our race has made in wisdom and in virtue be derived from the veneration paid to the immortal name of Washington!
—Lord Brougham

Thus 'mid the wreck of thrones shall live
Unmarred, undimmed, our hero's fame;
And years succeeding years shall give
Increase of honors to his name.
—William Cullen Bryant

Washington stands alone and unapproachable like a snow peak rising above its fellows into the clear air of morning, with a dignity, constancy, and purity which have made him the ideal type of civic virtue to succeeding generations. *—James Bryce*

Then honor to the day that gave him birth,
For it is also Freedom's natal day.
—Arthur J. Burdick

Crown, crown we the chief of the heroes eternal,
Whose honor was gained by his service to man!
—Hezekiah Butterworth

He gave us a nation to make it immortal;
He laid down for Freedom the sword that he drew;
And his faith leads us on through the uplifting portal
Of the glories of peace and our destinies new.
—Hezekiah Butterworth

Where may the wearied eye repose
When gazing on the Great;
Where neither guilty glory glows,
Nor despicable state?
Yes—One—the first—the last—the best—
The Cincinnatus of the West,
Whom Envy dared not hate,
Bequeathed the name of Washington,
To make man blush there was but one!
—Lord Byron

While Washington's a watchword, such as ne'er
Shall sink while there's an echo left to air.
—Lord Byron

Washington,
Whose every battle-field is holy ground,
Which breathes of nations saved, not worlds undone.
—Lord Byron

His great fame rests on the solid foundation that while he was careful to avoid doing wrong to others, he was prompt and decided in repelling wrong. *—John C. Calhoun*

Because he was a gentleman and a man of wise propriety, his acts became precedents that to this day gives the Presidency the great dignity it has. He shaped and molded that office to the contours of his own heroic stature. *—W. J. Cameron*

We see united in him the distinguished virtues of a good citizen, an experienced general, an upright senator, and a wise politician.
—William Paulett Cary

A stranger to profusion, yet generous in every instance where liberality was a virtue.
—William Paulett Cary

Washington served us chiefly by his sublime moral qualities.
—William Ellery Channing

When the storm of battle blows darkest and rages highest, the memory of Washington shall nerve every American arm, and cheer every American heart. *—Rufus Choate*

His strength was in himself, and he moved the world by the power of his character.
—Thomas M. Clark

Three times Washington's character saved the country; once by keeping up the courage of the nation till the Revolutionary War was ended; then, by uniting the nation in the acceptance of the Federal Constitution; thirdly, by saving it from being swept away into anarchy and civil war during the immense excitement of the French Revolution.
—James Freeman Clarke

The filial love of Washington for his mother is an attribute of American manhood, a badge which invites our trust and confidence and an indispensable element of American greatness.
—Grover Cleveland

So long as the spirit of democracy abides in the world, the fundamental principles which he defended. . . these will forever be an inexhaustable fount of inspiration for all peoples.
—Vicente Mejia Colindres

He understood human nature and he had the prophet's insight into difficulties and situations which were later to arise.
—Editorial. Collier's, Feb. 22, '36

Other men have had a great military genius, more intellectual capacity, more sympathetic influence over men, but of him it is to be said, "Better is he that ruleth his spirit than he that taketh a city."
—Rose Terry Cooke

If to set a mark upon the minds of men which changes the whole course of human events is teaching, then Washington ranks as a prince of teachers. *—Calvin Coolidge*

We can not yet estimate him. We can only indicate our reverence for him and thank the Divine Providence which sent him to serve and inspire his fellow men.
—Calvin Coolidge

Without bigotry, without intolerance, he appeals to the highest spiritual nature of mankind. His genius has filled the earth.
—Calvin Coolidge

Alone in its grandeur stands forth the character of Washington in history; alone like some peak that has no fellow in the mountain-range of greatness.
—John W. Daniel

By whom is he surpassed in physical and moral courage, in fiery energy, in tireless patience, in dogged and unyielding endurance, in personal modesty and absence of self-seeking, and in that rare sense of the true proportion of things which is the very crown of wisdom? *—John William Davis*

Blot out from the page of history the names of all the great actors of his time in the drama of nations, and preserve the name of Washington, and the century would be renowned. —*Chauncey M. Depew*

The superiority of Washington's character and genius were more conspicuous in the formation of our government and in putting it on indestructible foundations than leading armies to victory and conquering the independence of his country.
—*Chauncey M. Depew*

What a reward is Washington's! What an influence is his and will be! One mind and will transfused by sympathetic instruction into millions; one life pattern for all public men, teaching what greatness is and what the pathway to undying fame!
—*Charles W. Eliot*

Magnanimous in youth,
Glorious through life,
Great in death,
His highest ambition the happiness of mankind,
His noblest victory the conquest of himself—
Bequeathing to posterity the inheritance of his fame,
And building his monument in the hearts of his countrymen.
—*English Tourist in the Visitor's Book of Mount Vernon*

The defender of his country—the founder of liberty,
The friend of man,
History and tradition are explored in vain
For a parallel to his character.
—*Part of an Epitaph found on the back of a portrait of Washington sent to the family from England*

The character, the counsels, and example of our Washington. . .will guide us through the doubts and difficulties that beset us; they will guide our children and our children's children in the paths of prosperity and peace, while America shall hold her place in the family of nations. —*Edward Everett*

The greatest of good men and the best of great men. —*Edward Everett*

George Washington is one of the beacons placed at intervals along the highroad of history. *Orestes Ferrara*

His life was a hymn in praise of honor, uprightness, and patriotism.
—*Orestes Ferrara*

The form of Washington stands apart from any other in history, shining with a truer lustre and a more benignant glory. With us his memory remains a national property, where all sympathies meet in unison. Under all dissensions and amid all storms of party, his precepts and examples speak to us from the grave with a paternal appeal; and his name—by all revered—forms a universal tie of brotherhood,—a watchword of our Union.
—*John Fiske*

Washington's appointments, when president, were made with a view to gather all the talent of the country in support of the national government; and he bore many things which were personally disagreeable in an endeavor to do this. —*Paul Leicester Ford*

Illustrious man, deriving honor less from the splendor of his situation than from the dignity of his mind. —*James Fox*

One of the greatest captains of the age.
—*Benjamin Franklin*

He comes!—the Genius of these lands—
Fame's thousand tongues his worth confess,
Who conquered with his suffering bands,
And grew immortal by distress.
—*Philip Freneau*

O Washington! thrice glorious name,
What due rewards can man decree—
Empires are far below thy aim,
And sceptres have no charms for thee;
Virtue alone has your regard,
And she must be your great reward.
—*Philip Freneau*

The majesty of that life never grows old.
—*Melville Fuller*

Eternity alone can reveal to the human race its debt of gratitude to the peerless and immortal name of Washington.
—*James A. Garfield*

Conflict and pain, and fame immortal are his guerdon! —*Richard Watson Gilder*

Washington is, to my mind, the purest figure in history.
—*William Ewart Gladstone*

Washington it was who made the principle of the sovereignty of the people prevail for the good of the country, and who loved peace founded on justice and mutual respect.
—*J. V. Gómez*

The greatest man of modern times.
—*Sir Henry Grattan*

No nobler figure ever stood in the forefront of a nation's life.
—*John Richard Green*

George Washington is the typical leader of our American thought. His genius is American in every fibre. His thought is our hope, and his inspiration shall be our praise.
—*Frank Wakeley Gunsaulus*

Among a world of dreamers he was the only one whose vision in the slightest degree approached the great realities of the future. —*Edward Everett Hale*

From the life of George Washington one lesson stands forth that is to me of more interest than the great work he accomplished in winning the independence and liberty of his country. It is that in this great American is incarnate the type of statesman that is capable of converting his ideal of government into a practical and stable reality through the sheer strength of his uprightness and determination, without having recourse to secret machinations, to opportunism, or to that divergence between private and public morality of which the science and art of politics have been believed for many centuries to consist.
—*Enrique Olaya Herrera*

If from the vantage-ground of the present we survey the duties and difficulties that devolved upon Washington, we shall return from the outlook with the conviction that greater task was never laid upon the shoulders of statesman or ruler.
—*Newell Dwight Hillis*

Well hath he been called one of the architects of civilization.
—*Newell Dwight Hillis*

The universal consent of mankind accords to Washington the highest place among the great men of the race.
—*George F. Hoar*

Father! We, whose ears have tingled
With the discord notes of shame,—
We, whose sires their blood have mingled
In the battle's thunder-flame,—
Gathering, while this holy morning
Lights the land from sea to sea,
Hear thy counsel, heed thy warning;
Trust us, while we honor thee!
—*Oliver Wendell Holmes*

But over the sleeping volcano of his temper he kept watch and ward, until his habit became one of gentleness, generosity and shining simple truth; and, behind all, we behold his unswerving purpose and steadfast strength.
—*Elbert Hubbard*

His purity of purpose stands unimpeached; his steadfast earnestness and sterling honesty are our priceless examples. We love the man. We call him Father. —*Elbert Hubbard*

This was the man God gave us when the hour
Proclaimed the dawn of Liberty begun.
—*John Hall Ingham*

Washington, the brave, the wise, the good,
Supreme in war, in council, and in peace,
Valiant without ambition, discreet without fear,
Confident without presumption.
In disaster, calm; in success moderate: in all, himself.
The hero, the patriot, the Christian.
The father of nations, the friend of mankind,
Who, when he had won all, renounced all,
Then sought in the bosom of his family and of nature, retirement,
And in the hope of religion, immortality.
—*Inscription at Mt. Vernon*

To act justly was his instinct, to promote the public weal his constant effort, to deserve the affection of good men his ambition.
—*Washington Irving*

Truth will transmit his character to posterity in all its genuine lustre. —*John Jay*

It may truly be said that never did nature and fortune combine more perfectly to make a man great, and to place him in the same constellation with whatsoever worthies have merited from man an everlasting remembrance. —*Thomas Jefferson*

By giving an impetus to the struggle for the independence of his country, George Washington led the way to lasting emancipation. —*Augustin P. Justo*

Let him who looks for a monument to Washington look around the United States. Your freedom, your independence, your national power, your prosperity, and your prodigious growth are a monument to him.
—*Louis Kossuth*

A nobleness to try for,
A name to live and die for—
The name of Washington.
—*George Parsons Lathrop*

He was, in the highest sense of the word, a gentleman and a man of honor, and he carried into public life the severest standard of private morals.
—*William E. H. Lecky*

First in war, first in peace, and first in the hearts of his countrymen, he was second to none in the humble and endearing scenes of private life. —*Henry Lee*

Washington's is the mightiest name of earth —long since mightiest in the cause of civil liberty; still mightiest in moral reformation. On that name no eulogy is expected. It cannot be. To add brightness to the sun, or glory to the name of Washington, is alike impossible. Let none attempt it. In solemn awe pronounce the name, and in its naked deathless splendor leave it shining on.
—*Abraham Lincoln*

Behind the popular myths, behind the statuesque figure of the orator and the preacher, behind the general and the President and the historian, there was a strong, vigorous man, in whose veins ran warm, red blood, in whose heart were stormy passions and deep sympathy for humanity, in whose brain were far-reaching thoughts, and who was informed throughout his being with a resistless will.
—*Henry Cabot Lodge*

Broad-minded, higher-souled, there is but one
Who was all this and ours, and all men's,—
Washington.
—*James Russell Lowell*

Soldier and statesman, rarest unison;
High-poised example of great duties done
Simply as breathing.
—*James Russell Lowell*

The warrior, the governor, and the citizen, three times great, who was born two centuries ago for the good of the United States, for the honor of the new continent, and for the glory of the world. —*Gerardo Machado*

The quarry whence thy form majestic sprung
Has peopled earth with grace,
Heroes and gods that elder bards have sung,
A bright and peerless race;
But from its sleeping veins ne'er rose before
A shape of loftier name
Than his, who Glory's wreath with meekness wore,
The noblest son of Fame.
—*Isaac McLellan*

Time had no nobler son!
—*Edwin Markham*

He guided the passions of others, because he was master of his own.
—*Ebenezer Grant Marsh*

Resolute and undejected in misfortune, he rose superior to distresses, and surmounted difficulties, which no courage, no constancy, but his own, would have resisted.
—*Ebenezer Grant Marsh*

More than any other individual, and as much as to one individual was possible, has he contributed to found this, our wide spreading empire, and to give to the Western World independence and freedom.
—*John Marshall*

In youth through wildwood maze
Thy skill surveyed clear paths; and later, lo!
The way was straight because thou mad'st it so.
—*Geraldine Meyrich*

Ah, hero of our younger race!
Strong builder of a temple new!
—*Harriet Monroe*

George Washington was not only the father of the democracy of this great Nation but also a model of inspiring genius for the great liberators of the peoples of the American continent. —*Juan Esteban Montero*

It was his balanced intellect, understanding, and his greatness of soul that steadied and preserved the infant government against peril and prejudice.
—*James Shera Montgomery*

We would not visualize him as some half-mythical demigod, but rather as a courageous, strong, patient, intensely human person. We would visualize him as a man who worked, played, studied; sacrificed, fought, suffered; and lived to foster our infant republic into being. —*James R. Moore*

Nobility of character, a serene spirit, virile energy, and a heart full of sympathy, love, and humanity—these qualities which Washington possessed offer a magnificent examplar for the ready admiration of America and the world. —*Alfredo Baquerizo Moreno*

He had every title at command, but his first victory was over himself.
—*Gouverneur Morris*

Posterity will talk of Washington as the founder of a great empire, when my name shall be lost in the vortex of revolution.
—*Napoleon I*

Some men command the world, or hold its admiration by their ideas or by their intellect. Washington had neither original ideas nor a deeply cultured mind. He commands by his integrity, by his justice.
—*Theodore Parker*

In the war of the Revolution, when it was thought the cause was lost, men became inspired at the very mention of the name of George Washington. —*Horace Porter*

God give us the grace to prize his great example and, as we may in our more modest measure, to reproduce his virtues.
—*Henry Codman Potter*

Your presence led our fathers in the field,
Your spirit leads us still to that which lives
In Liberty and Peace.
—*John A. Prentice*

The character of Washington—in war, in peace, and in private life, the most sublime on historical record.
—*William H. Prescott*

His work well done, the leader stepped aside
Spurning a crown with more than kingly pride.
Content to wear the higher crown of worth,
While time endures, "First citizen of earth."
—*James J. Roche*

Great knightly soul who came in time to serve his country's need.
—*Margaret E. Sangster*

The more clearly Washington's teaching and example are understood, the more faithfully they are followed, the purer, the stronger, the more glorious will this Republic become.
—*Carl Schurz*

The flower imperishable of this valiant age,—
A true American!
—*Clinton Scollard*

By his inspiring light may we fare on!
—*Clinton Scollard*

George Washington—the highest human personification of justice and benevolence.
—*William H. Seward*

'Twas his ambition, generous and great
A life to life's great end to consecrate.
—*Percy Bysshe Shelley*

While Washington hath left
His awful memory,
A light for after times.
—*Robert Southey*

Happy was it for America, happy for the world, that a great name, a guardian genius, presided over her destinies in war.
—*Jared Sparks*

It is a happy combination of rare talents and qualities, the harmonious union of the intellectual and moral powers, rather than the dazzling splendor of any one trait, which constitute the grandeur of his character.
—*Jared Sparks*

He lives, ever lives in the hearts of the free,
The wings of his fame spread across the broad sea;
He lives where the banner of freedom's unfurled,
The pride of his country, the wealth of the world.
—*Alfred Tennyson*

The chief of a nation in arms, doing battle with distracted parties; calm in the midst of conspiracy; serene against the open foe before him and the darker enemies at his back; Washington, inspiring order and spirit into troops hungry and in rags; stung by ingratitude, but betraying no anger, and ever ready to forgive; in defeat invincible, magnanimous in conquest, and never so sublime as on that day when he laid down his victorious sword and sought his noble retirement—here indeed is a character to admire and revere, a life without a stain, a fame without a flaw.
—*William Makepeace Thackeray*

Washington represents the advent of republican democracy in the world, and that lofty principle in the realm of political ideals was developed and consolidated in modern times by the joint effort of all the nations of the New World when they became independent republics. —*Rafael L. Trujillo*

Let us go up with high and sacred love
To look on his pure brow,
And as, with solemn grace, he points above,
Renew the patriot's vow!
—*Henry Theodore Tuckerman*

May it please Heaven that his example shall continue to serve as a beacon to our Republics in their darkest moments of doubt and adversity. —*Jorge Ubico*

Let his countrymen consecrate the memory of the heroic General, the patriotic Statesman, and the virtuous Sage; let them teach their children never to forget that the fruit of his labours and his example, are their inheritance. —*United States Senate, 1799*

But why for him vain marbles raise?
Can the cold sculpture speak his praise?
Illustrious shade! we can proclaim
Our gratitude, but not thy fame.
Long as Columbia shall be free,
She lives a monument of thee;
And may she ever rise in fame,
To honor thy immortal name!
—*Unknown*

A great general like Napoleon may be produced in a military school. A great diplomat like Metternich may be developed in a court. A great philosopher like Hegel may be evolved in a university. But a great man like Washington can come only from a pure and noble home. The greatness, indeed, parental love cannot bestow; but the manliness is often a mother's gift. —*Henry van Dyke*

The prevailin' weakness of most public men is to Slop Over! . . . . G. Washington never slopt over. —*Artemus Ward*

I am not surprised at what George has done, for he was always a good boy.
—*Mary Ball Washington*

All the good, whether learned or unlearned, high or low, rich or poor, feel this day that there is one treasure common to us all, and that is the fame and character of Washington.
—*Daniel Webster*

Washington is in the clear upper sky.
—*Daniel Webster*

Thank God! the people's choice was just!
The one man equal to his trust.
Wise without lore and without weakness good,
Calm in the strength of flawless rectitude.
—*Whittier*

How felt the land in every part
The strong throb of a nation's heart,
As its great leader gave, with reverent awe,
His pledge to Union, Liberty, and Law!

—*Whittier*

The Republic may perish, the wide arch of our Union may fall; star by star its glories may expire; stone by stone its columns and its capitol may moulder and crumble; all other names which adorn its annals may be forgotten; but as long as human hearts shall anywhere pant, or human tongue shall anywhere plead, for a sure, rational, constitutional liberty, those hearts shall enshrine the memory and those tongues shall prolong the fame of George Washington.

—*Robert C. Winthrop*

Nor must it be supposed that Washington owed his greatness to the peculiar crisis which called out his virtues. His more than Roman virtues, his consummate prudence, his powerful intellect, and his dauntless decision and dignity of character, would have made him illustrious in any age. —*William Wirt*

AUTHOR INDEX